"*Becoming Beholders* gives the reader amazingly practical advice on how to entice busy and normally reactive college students to change modes and instead learn to be deliberatively reflective. With examples from disciplines as diverse as abstract mathematics and chemistry to communication studies and literature and writing, I walked away with several ideas to transform my teaching and of how to answer a question I've always struggled with: how can my ordinarily secular physics courses become so much more in light of the Catholic intellectual tradition? *Becoming Beholders* helped me conceive of new ways to help my physics students look at nature and the world and see, as Michael Himes, SJ, puts it so eloquently, the omnipresence of grace—'the love that undergirds all that exists.'"

> Gintaras Duda
> Associate Professor of Physics
> Creighton University
> 2013 Carnegie/CASE US Professor of the Year

"The editors write of the need for spaces where learning has meaning and purpose. Teachers don't create those kinds of spaces with their knowledge of the content or a sophisticated repertoire of pedagogical techniques. They do so with an imagination that sees what and how they teach in a life-enveloping context. That's what these essays showcase. You see how teaching looks when it's infused with a bit of divine perspective."

> Maryellen Weimer
> Professor Emeritus of Teaching and Learning
> Penn State University

Becoming Beholders

Cultivating Sacramental Imagination and Actions in College Classrooms

Edited by

Karen E. Eifler and *Thomas M. Landy*

A Michael Glazier Book

LITURGICAL PRESS

Collegeville, Minnesota

www.litpress.org

A Michael Glazier Book published by Liturgical Press

Excerpts from documents of the Second Vatican Council are from *Vatican Council II: The Basic Sixteen Documents*, by Austin Flannery, OP, © 1996 (Costello Publishing Company, Inc.). Used with permission.

Unless otherwise indicated, Scripture texts in this work are taken from the New Revised Standard Version Bible © 1989, Division of Christian Education of the National Council of the Churches of Christ in the United States of America. Used by permission. All rights reserved.

"Daffodils," from *No Heaven*, by Alicia Suskin Ostriker, © 2005. Reprinted by permission of the University of Pittsburgh Press.

"My Name Is Not 'Those People,'" from *My Name Is Child of God . . . Not "Those People,"* by Julia Dinsmore, © 2007. Reprinted by permission of Augsburg Fortress.

"Finding God in All Things: A Sacramental Worldview and Its Effects," by Michael J. Himes, © 2001. Reprinted by permission of Collegium.

"Practice Makes Reception: The Role of Contemplative Ritual in Approaching Art," by Joanna Ziegler, © 2001. Reprinted by permission of Collegium.

1	2	3	4	5	6	7	8	9

Library of Congress Cataloging-in-Publication Data

Becoming beholders : cultivating sacramental imagination and actions in college classrooms / edited by Karen E. Eifler and Thomas M. Landy.
pages cm
"A Michael Glazier book."
ISBN 978-0-8146-8271-5 — ISBN 978-0-8146-8296-8 (ebook)
1. Catholic universities and colleges. 2. Universities and colleges—Religion. 3. Catholic Church—Education. I. Eifler, Karen E., editor of compilation.

BX922.B43 2014
230.07'32—dc23

2013050527

Contents

Part 3:
Word and Sacrament

Part 4:
In Places of Struggle and Challenge

Part 5:
Appreciating Where We Stand and What Others See

Preface

The last twenty or so years have seen something of a renaissance in terms of attention to the mission of Catholic higher education and the value of preserving it as a distinctive contribution to the American educational landscape. In many ways, the conversation began by encouraging faculty at Catholic colleges and universities to see themselves not as guests on their campuses but as fully invested stewards and collaborators, sharing in the privilege and responsibility of carrying on the unique charism of the place. As the physical presence of vowed religious men and women diminishes on Catholic campuses, the yearning to keep vivid the visions of the institutions' founding orders in the work of education and formation takes on a new imperative for the lay boards and faculty now in place.

What has been missing for most lay faculty is a clear framework that allows teachers of all disciplines to situate their work in the twin animating spirits of Catholic higher education: immersion in the rich, ancient intellectual tradition and sacramental imagination of Catholicism. For indeed, more than anything, sacramentality is a religious *imagination*, offering a perspective on one's discipline and its value. It is a deeply Catholic perspective on the world, one that sees God manifest throughout the natural, created world.

Catholics may be accustomed to think in terms of just seven sacraments, but underlying these seven sacraments is the staggering possibility that God might communicate God's self through the water of baptism, or the oil of anointing, or the bread of the Eucharist. Sacramentality conceives of God as active in, and through, the material world. To some religious sensibilities, that claim might seem blasphemous—for them, the Creator is radically higher than—and different from—a world that might be variously seen as simply fallen or profane. But in terms of a sacramental imagination, learning to see, learning to pay attention— teaching students to become beholders—is a fundamental religious good, and a primary educational task. "Learning to see" means learning to see a thing, or a person, or a social system in all its complexity, as it is. Botanists, poets, historians, nutritionists, and art historians all seek to untangle the webs of their disciplines with students in unique ways, and each field has its own distinct "grammar" and "syntax" to be mastered for genuine understandings to coalesce. While the disciplines and courses taught at Catholic colleges and universities are overwhelmingly, and appropriately, nontheological, approaching that enterprise through a sacramental imagination provides connective tissue that can lend a crucial kind of unity to any course of study. Undertaken in the context of sacramentality, students receive a cohesive, vigorous, and ultimately positive approach to their world, rather than a disconnected amalgam of classes.

But professors cannot teach what they do not know; this is as true of a sacramental worldview as it is of biochemistry. As Catholic higher education confronts tectonic shifts in every conceivable aspect, it behooves us to heed these words of Eric Hoffer, who borrowed substantively from the Rabbi Jesus: "In times of change, the learners will inherit the earth, while the learned will find themselves marvelously equipped for a world that no longer exists."

This book is intended for learners in all disciplines who find themselves, perhaps a bit surprised, embarking on a teaching career at a Catholic college or university. They might be in their first few terms of an assistant professorship, slogging through the usual battle simply to stay a chapter or two ahead of their students. Or they might be well on their road to tenure and pondering the fuzzy question of their "fit with institutional mission," understanding perfectly well how their theology faculty colleagues contribute to the Catholic nature of the place they are establishing a career, but less clear on what they might bring as a teacher of mathematics or psychology. Even with tenure secured, thoughtful veteran faculty can find themselves in the relatively luxurious position of embarking on new phases in their careers as elders of the local community, charged with inculcating a sense of mission and possibility in their young colleagues. Still others grow restless for new ways of approaching the 112th iteration of a survey course.

As student populations change and higher education is increasingly under pressure to prove its value in the face of crushing tuition costs, it is not unusual for later-career academics to reconsider their roles in the classroom. Reflective practitioners look at the heavy-lidded, slouched posture of their students, who seem to be saying "go ahead and teach me; I dare you," and assert influence in the only place they can: their own efforts. Rarely do college faculty members outside schools and departments of education receive formal pedagogical training as part of their doctoral programs. While some may wear this as a badge of distinction, the growing numbers of centers for teaching excellence on campuses across the country suggest that a large percentage of college faculty hunger for resources to help them hone their effectiveness in the classroom. Even more profoundly, they may seek not simply to discharge their teaching responsibilities more competently, but to create for their students and themselves a space of meaning and purpose. This volume is for the latter. Operating under the assumption that Christ is refracted in every academic discipline, we have assembled a collection of essays from nearly every corridor of the academy. Each contributor is a successful teacher within their discipline, and this will come through in their practical pedagogical suggestions. On the one hand, it is clear that these people know their students and the content they were hired to teach through and through. On the other hand, and more saliently, these professors, who comprise the entire faith spectrum—cradle Catholics, members of other and of no religious or spiritual traditions—provide a rich array of answers to crucial questions:

> "OK, I buy the premise that I share some responsibility for participating in the Catholic mission of my institution. How can *what* and *how* I teach contribute to that?"

> "I think I may actually be beginning to grasp what my Vice President for Catholic Mission and Identity means when he talks about a 'sacramental worldview.' If God can be found in all things, that must mean God is present in my literature course. What are the implications for engaging my students in the quest to find God there? How about in my research methods course?"

> "No one ever taught me my discipline with the intention of nurturing a sacramental worldview, so I have no models to draw upon, even though I want to do this thing. And it's well-known that, for better or worse, teachers teach as they were taught—so what are some practical ways I can become bilingual in these secular and religious languages, and help my own students do the same?"

The burgeoning of service learning has made the venerable tenets of Catholic social teaching familiar to many faculty on college and university campuses. Even in our nation's deeply partisan political milieu, the prophetic and Gospel exhortations to feed the hungry and clothe the naked are not hard sells in Catholic institutions. For many newcomers to Catholicism, Catholic social teaching is the perfect "appetizer course," inviting further explorations of the other rich dimensions of Catholic intellectual and spiritual life. Many faculty on Catholic campuses have, with relative ease and even a good deal of relish, incorporated service learning projects into their academic curricula. The prevalence of service learning as a gateway into Catholic traditions is reflected here in the presence of three essays that detail particular service learning projects that have been folded into academic enterprises. The authors of those pieces provide helpful details on how they have provided the intellectual scaffolding to move their students beyond the considerable power of experiential learning into understanding the graced nature of that work, fostering links between the human logic of social justice and the divine nature of looking at those we serve through a sacramental lens.

Each essay was selected for its ability to illuminate in very practical ways Gerard Manley Hopkins's ever-startling insight from his poem "Hurrahing In Harvest" that lends its name to the entire volume: "These things, these things were here and but the beholder/ Wanting; which two when they once meet/The heart rears wings bold and bolder/ And hurls for him, O half hurls earth for him off under his feet." We take it as given that teachers at Catholic colleges and universities are stakeholders in the quest to nurture in their students the capacity to become beholders themselves. Further, we have found teachers who realized that the capacity to do so, like the Divine Presence itself, is always there, wanting only a beholder to see and share it. In other words, the strategies unpacked in these essays are not divine revelations that can only be understood by fellow preternaturally gifted teachers. Rather, each author has unfolded for all readers a particular, straightforward practice for anyone teaching in a Catholic institution.

This is not to suggest that the volume contains recipes that, if followed faithfully, will result in perfect realization of the end goals. Great teaching does have an inchoate sense of grace to it, and each practitioner will render results unique to herself and the content area in which the idea is implemented. But for readers interested in finding assignments, ways of approaching texts or manners of interacting with learners that have been successful in helping nurture a sacramental worldview, this volume will be a useful tool. And while each piece reflects the expertise of a single discipline, readers should also find that most of the ideas are portable to other content areas, with a few disciplinary tweaks. As "all of us are smarter than one of us," it would be useful to read essays as a member of a faculty reading group and weave in a discussion as to how a given pedagogical strategy related in this volume might be adapted in a different department. We recommend doing this over wine and cheese. Still other readers may find the principal value here is simply giving them the language to comprehend what is meant by the daunting exhortation to teach from the perspective of a sacramental worldview, to contribute to the mission of their institution as a chemist, mathematician, or linguist.

Finally, this collection of essays is not intended to promulgate indoctrination or evangelization. It is not religious education, catechesis, or spiritual development. The intellectual integrity of calculus, social sciences, and the humanities is fully respected in each piece, even as the authors suggest that in any area of human learning, there is more going on than meets the eye. Catholic institutions of higher education are in a unique position to tap into that "something more," which we have labeled as sacramentality, the potential finding of God in all things. At the same time, we echo the hope of St. Paul that in exploring our own disciplines through a sacramental lens, it will not lessen our intellectual acuity but rather allow us to approach knowledge, mystery, the Divine Presence "in a manner that is worthy of thinking beings" (Rom 12:1).

Karen E. Eifler and Thomas M. Landy
February 2014

Part 1

The Sacramental Imagination
as a Theological Perspective

Finding God in All Things:
A Sacramental Worldview and Its Effects[1]

Michael J. Himes

What is it that makes Catholicism Catholic? There are, after all, many ways of being Christian: the rich Orthodox traditions, the Anglican tradition, the Lutheran tradition, the Reformed traditions, and the Evangelical traditions, to name the most obvious. All of these traditions have wonderfully wise, insightful, powerful things to tell us about Christianity. And there is the Catholic tradition. What has Catholicism to tell about Christianity? What makes Catholicism Catholic? I suggest that the most important answer to that question is the sacramental principle. I must offer a provisional statement of the sacramental principle, one which will, I hope, become clearer as we go on: the sacramental principle means that what is always and everywhere the case must be noticed, accepted, and celebrated somewhere sometime. What is always and everywhere true must be brought to our attention and be embraced (or rejected) in some concrete experience at some particular time and place.

Talking about God

To explain why I think that this sacramental principle is so important, I must ask your indulgence while I lay some deep foundations. Consider the word "God." "God" is the theological shorthand that we use to

---

[1] This essay first appeared in *As Leaven in the World: Essays on Faith, Vocation, and the Intellectual Life*, ed. Thomas M. Landy (Franklin, WI: Sheed & Ward, 2001).

designate the Mystery which grounds and undergirds all that exists. One could call it something else, if one likes, but "God" is handy. It is short, three letters, one syllable, it has been around for a good while, and it has the advantage of familiarity, so let us use it. If we are talking about God, the ultimate Mystery, that which grounds all that exists, then we are speaking about that which is itself not grounded on or in anything else. The ultimate Mystery is *ultimate*, not itself dependent on another. Everything that exists and is not that ultimate Mystery is the universe. Thus we cannot account for the universe's existence in such way that it is understood as giving something necessary to God.

I teach at Boston College, a Jesuit university. Perhaps for that reason, I think in this context of the familiar Jesuit motto, *Ad majorem Dei gloriam*, "For the greater glory of God." As a description of the motive of our actions, that motto is very powerful and very challenging, indeed. But it ought not be taken as a theological statement, i.e., a statement which tells us something about God. God does not need greater glory; God has tons of glory. God is never going to use up all the glory God has. God has closets full of it. God does not require creatures to tell God that God is great. Presumably God has noticed. God does not need us to glorify God. Why does anything other than God, i.e., the universe, exist? Not so that it can give something to God but so that God can give something to it. The universe (or, as we more often call it in religious language, creation) exists as the recipient of a gift.

What is it that God, the ultimate Mystery, gives to creation, the universe whose being is grounded in that Mystery? There are only two possibilities: either God gives something other than God, which would simply be more of the universe, another creature, or God gives God. Here is the great Christian claim about the universe's origin in Mystery: creation exists so that God can give God's self to it. Creation exists so that God can communicate God's self to creation. That gift of self is what is meant by *agape*, love. Creation exists because it is the object of love. Love, agape, is the only ground for its existence. So deep is this claim in the Christian tradition that Christianity actually insists that it is the least wrong way to understand what we mean by the Mystery which grounds and surrounds all that exists.

I tell beginning students that theology, certainly Christian theology, is always done between two poles. One pole is probably best summed up by Ludwig Wittgenstein. The final proposition in the only book published by Wittgenstein during his lifetime, the *Tractatus Logico-Philosophicus* (you may have seen the film) is arguably the most famous single sentence

in twentieth-century philosophy: "of that about which we can say nothing, let us be silent." If I may paraphrase less elegantly, "if you don't
know what you're talking about, shut up." That is an enormously important religious counsel. If God is Mystery, then let us not natter on
about God like we know what we are talking about.

A great problem of religious language and imagery is that we use it
too confidently. We speak as if what we are talking about—God—is
perfectly clear and fully intelligible. Any language about God which is
perfectly clear is certainly wrong. We are, after all, daring to speak about
ultimate Mystery, and whatever we say, we must not under pain of
blasphemy lose a profound sense of awe before the Mystery that undergirds all that exists. The first commandment of the Decalogue in both
Exodus and Deuteronomy is not to fabricate any image of God: "I am
the Lord, your God, you shall have no strange gods before me; you shall
make no graven images of me." That is a commandment to be taken to
heart by all religiously interested people, because it counsels against the
too easy idolatry of religious language. For we all make images of God.
For several pages now I have been referring to "God," yet I suspect that
no one reading this has stopped to ask, "Who is he talking about?" We
begin with some idea of what the word means or might mean. When
I say the word "God," something goes on in your mind. Now, however
wonderful, however deep, rich, powerful, consoling, however philosophically informed, however metaphysically precise, however traditionally grounded, however scripturally sound, however magisterially
orthodox, whatever that idea in your mind is, it is not God. And that is
the most important thing to know about God: that what you have in
your mind when you hear or speak the word "God" is an image of God,
and the first commandment is against the making of images of God.
So we must be very cautious not to confuse what we think when we hear
or speak the word "God," with God.

The second commandment of the Decalogue, of course, flows directly
from the first. The second commandment, as you recall, is, "You shall not
take the name of the Lord your God in vain." We have done terrible things
to this commandment. We have diminished it into a commandment
against profanity: "Don't use bad language." (Should you be asked what
Himes's position is on profanity, you can answer that I am against it. But
I strongly suspect that Moses had more on his mind at Sinai than how
colorfully the Israelites were swearing at the foot of the mountain.)

The second commandment is not about profanity. It states the obvious
consequence of the first commandment: do not take the name of God in

vain. Do not talk about God like you know what you are talking about. Far from a commandment against profanity, it is a warning against over-confident theology and too-simple preaching. We need to be very, very cautious about how we use the word "God" because, much more often than not, we use it in vain. If one speaks of Mystery, one must acknowledge that finally one does not know what one is talking about. Wittgenstein's caution is immensely important.

This caution, however, must be balanced by another pole. And the statement of that other pole I borrow from T. S. Eliot. (Eliot was talking about poetry, but I think I can borrow the statement and apply it to religious language without distorting it too much.) Eliot wrote that there are some things about which we can say nothing and before which we dare not keep silent. There are some things about which we know in advance that whatever we say will ultimately be inadequate. But these issues that are so important, so crucial, that we dare not say nothing. Let me offer an image taken from a Woody Allen film. (I am a New Yorker, indeed, a Brooklynite, by origin. All New Yorkers have an immediate affinity with Woody Allen films. Elsewhere people think Woody Allen makes comedies; New Yorkers know Woody Allen makes documentaries. He sets up a camera on the Upper West Side and films what is going on. The rest of the world thinks it is funny; New Yorkers know it is life.)

In one of his films, *Manhattan*, Allen plays a man in love with a younger woman. One night, while on a horse and carriage ride, the woman asks him if he loves her. The Allen character answers yes, but immediately catches himself and adds "I llllllove you. No, no. I looooove you." He proceeds to go through a dozen different ways of saying precisely the same three words. Why? The point of the scene is, I think, that the moment he says those three words, "I love you," he knows how hopelessly inadequate they are. They are such a cliché, so banal. They have been so used and misused and overused in the English language that to say "I love you" does not begin to convey what this man wants to say to that woman. Were Wittgenstein looking over Allen's script, he would have advised him to end the film at that point. If it cannot be said, be silent. If you do not know how something can be said correctly, do not say it. But Eliot wisely knows that there are some things that are so important you dare not keep silent. You know that you cannot say, "I love you," in any way that is adequate, but you also know that you cannot simply be silent, that you have to try to say something, however badly. There are those things so important that one cannot be silent about them. This is preeminently true when we speak of God.

At this point I should add a caution. When the Christian tradition speaks of God, it does not mean a great big person out there somewhere, older, wiser, and stronger than you and I. That is Zeus, not God. One can baptize Zeus, but Zeus always remains Zeus. A baptized Zeus is not what a Christian means when he or she talks about God. I often tell students that to demonstrate that the Christian statements about God are ways of answering the question, "Do you think that there are meaning, purpose, and direction to your life, and do you think that you are not the one who decides that meaning, purpose, and direction?" That question, however it is answered, is the question of God. Does my life have meaning, and if so, do I create and impose that meaning or do I discover it? How you answer that question is how you answer the God question. It is an unavoidable question. One cannot dismiss it as too difficult or impossible of final and sufficient resolution and so decline to ask it. One cannot not ask that question, implicitly or explicitly. It cannot be answered finally, but it is too impossible not to answer it in some way. That is where we find ourselves in religious language, language about Mystery. Theology, like all religious language, is caught between Wittgenstein's caution and Eliot's insight.

How, then, do we talk about God, recognizing that we cannot speak of God adequately but must say something? We do what the great users of language, poets, do when trying to say the unsayable: we pile up metaphors. Let me use my favorite example of this from Shakespeare, certainly by anyone's standard a great user of language. I call to your recollection act 5, scene 5 of *Macbeth*. Macbeth's world is falling apart. The English and the Scottish rebels are drawing closer to Dunsinane. As Macbeth gives his frantic orders for defending the castle, there comes a scream from offstage. To learn the cause of the cry he sends his servant who shortly returns and announces, "The queen, my lord, is dead." Then Shakespeare does what he often does at such moments in his plays: he has a character say that he cannot speak about the crisis. For example, Hamlet dies saying that "the rest is silence." Othello kills himself while talking about an irrelevant action long ago in Aleppo. King Lear's last words dissolve into sound and rhythm.

When Macbeth hears of the death of his wife, he says, more to himself than to his servant, "She should have died hereafter;/ There would have been a time for such a word." There are no words for Lady Macbeth's death, at least not at that moment. He cannot talk about it. But, of course, he does. He launches into his great soliloquy: "Tomorrow, and tomorrow, and tomorrow / Creeps in this petty pace from day to day . . ." And we come to the extraordinary moment when Macbeth says, "Life is . . ." Realize what the death of this woman means to this man. She was not only his wife; she was the only other human being who shares the guilt, the only other person who knows all the horror—and she is gone. Macbeth is now utterly alone, alone as few, if any, are ever alone. So the loneliest human being in the world is about to tell us what life is like for him. How does he do it? He gives us three metaphors. "Life's but a walking shadow." A shadow, nothing, merely the absence of light. But a walking shadow—animated nothingness. Hold that image in mind. Shift your angle of vision, as it were. Life is also "a poor player/ That struts and frets his hour upon the stage/ And then is heard no more." A bad actor—Shakespeare had probably known many. An actor who gets onstage and flubs his lines and muffs his gestures and bumps into the props. The audience wants him to get off so that the play can go on; he exits and they forget him.

Hold that image in mind, too. Shift your perspective to still another angle. Life is "a tale/ Told by an idiot, full of sound and fury,/ Signifying nothing." I suspect that most of us, if not all, have had the experience of being harangued by someone who was overwrought and out of control, who spluttered on about—what? Something, nothing, whatever it was, we did not understand it. A moment of pure frustration. A tale full of sound and fury told by an idiot. (Teachers have probably had such experiences. Believe me, anyone who has spent any time in ministry knows what it is like to be buttonholed by someone who carries on at length about something that apparently means a great deal to him or her and that remains thoroughly impenetrable to the captive listener.) Three images. Draw out the lines of those three perspectives and, where they intersect, that is how life looks to the loneliest human being on earth. When trying to say the unsayable, we pile metaphor on metaphor on metaphor. Shakespeare, of course, does it better than the rest of us.

That is precisely what we do in religious language when we try to speak about God. And so we say that God is creator, judge, parent, spouse, shepherd, king, lawgiver, rock, leader in battle, savior, and on and on. We pile image on image on image on image, metaphor after metaphor after metaphor. But there must be some control on these metaphors. After all, some ways of describing God are simply abhorrent to the Christian tradition, e.g., God is evil, or God is hatred. Is there some fundamental metaphor for God according to the Christian tradition which can provide a guideline for talking about God, a metaphor with which all other metaphors must be in accord in order to be deemed acceptable? Granted, no way of talking about God is the fully adequate way, so is there some way of talking about God that is less hopelessly inadequate than other ways? The Christian tradition says yes. There is a fundamental metaphor for talking about God with which all the other metaphors we use for God must fit. (I suspect, by the way, that this idea of a fundamental metaphor for ultimate Mystery is applicable to all great religious traditions, but at this moment we are interested in Christianity, especially in its Catholic form.) The fundamental metaphor for God in the Christian tradition is suggested over and over again in the New Testament but finds its clearest, sharpest, most succinct statement in one of the last documents of the New Testament collection written, what we call the First Letter of John, at 4:8 and again at 16: "God is love."

A Fundamental Metaphor for God

But this love which is offered as the fundamental metaphor for God is a peculiar kind of love, *agape*. This is not the usual Greek word for "love" in the New Testament era. That would be *eros*, a perfectly fine word and a marvelous concept, but not the one which early Christians chose as the metaphor for the ultimate Mystery. *Eros* is a love that seeks satisfaction from the person or thing loved. Thus it clearly includes what most of us think of first when we hear of erotic love, i.e., sexual love. But it also means what we refer to in English when we say "I love that movie" or "I love playing tennis." These are instances of what the Greek-speaking world called erotic love because the lover finds satisfaction and pleasure in that which is loved. There is certainly nothing wrong with *eros*; it is simply something other than *agape*. *Agape* is love to which satisfaction is irrelevant. The lover seeks nothing from the beloved, not even gratitude. The lover simply gives the lover's self to the beloved. Rather than "love," which has become a word with so many (probably too many) uses in English, I prefer to translate *agape* as "self-gift," the gift of the self to the other asking nothing in response. *Agape* is pure gift of self to the other. This is what the Christian tradition claims is the least wrong metaphor for God.

The whole Christian doctrinal tradition is an expansion of this fundamental claim, that God, the ultimate Mystery which undergirds the existence of all that is, is least wrongly thought of as pure and perfect self-gift. I might exemplify this at great length, but you will be thrilled to know I shall not. But we should note that, while the fundamental Christian metaphor for God is *agape*, pure other-directed love, "love" is not the name of a person but rather of a relationship among persons. So we are saying that the least wrong way to think about God, the foundational mystery that grounds and surrounds all that exists, is not first and foremost as a person but as a relationship. You may well think that this is a bizarre claim, and in many ways it is. But I am sure that it is scarcely a claim which you have not heard before, although perhaps not in quite these words. In fact, among Christians—certainly Catholic Christians— we make this claim all the time. We often affirm that we do or say something "in the name of the Father and of the Son and of the Holy Spirit." When we do so, we assert that God is to be thought of first not as "the one," but as the relatedness of "the three." The central point of the doctrine of the trinity is that God is least wrongly understood as a relationship, as an eternal explosion of love.

When he wrote *De Trinitate*, Saint Augustine acknowledged that the church had language for the Trinity from the New Testament itself. At the end of the Gospel of Saint Matthew (28:19), we find the command to go out and baptize all nations "in the name of the Father and of the Son and of the Holy Spirit." But Augustine suggested that however biblically rooted such language may be, it is not especially helpful in trying to show the meaning of the Trinity for people's lives. After all, he reasoned, if we are created in the image and likeness of God and God is Triune, then ought we not be able to see traces of the Trinity in our own experience? So he set out to find alternate terminology that might better convey the meaning of the Trinity. He came up with two sets of terms that he seems to have particularly liked, and I must confess I like them too.

Augustine suggested that perhaps more useful for teaching and preaching than "Father, Son, Spirit," might be "Giver, Recipient, and Gift given," or as yet another alternative, "Lover, Beloved, and the Love between them." This is what Christians mean when they talk about God: from all eternity the Mystery at the root of all that exists is endless self-gift, endless outpouring of self; for all eternity the Mystery is endless acceptance of the gift of that outpouring and rejoicing in it; and for all eternity the Mystery is the outpouring. God is the Lover, the Beloved, and the Love between them, the Giver, the Recipient and the Gift given. When we use the word "God," the Mystery that grounds and surrounds all that exists, we speak of the infinite and eternal explosion of self-gift.

That allows me to pose another question: why does God create? Think with me for a moment about the question that Martin Heidegger maintained was the beginning of all metaphysics, i.e., of all accounts of how things finally fit together: why is there being rather than nothing? There are many ways in which that question has been answered, many metaphysical ways. The Christian tradition's answer, as I understand it, is, "Because it is loved." The reason that anything exists is that it is the object of love. All things that are, are loved into being. The fundamental ground for anything is that it is called into being because God loves it. As I noted earlier, the universe gives nothing to God, rather God gives something to it, namely, God's self. Why? Because God gets a kick out of it. Because that what God is like: overflowing love. Please notice: I am speaking about the reason *anything* exists, not only *anyone*. This overflowing love is the reason not only for your existence and mine but for the existence of the chair on which you are sitting and the pen you are holding, the existence of the leaves on the trees and your pet cat and your favorite rhododendron and the farthest supernova. It is the ground of the existence of the universe, everything that ever has, ever will, or ever can exist. Why does anything exist rather than nothing, in Heidegger's question? The Christian tradition's answer is because it is loved.

What makes us unique as human beings (at least, as far as we know) is that we are the point in creation that can acknowledge that we are infinitely loved and either accept or reject it. We can embrace being loved or deny and turn away from it. This podium at which I am standing cannot know that it is loved; it cannot accept or refuse being loved. It is, however, as truly and perfectly loved as I am. Please notice: everything is loved perfectly because God, being God, does nothing imperfectly. God is God and therefore always acts in a Godlike way, which is to say, God does everything perfectly. God does not love a little today and a bit more tomorrow and perhaps a bit less the day after. It is simply not the case that God loved you on Tuesday, but then on Wednesday you sinned, so God loved you less, but then on Thursday you repented, so God loves you again. That is pure mythology. God has been reduced to Zeus or Odin. God loves everything in a Godlike way, perfectly, completely, one hundred percent. Not every creature can know and accept this love. The podium is loved perfectly, and so is Himes. The difference is that Himes knows it and the podium does not. Sometimes Himes accepts it, and sometimes, tragically, he refuses it. But God remains God.

Nothing you can do can make God not love you. If there were, then you would be more powerful than God in that you could cause God to change. I sometimes use this image when I preach. It ruffles some feathers, but feather-ruffling is by no means a bad thing to do in the pulpit. Let me dare to make a claim about how things look from God's perspective: from God's point of view, there is no difference between Mary and Satan; God loves them both perfectly. The difference is on the side of the two creatures: Mary is thrilled and Satan hates it. In the *Summa Contra*

Gentiles, Saint Thomas Aquinas raises a question: if God is everywhere, is God in hell? His answer is that, indeed, God is in hell. Of course, his next question is, "And what is God doing there?" Thomas's answer is that God is in hell loving the damned. The damned may not love God, but the damned cannot make God not love them. Since perfect love—which is the least wrong metaphor for God—is the reason for our being, the opposite of being loved by God is not damnation, but nonbeing. Not to be loved by God is not to exist. Everything that is, to the extent that it is, is loved.

The Sacramental Principle

Let me introduce another piece of theological shorthand: grace. "Grace" is the word by which we traditionally designate the *agape* of God outside the Trinity, the *agape* of God calling all things into being. In Christian theology grace is the self-giving of God outside the Trinity bringing all things into being. With the introduction of that word, I want to turn our attention to a difficulty. Consideration of the difficulty for a moment will lead us back to the sacramental principle. If the agapic love of God or grace is omnipresent, if everything is loved or engraced, if everything we are and everything we encounter is rooted in grace, grace may go unnoticed. What is omnipresent is more often than not unnoticed. For example, the whole time you have been reading this, you have been blinking. Now, unless this essay has been preternaturally boring, you have not been counting your blinks. After all, who thinks about blinking?

This example first struck me a few years ago when I was hit with a bout of Bell's palsy. The left side of my face froze, and one of the consequences was that my left eye could not blink. Throughout the day, I had periodically to hold my left eyelid down, and at night I taped the eye shut. One becomes very conscious of blinking when one cannot do it. I never thought about it at all until Bell's palsy called my attention to it. What one does all the time, one seldom, if ever, thinks about. What is always there gets little or no attention. You never think about the oxygen in a room until the air starts to become stale. You do not think about your heart beating, although if it stopped, we would notice as you slump to the floor. So if grace is omnipresent, grace is likely to go unnoticed. We require occasions when grace is called to our attention, when it is made concrete for us, when that which is always the case is made present in such a way that we cannot help but notice it and may either accept or

reject it and, if we accept it, celebrate it. Let me remind you of my pre-
liminary description of what I called the sacramental principle: that
which is always and everywhere the case must be noticed, accepted, and
celebrated somewhere, sometime.

In the Catholic tradition we call the occasions when grace is made
effectively present for us sacraments. I am not referring here primarily
to the seven great public rituals that Catholics celebrate (although I am
by no means excluding them). By "sacrament" I mean any person, place,
thing or event, any sight, sound, taste, touch, or smell that causes us to
notice the love which supports all that exists, that undergirds your being
and mine and the being of everything about us. How many such sacraments are there? The number is virtually infinite, as many as there are
things in the universe. There is nothing that cannot be a sacrament,
absolutely nothing—even, as St. Augustine observed, sin. Within the
context of repentance, sin can become an occasion when one discovers
how deeply loved one is. This is what he meant by calling the sin of
Adam and Eve *felix culpa*, a happy fault, a phrase which the church still
sings in the Easter Proclamation every Holy Saturday. There is nothing
that cannot become a sacrament for someone, absolutely nothing.

We all have our personal sacraments. For all of you who are married,
I hope that one of the deepest, richest, most profound experiences of the
fundamental love which undergirds being is your spouse. For those who
are parents, I hope that your children are such experiences. To your
neighbors they may be the little pests who live next door, but to you they
are sacraments. We all have our own array of sacraments that are absolutely necessary for us.

This, by the way, is an important element in Catholic liturgy. The
fundamental principle of Catholic liturgy is that everything and the
kitchen sink have a place within it. Why? Because everything is potentially sacred. Everything is engraced. So everything is fair game for
liturgy. So we sing, we dance, we parade, we wave banners, we ring
bells, we play organs, we blow horns, we sound trumpets, and sometimes, we are still and silent. We eat, we drink, we bathe you in water,
we pour oil on you, we put you to bed when you get married and into
the earth when you die. We waft incense, we hang paintings, we put up
mosaics, we erect statues, we construct extraordinary buildings and
illumine them through stained glass. We appeal to sight, sound, taste,
touch, and smell. Historically the principle on which the liturgy oper-
ated was, "If it works, throw it in." The reason for such inclusiveness is
the deep Catholic conviction that nothing is by definition profane. Everything is potentially sacramental.

The great nineteenth-century English Jesuit poet Gerard Manley Hopkins has an especially beautiful phrase for this. It is a line in one of his best-known and most frequently anthologized poems, "Hurrahing in Harvest." At the time of the poem, Hopkins was teaching at a Jesuit boys' school in Wales. At the opening of the poem it is the fall and Hopkins is disheartened by the disappearance of the summer's beauty and the coming onset of winter. But he begins to consider the clouds scudding across the sky, the way the wind blows off the Irish Sea at that time of year in Wales, the joy of people bringing in the harvest and the changing color of the leaves. How beautiful it all is, yet he does not notice it while he worries about what is gone and dreads what has not come. All the while, he fails to notice what is here at the moment. In what is, in my opinion, the single most beautiful statement in English of the Catholic sacramental principle (and Hopkins was Catholic to the tips of his fingers), the poet wrote, "These things, these things were here and but the beholder/ Wanting." The leaves have not suddenly changed their colors at that moment, nor has the sky been transformed. All that beauty was already there. What changed? Hopkins. The splendor was there, but he did not notice it. He has become a beholder and sees what is there to be seen. The whole Catholic sacramental life is a training to be beholders. Catholic liturgy is a lifelong pedagogy to bring us to see what is there, to behold what is always present, in the conviction that if we truly see and fully appreciate what is there, whether we use the language or not, we will be encountering grace. We will see the love which undergirds all that exists.

Those who have been fortunate to have seen the film *Babette's Feast* might recall how the little band of Lutheran sectarians learn to appreciate what has been placed there before them by the French chef, Babette. They learn to savor the taste, the aroma, the color of the food and drink, and in discovering the goodness of the physical world are led to reconciliation with one another. At the end of the extraordinary meal, they go outside into the little square of the village where they have stood countless times. They look up at the stars, join hands and begin to sing. At one marvelous, closing moment, one of the two elderly sisters says to the other, "The stars look very close tonight," and the other replies, "Maybe they are every night." That night they could see what was there every night because Babette's feast had made them beholders. That is what sacramentality does.

But what has all this to do with education and the intellectual's vocation? As a Catholic and an educator, I think that it may suggest a very important perspective on education. If we accept what I have said about the sacramental principle, then anything that awakens, enlivens, and expands the imagination, opens the vision, enriches the sensitivity of any human being is a religious act. Although we may not use this language, education is or can be training in sacramental beholding.

At the very beginning of the century just ended, one of the most profoundly Catholic people of the twentieth century, Baron Friedrich von Hügel was invited to give a talk to a Christian students' association at Oxford. (Despite the Austrian name he was, in fact, an Englishman. His father had been an Austrian and a baron of the Holy Roman Empire, but his mother was a Scot. He was brought up in England and English was his first language.) In his lecture to this group of presumably earnest Christian students, von Hügel spoke of asceticism, self-discipline, as a traditionally important part of the Christian life. He asked a rhetorical question: who is the most striking example of asceticism in the nineteenth century, which had just ended? I suspect that his answer must have shocked those sober young Christian gentlemen in Oxford, for he said that he thought, beyond doubt, the great example of asceticism in the nineteenth century had been Charles Darwin. Darwin, according to von Hügel, had with immense discipline, over a long period of time, subordinated his extraordinarily keen, powerful intellect and astonishing energy to the painstaking observation of the varieties of barnacles and the shapes of pigeons' bills. With astonishing clarity and intensity, Darwin had forced himself to observe what was there. And that, claimed von Hügel, is what asceticism is all about. Asceticism is not self-denial in order to please a mildly sadistic deity. Its goal is to discipline oneself sufficiently so that one can move beyond one's hopes, dreams, fears, wants, and expectations to see what is, in fact, there.

Asceticism is a training to see reality, not what I expect, hope, or fear to see. I have often told students that the point of asceticism is to stop looking in the mirror long enough that one might look out the window, to stop gazing at oneself long enough to see something else. The Catholic conviction is that if we see what is there to be seen, we will discover grace, the love that undergirds all that exists. The ascetic beholds the omnipresence of grace.

Where do people today learn that kind of self-discipline? There are, I think, many ways in which life teaches us asceticism. Marriage is a splendid school of self-discipline for those who live it well and wisely, as is parenthood. Paying off the mortgage and managing one's credit cards can be excellent paths of ascetical training. They are all ways of coming to grips with what is there, not what we would like to be there. And certainly one of the most rigorous and effective ways of self-discipline is science. Following von Hügel's claim about Darwin, I suggest that there is a profoundly sacramental dimension to all the sciences because they are all a form of training in intellectual self-discipline. After all, we often call our fields of study "disciplines." When we study anything, we discipline ourselves.

Anything that expands the imagination, enriches the vision, liberates the will, frees the vision, and disciplines the attention, is a profoundly religious act. Indeed, so convinced am I of this that I could have come at this same point from an entirely different angle from the way I have done so thus far. I could have developed this same conclusion starting from a consideration of what Christians mean by the incarnation. Catholics try to hold this belief radically, insisting that in Christ, God does not merely seem to be human or act in a human way, but has *become* human. In the words of an ancient hymn quoted in Philippians 2:6-11, he has become human as all human beings are human, that he is like us in all things except sin.

The Catholic tradition has recognized that if this radical claim of the incarnation is true, then you and I and God share humanity in common! Therefore, to become like God, we should be as fully human as we can. Thus whatever enriches and deepens our humanity, whatever makes us braver, wiser, more intelligent, more responsible, freer, more loving, makes us holy, i.e., like God. Thus education, which certainly should aim at making human beings braver, wiser, more intelligent, more responsible, freer, and more loving, is a work of sanctification. This is why the Christian community has always been involved in education and not only in catechetics. A good Catholic university or college is not a place where we allow people to study mathematics or history or literature so that we can get them to sit through a religion course. We do not admit people to the business school so that we can require them to take a minimum number of credits in theology. Any and every field of study is ultimately religious in nature if everything rests on grace and humanity is shared with God in Christ.

This sacramental conviction shapes Catholicism at its best. Of course, Catholicism is not always at its best. It therefore does not always act in accord with its sacramental vision. But were we all to require ourselves to live up to our best vision all the time, who of us would have gotten out of bed this morning? Still, at its best and wisest, Catholicism is shaped by the conviction that grace lies at the root of all reality. And if that conviction is true, all the humanities as well as all the sciences become religious enterprises.

Let me offer a closing image. In the *Divine Comedy*, you will recall that Dante allots hell, purgatory, and heaven thirty-three cantos each. The whole of the great poem is completed with a hundredth canto in which Dante attempts to do what Wittgenstein would have told him he should not even try, to describe to the reader the vision of God. In the ninety-ninth canto of the poem, the thirty-third of the *Paradiso*, Beatrice has conducted Dante to the highest circle of heaven. She points him toward Bernard of Clairvaux, a symbol of all that was richest and best in the spiritual tradition of the Middle Ages. Looking in awe at Bernard, Dante realizes that Bernard is gazing steadily across at someone else, and he follows Bernard's gaze to Mary. And he is overwhelmed with the sight of Mary until he sees that she has her look fixed steadily upward. Dante follows Mary's glance and beholds at the end of canto 99 the vision of God. In canto 100, he tries to do the undoable. Needless to say he fails, but Dante's failures are more interesting than almost anyone else's successes. He says that he was dazzled by a light which blinds him initially. But as the intense light burns his eyes, it heals them so that he begins to discern that the light is actually the interaction of three concentric globes of three colors, his image for the Trinity. As his eyes were simultaneously seared and strengthened, he could look into the very depth of the light, and there he saw one exactly like himself. In one of the greatest statements of the Catholic humanist tradition, Dante saw that, as a result of the incarnation, at the heart of God is one like him and you and me. And so, in the great final line of the great poem, the line to which the whole *Divine Comedy* has been leading, his recognition of "*l'amor che move il sole e l'altre stelle*," "the love that moves the sun and other stars." This is Dante's statement of the sacramental principle: the universe, the sun and all the stars, is grounded and governed by love. It exists because of infinite self-gift. That is what enlivens the Catholic tradition at its best.

Detectives of Grace in the Adventures of Scholarship

James Corkery, SJ

The Ireland in which I grew up was more attuned to invisible realities than to visible ones. A West of Ireland sky is an ever-changing canvas, with rolling clouds—now hiding the sun, now letting it peep through—so that the landscape, for an instant bathed in splendour, is suddenly dimmed by shadow. "Now you see me, now you don't," this world flirtatiously seems to taunt, tantalising as a young woman/man newly alive to her/his charms and eager to bestow them one minute, only to withdraw them the next. The sense of mystery is heightened—of things seen, yet unseen, reached, yet beyond reach—and the heart gasps for the object of its longing disclosed to it in a scarce-glimpsed hope. This is painful and lovely, present and elusive, here and beyond. And it pulls us outside of ourselves—into the realm of *wonder*.

There is a kind of imagination that sees beyond *visibles*. There are certain circumstances and settings that, like the Ireland I just described, tilt one's vision in a more mystery-oriented direction. People in sailboats, Bertrand Russell once observed, find it easier to believe in God than people in motor boats. I am not (yet, anyway!) speaking about belief in *God* here, but I do agree with Russell that closeness to nature can heighten people's sensitivity to the unpredictable, to the uncontrollable, to the mysterious. Nonetheless I have always also been convinced that, just as in premodern societies, so too in modern and even in postmodern ones, it is possible to see beyond surfaces and pick up the deeper message that things send out. This is the case even when immersed in technology (and surrounded by positivist ways of thinking). Indeed, technology itself can make us marvel and wonder more! Not so, however, if it is assimilated and adapted to uncritically! That is why the thought-forms to which it gives rise can benefit from engagement with another way of seeing the world, one that takes us away from a functional or strategic pattern of relating—away, that is, from the "McDonaldization" (marked by efficiency, calculability, predictability, and control)[1] that tends to hold sway if technology is left entirely to its own devices—into spaces where surprise and *un*predictability may still have their chance in a landscape of unscripted exchanges.[2]

The way of seeing I have in mind here is referred to by Catholic writers as the "sacramental imagination." It lies behind the Catholic attempt to understand the human world in its many dimensions—beyond the directly religious—and it embodies the spirit that animates its enthusiasm to probe the depths of things. My task here is to say something about how it may enrich our scholarly lives as we pursue our subjects through sharing their gems (that's teaching!) and through uncovering their hidden depths (that's research!). I hope to shed some light on how these scholarly ventures—adventures!—can be enhanced by this lively vision of things that inspires Catholic Christianity to explore the entire world.

A Way of Seeing, A Vision of Things

Yoko Ogawa, in her stunning novel *The Housekeeper and the Professor* (2003), takes her readers to the world behind the beauty of mathematics through the charming story of the relationship between a young housekeeper and her son with a Professor, who lives (as the result of an accident) with only eighty minutes of short-term memory. As they care for him, and he shares mathematical marvels with them, a world opens up—sometimes referred to by the Professor as "the truth" (p. 115) or as "God's notebook" (p. 153)—that is detected behind the beauties of mathematics, a world that is not visible (the Professor, pointing to his chest, often says "it's in here" [p. 3, p. 115]) but that *is* real. At one point, having taught the housekeeper that the (inevitably limited and two-dimensional) line-segment that she draws merely gives expression to the real line that is

---

[1] See John Drane, *The McDonaldization of the Church* (London: Darton, Longman & Todd, 1999), 28–29.

[2] See Richard R. Gaillardetz, *Transforming Our Days* (New York: Crossroad, 2000), esp. 57–61.

eternal, one-dimensioned, and beyond the power of any segment to capture, he leaves her reflecting thus:

> As I mopped the office floor, my mind churning with worries about Root, I realized how much I needed this eternal truth that the Professor had described. *I needed the sense that this invisible world was somehow propping up the visible one*, that this one, true line extended infinitely, without width or area, confidently piercing through the shadows. Somehow, this line would help me find peace.[3]

The early Fathers of the Christian Church (and some Mothers, too, we are now more aware), writers who followed not long after Christianity's period of infancy, were animated by the desire to pass from the visible to the invisible (*per visibilium ad invisibilium*). This desire had roots mostly in their belief that God was truly present in Jesus—the invisible in the visible: Christianity's doctrine of the incarnation. They believed that the eternal had decisively burst in upon the temporal because, after Jesus' ignominious death, God had raised him up: Christianity's doctrine of the resurrection. Many of these early Christian writers used Platonism and (Plotinian) Neoplatonism to give density to their arguments. They drew on persuasion and poetry to fire the imaginations of their listeners, to guide them into a vision of things that could give them hope amid the ordinary, color amid the monochrome. Thus the author of *1 Clement* (in #24 of this letter addressed to the Corinthians around AD 80) invited his readers to step closer to the resurrection of Jesus through observing resurrection in nature:

> Let us consider, beloved, the kind of resurrection that occurs at regular intervals. Day and night give us examples of resurrection. The night sleeps, the day rises; the day departs, the night comes on. Let us take the crops. The sowing—how and in what manner does it take place? The sower goes out and puts each of the seeds into the soil: when they fall on the soil, they are dry and bare, and decay. But once they have decayed, the Master's wondrous Providence makes them rise, and each one increases and brings forth multiple fruit.

---

[3] Yoko Ogawa, *The Housekeeper and the Professor*, trans. Stephen Snyder (London: Vintage Books, 2010; original Japanese 2003), 116. Italics mine. (The reference to "Root" is to her son.)

Or Minucius Felix, a lawyer, writing about AD 226 (see *Octavius* 34:11-12) said:

> See, too, how for our consolation all nature suggests the future resurrection. The sun sinks down, but is reborn. The stars go out, but return again. Flowers die, but come to life again. After their decay shrubs put forth leaves again; not unless seeds decay does their strength return. A body in the grave is like the trees in winter: They hide their sap under a deceptive dryness. Why are you in haste for it to revive and return, while yet the winter is raw? We must await even the spring of the body.

These words remind me of the unforgettable scene in the film *Dr. Zhivago*, in which the dreariness of winter is replaced by the growth-bursts and colour-bursts of spring. The quotations from Clement and Minucius Felix indicate something of their *sacramental* view of the world, fed by what God has done in the human life and activity of Jesus. They speak of going (taking the incarnate Christ as their cue) from the visible to the invisible. And their manner of thinking has continued, with adaptations, in a number of Christian spiritual traditions, not least the Franciscan. Francis, a "poet of the ontological" (thus Leonardo Boff), knew how to find God's traces in the created realities of the world. His seventh successor, St Bonaventure, expressed the Franciscan vision in these words: *hoc totum quod fecit fuit gratia* (all this that he made was grace). Indeed, Bonaventure grasped that creation itself was not only God's free gift but that it was also God's most excellent "medium" for making the divine self available and generously present in the world. God creates with a view to self-communication: this self-communication is "grace" (thus Karl Rahner, centuries later), mediated to us through God's "disguised" (alloyed) presence in the world—in things, events, and persons. I hinted already, in the title I gave to this essay, of the possibility that we might become "detectives" of this mediated presence of God through our scholarly adventures (and I shall have more to say about this shortly). This presence-of-God-in-the-world is what the Christian word "grace" really refers to; and it occurs *sacramentally* as the invisible becomes visible in the created realities round about us.[4] From his

[4] See Michael Leach, *Why Stay Catholic? Unexpected Answers to a Life-Changing Question* (Chicago: Loyola Press, 2011), 4: "A sacrament points to and opens what is invisible but real." (Needless to say, there are sacraments with a big S—Catholicism's seven, for example—but also countless sacraments with a small s).

Catholic viewpoint (I am aware that there are others), Michael Leach expresses it thus:

> Catholicism is about seeing what the eyes cannot see and under-standing what is at the heart of things: truth, love, mercy, goodness, beauty, harmony, humility, compassion, gratitude, joy, peace, salvation. *It's about seeing the ordinary and perceiving the extraordinary at the same time*: the midnight glow of Easter candles that are, in truth, a thousand points of light; the stories of saints, the saga of sinners, and the rumours of angels that inspire and heal us. "It is only with the heart that one sees rightly," wrote Antoine de Saint-Exupery. "What is essential is invisible to the eye."[5]

All this is true, but there must be "controls" lest the vision become naïve and blind to what Leonardo Boff has called "dis-grace" in our world. For this reason, while holding fast to the great possibilities for God's presence in the human world—for grace, that is—we must attend also to what is needed for a reliable discerning of this presence.

Remaining Vigilant While Seeing Sacramentally

The sacramental perspective is not naïve, finding traces of God every-where while blinding itself to injustice and evil. Many who take their inspiration from Francis of Assisi, for all their appreciation of the pres-ence and traceability of God in created reality, are not naïve about the need to discern this presence wisely. A contemporary Franciscan writer, Leonardo Boff, situated as he is amid the glaring social injustices of his native Brazil, is well aware that, at the level of concrete history, created realities can be manipulated to become bearers not of the traces of God, but of what is out-of-step with God's intent for the human world. Boff speaks beautifully, but with nuance, about the reality and presence of grace in the world:

> We can never talk about grace in itself because it shows up in this particular thing or that particular thing. It has a sacramental struc-ture, if we do not restrict the term "sacrament" to the seven chief signs of faith usually considered under that term. Here that term refers to all the mediations through which we arrive at God and his love. In other words, there are things, situations, persons, cultural

---

[5] Ibid., 3–4 (italics mine).

data, and relationships that may be grace-filled or not, that may carry grace or not, that may be sacraments of grace or not.

Grace is not something isolated in itself that stands apart from other things. Grace is a mode of being that things take on when they come into contact with the love of God and are suffused with his mystery. In that sense the whole world is related to grace.[6]

These words indicate that the world can be transparent of God, that (thus Teilhard de Chardin) "there is no reality that is only profane for those who know how to look,"[7] and that grace—God's real but hidden presence in the world—is generously offered. But they also indicate that grace can be blocked by refusals or rejections on our part, so that whether or not it is present needs to be discerned and requires "detectives" who are sensitive to its incarnations (and also its absences). Like people with an ear for music, there are those, said Woody Allen (amazingly), who have an ear for the Transcendent (he was not among them, he added, although he had met them). If genuinely musical, if they are genuine "detectives," their *ear* always includes a capacity to recognize that which is out of tune also.

St. Ignatius of Loyola, father of the Ignatian and Jesuit tradition, developed a spirituality of finding God in all things that is (like that of Francis) closely linked to the Christian doctrines of creation and incarnation. He was intuitively aware that if a tracing of the divine presence at the depths of human realities[8] was to have any foundation at all, then it had to begin with the incarnation, with God's leaving of his own footprints on the human earth. He knew also that there was no place to which grace could not penetrate—and that there were many realities that had particular need of its healing and warmth. Thus, for Ignatius, the possibility of finding God in all things—even in darkness and sin— was real, with the proviso that this divine presence had to be very carefully discerned.

The word *discernment* has become a Jesuit buzzword; but it will remain because the spirituality that it embodies—allowing wheat and weeds to grow together (cf. Matt 13:24–30) until the time of reaping permits their separation—will remain also. Four hundred fifty years after Saint

---

[6] Leonardo Boff, *Liberating Grace* (Maryknoll, NY: Orbis Books, 1979), 28.

[7] Pierre Teilhard de Chardin, *Le milieu divin* (London: Collins, 1960 [1957]), 66, as referred to in Decree 2: *A Fire That Kindles Other Fires: Rediscovering Our Charism*, in The Society of Jesus, *Decrees and Documents of the 35th General Congregation* (Oxford, UK: Way Books, 2008), 36–52, paragraph 10, p. 41.

[8] See *A Fire That Kindles Other Fires*, paragraphs 5–7.

Ignatius founded the Jesuits, a British Jesuit editor, Michael Barnes, articulated the "one conviction" (that has now become ecumenical) accompanying all sacramental thinking—all "reading" of God's traces in the human world:

> God is not an occasional visitor, interrupting the dark story of human tragedy with occasional flashes of brilliant light. God lives in the very darkness itself, transforming it from within. Such is the implication of a radically incarnational faith. Any spirituality which ignores the signs of transcendence in the world—those revealed in the privileged moments ordained by the Church *and* those more distantly appre-hended in the joy and sadness of people of all faiths and none—will lack the power to transform ordinary human living.[9]

Notice here that Barnes links the signs of transcendence to darkness and to sadness as well as to the joys of people. This indicates that grace is not about what is comfortable, cosy; it is about God's ubiquity—in weal and woe. Furthermore, it is not only theologians who are interested in this and who search out "signs of transcendence." Way back in the late 1960s, the sociologist Peter L. Berger (who is still alive and active today), fearing that in his book, *The Sacred Canopy* (1967), he might have left in-sufficient space for the possibility of a justified faith in things invisible, things divine, wrote a sequel called *A Rumour of Angels*, in which he sought to detect, in the circumstances of his time, what he referred to as "signs" or "signals" of transcendence: pointers to the dimension of tran-scendence amid ordinary, everyday life. Here, availing of a "sacramental vision" (because Berger, the sociologist, was also a religious person), he managed to bring to bear on the world as he saw it a vision not resident in sociology itself but not inimical to it either. And he found a number of "arguments" for transcendence, among them the argument from *order* ("everything will be alright"), the argument from *play*, the argument from *hope*, and the argument from *damnation* (intuiting that, somehow, the world's great evildoers will ultimately get what they deserve).[10] Humor, if I remember correctly, was highlighted as a signal of transcendence also. In such human activities as: trusting in an overall order despite the sur-rounding anxieties; suspending the apparent fixities of life in a willingness to enter the imaginative world of play; hoping against hope, even in desperate situations; and relying on an ultimate justice that is not yet

---

[9] Michael Barnes, SJ, "Editorial" in *The Way Supplement* (1999:1): 7–8, at 8.
[10] See Peter L. Berger, *A Rumour of Angels* (New York: Doubleday Anchor, 1970), 66ff., 72ff., 75ff., and 81ff.

evident, Berger detected "pointers" to transcendence lying at the very heart of how people ordinarily and spontaneously live.

Peter Berger did it his way (I am echoing Frank Sinatra here). Without prejudice to his sociologist's craft, he invoked a more overall vision, a worldview greater than what sociology itself was able to provide, and he was aware that he did so; indeed, it expressed his wider *Weltanschauung*, his overall take on things, his philosophy (or metaphysics, even), since nobody is without such. For Berger, for everyone, the important thing is to be aware of one's worldview and to place one's cards on the table about it. If one operates with some kind of sacramental vision such as we have been talking about here, one must be equally up front about it—but one is not required to have no such vision, much less to live un-animated by it, since having no such overall take on things is impossible in any case. I shall return to this matter in a final, critical reflection.

Having a Go:
Exercising a Sacramental Way of Seeing as Scholars

An active detecting of grace in the adventures of scholarship is needed at this juncture. This section will necessarily be more narrative/personal. My efforts to be a "detective of grace" will be concentrated mainly in three places, in three Cs:

- in **curiosity**, which reveals our self-transcendence, our orientation to discovery (and even to *mystery*), how we are "open at the top";[11]

- in **conversion**, which reveals our desire to understand properly and to reach reliable knowledge, thus to shun hasty conclusions and be willing, rather, to pay careful attention, to submit to rigorous intellectual asceticism,[12] and even to allow ourselves to be transformed by what confronts us;[13]

- in **celebration**, as we find delight in understanding and joy in our journeys of discovery.

[11] See Elizabeth A. Johnson, *Consider Jesus: Waves of Renewal in Christology* (New York: Crossroad, 1990), 21–25, at 24.

[12] See Bernard J. F. Lonergan, *Method in Theology* (New York: Seabury Press, 1972), 231 (on achieving appropriate detachment through rigorous adherence to the four transcendental precepts in the attempt to know).

[13] See Richard R. Gaillardetz, "The Church as Sacrament: Towards an Ecclesial Spirituality," in *The Way Supplement: Spirituality and Sacramentality* 1 (1999): 22–34, at 28–29.

Curiosity

The theologian Karl Rahner (1904–1984) was an inveterate, indeed an insatiable, questioner. It took two hours to walk a couple of blocks of a city street with him. Tugging at his companion's elbow, poking at window displays, peering all around him, he always wanted to know; he was unrelentingly curious. As teachers and researchers we may recognise something of this drive or thirst in ourselves. As a young kid (my mother told me later) I was very annoying, asking "what—why—how" relentlessly. Mr. Doyle across the road, who was so quiet that he hardly even spoke to his wife, would be pummelled with questions by irritating little me as he fixed his car or trimmed his rosebushes. Children are like this, open at the top, each question but the springboard for the next inquiry. I never really thought much about it all—until about ten years ago when, cajoled into a bit of reflection, I caught a glimpse of something arresting. I had been teaching theology, happily, for over a decade at that time, and suddenly I was asked to write a few paragraphs about being a Jesuit as I actually experienced it, concretely, for some promotional/vocational literature. This is what tumbled out of me—about the scholar's "vocation" *within* the Christian, Jesuit one that had found me, very much to my surprise, in my life as it had unfolded:

> I have been in the Jesuits since 1972—imagine, thirty years! I spent many of those years studying and the last eleven teaching theology at the Milltown Institute in Dublin. During all that time I had lots of ups and downs, even some really challenging times, but there was an unbroken thread of consolation through it all. You might think this thread was some great spiritual thing, some mystical lifeline, but it wasn't. It was simply the joy that came from learning, from studying and understanding things, from having the assignment to, and the inclination for, serious heartfelt study.
>
> I'm not an egg-head, or what Americans call a "nerd"; I never expected this joy in learning. I hadn't even been particularly studious at school. But later on, mysteriously, the experience of learning brought light and life to me. Now, well finished with formal studies and working as a teacher, I still think of myself as a student and a learner, although my own students roll their eyes at this! One bright August day I met one of these students as I sat reading a theology book outside a café. She stopped, bent my book upwards to see its title, and snorted amiably: "I might have known." I laughed then— and we had a cup of coffee together. But I hesitated to tell her what had happened just before she appeared.

> I had been reading, with the sun warming my face and the book warming my heart. All at once there stole over me the sense that, even if I was not Karl Rahner or some other theological giant, there was a rightness about what I was doing and a kind of joy in it that could never be taken away. I became aware that this activity, this ministry, was God's gift to me. I didn't quite know why—I still don't—but I knew for certain that, in some form, this gift was mine for keeps, but not *to* keep (the student was a reminder of that). Often, still, I recall fondly that August day, and that mischievous student, and that engaging book, and I rejoice in the freshness, in the relationships and the consolations that I have known over the years through the ministry of shared learning.[14]

I still subscribe to these words, even a tired decade later. There is immense joy in questioning, probing, poking, discovering . . . even when it is painstaking and difficult and sometimes downright intractable. I am reminded of Kierkegaard here: the understanding seeks an object on which it can founder. The experience of writing this very essay had all of that in it because I know I have one chance to say something useful here—about material that really matters to me[15]—but also that the perspective I am working from has to be critically reflected upon and has to be expressed in a way that makes it accessible in our current, postmodern cultural circumstances if it is to succeed in commending itself at all. So there is a lot at stake here—there always is as one writes, because one is always writing for people. Ultimately our work is relational; and that is what spilled out of me ten years ago also. Scholarly work is a gift to the scholar—but not *for* the scholar. It has to do with engagement with a whole host of persons; with students as one teaches and with colleagues and even wider audiences as one writes and publishes.

Having begun with curiosity, we have now reached relationship and service. An older Jesuit who taught me mathematics once showed disappointment that I would not be assigned to work in a high school. He felt that the world of theology would prove arcane and disconnected. He said, provocatively: "I'd give up all the philosophy and theology I know if I could just play the accordion" (meaning that at least *that* activity would

---

[14] Taken almost verbatim from: Jim Corkery, SJ, *Jesuit Lives: 'Let God Be Present in Our Midst'* (Dublin: Irish Province of the Society of Jesus, 2002), 18.

[15] I recall here a discussion with a colleague about how the sacramental way of seeing things and the rich treasury of "jewels" of the Christian tradition are what keeps us hanging in at the present time of difficulty for faith and church.

enable him to draw people together and help them to enjoy one another!). In a flash of genius (under pressure!), I replied: "Would you give up mathematics?" His face fell—because he loved the subject and taught it superbly. "Ah, I said; so your heart is given too." He replied: "I'm not so attached to mathematics *as such*; but I love what teaching the subject enables me to do. I can connect, reach people, convey an enthusiasm and open up wonder." To which I said: "And what if theology were like that for me—not just a domain of knowing but something that spills over into relationship, connection, service?" "Hmm," my old master said reluctantly, "I fear I see your point; you had better do theology!"

In all of this, there is real wisdom—and some serious "sacramental thinking" too—because through the loved subjects something more is reached and experienced. Through taking theology, or mathematics, or history, or poetry, or whatever, in all their richness, fully seriously, more becomes possible, as the Professor illustrated in the novel of Yoko Ogawa that I referred to at the start. This *more* is what I have been trying to get at in speaking about the "detecting of grace."

There is one final thing about curiosity. Perhaps, more than anything else, it shows how the scholar's life can be graced. To be relentlessly questioning, interrogative, searching, is to express a fundamental anthropological fact: that we are (as alluded to earlier) beings of openness, other-oriented, "open at the top," as Elizabeth Johnson (drawing on Karl Rahner) puts it. She views the unstoppable, insatiable questioning of our dynamic spirit as revealing an infinite thirst for truth on our part that will never be quenched, never be fully satisfied. And she notices and teases out a similar thirst in our experiences of hoping and loving. From this observed dynamism that marks us, so that "we go off into the infinite by the very way that we are made," she makes a link to the famous observation of Augustine: "You have made us for yourself, O God, and our hearts are restless until they rest in Thee." Johnson sees here that it is for what lies beyond us that we are made and observes that Christians find this to be no accident, saying: "God graciously made us this way precisely in order to be able to be our fulfilment."[16] Thus, by attending to how we visibly are, Johnson uncovers the invisible hidden in, and animating, all our human strivings—including, we may add, our impassioned scholarly quests.

---

[16] Elizabeth A. Johnson, *Consider Jesus*, 24 (for all the Johnson material here, see 21–24).

Conversion

One could be tempted to label the sacramental way of seeing things "Platonism": penetrating the shadows of the temporal to reach the reality of the eternal. One might even see it as make-believe. Or perhaps some would be willing to accord it a kind of "in-between" status, something that tempers longing with a measured scepticism but without being so foolish as to still the hungers of the heart entirely.[17] Hunger/desire has its place in all human undertakings—otherwise we would not bestir ourselves at all—but this does not mean that we pursue our ventures, particularly our scholarly adventures, blinded by them. Not at all! And here is the critical bit! In spite of the committed character (religiously speaking) of the sacramental worldview, and the motivation it provides for loving and probing the world, it can, indeed must, exist in companionship with responsible knowing and complete respect for the autonomy of secular disciplines and their methods. In fact, the delight in and responsibility toward created reality that is embodied in the sacramental worldview—the stance of *per visibilium ad invisibilium*—should lead us to pursue our research with all the care and transparency demanded by the methods of our disciplines *and*, at the same time, with all the passion and engagement demanded by our relentless curiosity and our desire to understand and appreciate what we are probing.

As scholars and teachers, we are first and foremost concerned with knowing—with seeking to know reliably. Simone Weil said: "The most important part of teaching is to teach what it is to know." Human knowing is a very careful, but not a disengaged, enterprise. We only find things out because we ask questions and desire to understand.

Where disengagement does occur, this lies in *methodically* setting aside the biases and inclinations of our own limited horizons so that that which is the case may better reveal itself. I think here of the transcendental precepts of Canadian Jesuit theological-methodologist Bernard Lonergan: be attentive, be intelligent, be reasonable, be responsible.[18] One is disengaged from self if one follows these, but one's self is not disengaged in the process of so doing because these precepts embody a commitment to discovering what is the case. They embody an intellectual conversion (thus Lonergan) that fully engages the knower, while at the same time

---

[17] A phrase I owe to Tom Waldron's "Hope and the Hungers of the Heart," *The Furrow* (October 1992): 523–30.

[18] Recall Bernard Lonergan, *Method in Theology*, 231 (and footnote 12 above).

ensuring that she is less likely to fall into error—once said by Descartes to occur because the intellect is outstripped by the will in the knower's enthusiasm to arrive at a conclusion! Lonergan's precepts involve a commitment to what is invisible—I spoke of that which is the case *revealing* itself (it is not yet fully known)—and asks for an intellectual conversion on the part of the knower who is, in the process, at once fully humanly committed and, at the same time, radically open to what is *other*. (There is something quite postmodern about that!) Richard Gaillardetz speaks of this when he notes how the sacramental route of discovery must pass through that of conversion and transformation also, as one is challenged by what Edward Schillebeeckx might call the "refractoriness" of the real.[19] The same point is made, albeit somewhat differently, when Simone Weil points to the generosity (ascetical and self-disregarding) that accompanies the giving of one's attention.

Celebration

There is joy in study and learning; we mentioned this already. It is even the case that, having spent the morning exploring a really good book or trying to appreciate the intricacies of a colleague's position, I emerge (in the short term anyway!) something of a better person, more attuned to the richness of things because of what I have been probing and thus more open to the richness of what I might meet when I venture forth. Doing my doctorate in Washington, DC, I used to sometimes work in the Library of Congress. After a day there, I was invariably happy; I had a heart for those on the subway and even on the street corners afterward, too. When a bunch of us were doing our doctorates, some used to moan "When will we finish?" as if those were the most awful days of our lives. I found the time that we had for dedicated study and research a great blessing (knowing we would struggle for such time in our later, busy lives). And wonder not infrequently replaced drudgery in those un-dreary days; and there was a sense of adventure and discovery too.

Grounded by a sacramental vision, scholarship can come to life. It can even be transformed by the "shimmer" of the Catholic sacramental tradition that always illumines the life and activities of a Catholic college or university, be it Franciscan, Benedictine, Jesuit, Dominican, or whatever,

---

[19] See Richard Gaillardetz, "The Church as Sacrament," 28–29 (and footnote 13 above).

because the pursuit of scholarship there—especially of exploring the depths of created human reality as represented in disciplines such as physics and history, biology and psychology, chemistry and literature—will inevitably have its *raison d'être* in a vision of the world as being "charged with the grandeur of God" (Gerard Manley Hopkins). To catch sight of this charge requires imagination—once spoken of as lying halfway between reason and faith—and this is as evident in the (relatively unbelieving) Einstein as it is in the mystics and contemplatives. Daniel J. O'Leary writes:

> Einstein cherished "a feeling of utter humility towards the unattainable secrets of the harmony of the cosmos" and saw himself, before the mystery, as he put it, "in the position of a little child entering a huge library filled with books in many languages." Here we have the wonder of the mystics, the silence of the contemplatives, the new images of a sacramental vision. Fearful religion, adrift from its source, blocks out God's mystical flow in and through all things. It cannot cope with a God so big.[20]

A modern version of that library image is when an Amazon package arrives and you just cannot wait to open it and to see, touch, page through, scan the index of whatever it is that you have bought; all the better if you cannot quite remember! You think of coffee (or wine!) and a comfortable chair: wouldn't that be paradise (I use the word advisedly!). Once, in Cardinal Avery Dulles's office, when the poor man was dealing with the subtleties—or rather, the crass unsubtleties—of a chapter of my licentiate thesis, the department secretary dropped in an Amazon package and Dulles could hardly remain in his seat. "Go on, open it," I said. And then—to ensure he would feel free to, I added "I wouldn't mind seeing what's in there myself." Years ago, some friends gave me a sweatshirt with the words "So Many Books, So Little Time" emblazoned on its front! Most academics know this feeling! At its core are joy and celebration, not always equally felt, to be sure, but always a possibility. There is a "taking-delight-in" here, joy in a created reality. The Irish poet Pádraig Pearse, overwhelmed as he recalled the beauties of a long-shadowed evening on the very night before his execution, could write:

---

[20] Daniel J. O'Leary, *Unmasking God: Revealing God in the Ordinary* (Dublin: Columba Press in association with *The Tablet*, 2011), 57.

> Sometimes my heart hath shaken with great joy
> To see a leaping squirrel in a tree
> Or a red ladybird upon a stalk,
> Or little rabbits in a field at evening,
> Lit by a slanting sun.[21]

Do we not have such moments, and what happens to us as we become consciously aware of them?

Daniel O'Leary linked the joy of Einstein's wonder at the marvels of the cosmos to the awe of mystics and the silence of contemplatives. He saw in these what he called "the new images of a sacramental vision." And what he goes on to write indicates that this vision is rooted, for him (as for Francis and Ignatius) in the incarnation—the becoming human of the invisible God in the visible Jesus. It is because of this underlying coming-together of God and creation that *all* created things, events, enterprises—and not least the scholarly enterprise—can be vehicles for the divine in the human world. Of the incarnate Son, O'Leary writes:

> The heart of God and the heart of Creation beat in tune and time in his human heart. . . .
>   Here we have the fleshed love, extravagance and wild artistry of our devoted Creator now incarnate in this uniquely graced man. There is no gap, dislocation or dissonance between the innate God of our hearts, of nature, of everything beautiful, and the God of Jesus. Jesus brings a tangible focus and a physical presence to the hunches and intuitions of the human race from the very beginning.[22]

Seeing the world sacramentally means seeing it just as it has been made—and, through careful attention to this, seeing the God who made it: *per visibilium ad invisibilium*. Simone Weil speaks of attention as "the rarest and purest form of generosity," knowing that to attend to things as they are is to give them all the space they need to be *all* that they can be. Speaking of science, Weil deepens her point: its true definition, she says, is "the study of the beauty of the world" and then (in a further word about it) she adds: "a science which does not bring us nearer to

[21] Pádraig Pearse, "The Wayfarer," 1916. http://www.eirefirst.com/archive/pearse7.htm.
[22] O'Leary, *Unmasking God*, 57–58.

God is worthless."[23] Seeing sacramentally means picking up (as was mentioned earlier) the deepest message that things send out; and this is catching the divine through the human; it is detecting grace. One sign that we have done so is the presence, however fleeting, of that joy which I have been mentioning. Perhaps this is because we are oriented toward this grace which, above all through God's incarnation in Christ, is, from eternity, oriented toward us. Thomas Marsh, an Irish theologian, has reminded us of our *God-towardness*;[24] I would also like to highlight God's *us-towardness*. Joy meets joy here, or, if one prefers, *Cor ad cor loquitur*. And Daniel O'Leary reminds us that we are the objects of God's delight— "the Lord takes delight in his people" (Ps 149:4)—and then he adds: " 'God is sheer joy,' wrote St Thomas Aquinas, 'and sheer joy demands company.' "[25]

Imagination, said earlier to be located halfway between reason and faith, head and heart, is important for all knowing (recall Einstein), but in sacramental knowing it definitely has a place. Great religious thinkers—John Henry Newman, for example—are aware of this. From my own experience, I have the same view. When we doubt it, others urge us to it, like a challenging young woman, a scientist, whom I taught philosophy of religion to more than thirty years ago and who, while struggling with the sacramental way of thinking herself, growled at me at the end of the course that *I* should work hard to hold on to that vision. Other scientists—and many postmoderns—ask the opposite of us today, believing the sacramental way of thinking to be unsustainable and suggesting that it places us on a false trail. So, in a final section, a word will have to be addressed to their critical views.

Just like the position I advocate, so too do their positions involve adopting certain presuppositions—there is no presuppositionless position—and it is important that I bring mine into some contact with theirs. In the end, it is a question of what presuppositions, what "antecedent inclinations" (Newman) are anthropologically appropriate—appropriate, that is, to what we are as men and as women today. There is a need

[23] Simone Weil, *Gravity and Grace* (London and New York: Routledge Classics, 2002), 56 (originally published in Paris in 1947); see also "Simone Weil Quotes," accessed October 11, 2013, http://www.goodreads.com/author/quotes/18395.Simone_Weil; and see Terry Tastard, "Simone Weil's Last Journey," *America* 184, no. 12 (April 9, 2001).

[24] Thomas Marsh, *The Triune God: A Biblical, Historical, and Theological Study* (Dublin: Columba Press, 1994), 9.

[25] O'Leary, *Unmasking God*, 41.

therefore to choose, and to be up front about, our presuppositions, and to do so with solid criteria. The journalist Martyn Harris, before his premature death from cancer, found himself forced to choose, to take a stance, in an agonising and heartrending way, with regard to how he believed things would ultimately be. And he did so with startling courage, attending fully and honestly to all that he had experienced during his illness and writing, as the final sentences of his article: "Put the gun to your head Harris, and say it: Yes. I think so. I don't know. No. I hope so. Yes."[26] No one completely escapes facing such a choice; it belongs to our very humanity to have to confront it at some point.

But Is It Permissible?
Probing the Sacramental Thought-Form

Sacramental (Catholic) analogical thinking—the "sacramental imagination"—is: having the lover's eye for the Beloved. It engages the whole person and is not, therefore, mere head-knowledge, but also a knowing with the heart—always rooted in the experience, the *praxis*, of relationship. It bespeaks relationship and furthers relationship. It represents a certain take on reality, a vision of how things *are*. As such, it is metaphysical/ontological in character: an all-embracing worldview that "stands behind," or transcends one's approach to particulars. Like any worldview (and what thought-system, or even individual, can manage entirely without one?), sacramental thinking has to declare its presuppositions and allow them to be seen and discussed by others.

Its presuppositions are these: it rests on the view that human beings and the Earth and the cosmos are not the products of chance but have their origin in a creative love, a *Logos*, whom/which Christians call "God."[27] The sacramental imagination sees a loving Creator as standing at the origin of all that is (this is the Christian doctrine of creation) and understands this same originating Love to have taken flesh in the one called Jesus, who is thus its sacrament: the visible presence of the real but invisible reality of the loving God-with-us. It is he who preeminently

---

[26] Martyn Harris, "Something Understood," *The Daily Telegraph* (Weekend), Saturday, May 25, 1996, 1–2, at 2.

[27] This actual formulation is close to what is found in the eschatological writings of Joseph Ratzinger but represents also the basic belief of several other Catholic theologians including Thomas Aquinas, Karl Rahner, and Edward Schillebeeckx.

confers the sacramental/incarnate structure on the divine-presence-in-the-world, the presence I have been referring to as grace. This grace, as we see, for example, in the 1987 movie *Babette's Feast*, is never clearly and unambiguously "nameable" because it always turns up or appears in tandem with some created reality, some "vehicle" that is its bearer.[28]

So yes—the Christian sacramental worldview rests on presuppositions that must be named and cannot always be assumed to be those of everybody and that Christians cannot ask that everyone share. What Christians can (indeed must) do is give some account (recall 1 Pet 3:15), as best a reasoning faith can, of why they live out of these presuppositions, drawing on lives as they have actually been lived and on stories/experiences of the Mystery as this has touched them. Believers can also argue that it is more intellectually defensible to posit an ultimate intelligibility than to deny it;[29] but even in so doing, believers are still a distance from the named God of Christian revelation. So Christians must be open, entering discussion and subjecting faith to the scalpel of reason, never simply assuming that their positions are ones that others can straightforwardly share.

Today, in many far-flung sections of the globe, we live in a pluralist cultural space that, for want of a more precise term, may be referred to as *postmodernity*. The attitudes and thought-forms of this era do not cohere easily in many respects with some of the presuppositions I have pointed to as belonging to Christian faith. So, *in* the postmodern, Christians meet the "other"; but *from* the postmodern, Christians have learned much about how to treat the other, to "welcome the stranger." Strands of Christianity, more Augustinian in character, will see Christian faith and postmodern culture as being more in opposition than in agreement. Thus in their view the culture will need to be "slit" by the Gospel for its impurities to be drawn.[30] However, strands of Christianity more Thomistic in character will conceive the relationship between faith and culture—here, between Christianity and postmodernity—more amicably, with the former seeking (and finding!) in the latter much that it can value and from which it can learn. Here what I have been saying about being *detectives of grace* shows itself in bold relief: this detecting is an attitude of

---

[28] This is basically Leonardo Boff's language and insight.

[29] This is because denying it requires positing it *sotto voce*!

[30] See Joseph Ratzinger, "Communication and Culture: New Methods of Evangelization in the Third Millennium," in *On the Way to Jesus Christ* (San Francisco: Ignatius Press, 2005), 42–52, at 46–48 especially.

searching the world, searching it avidly, for what is good, salvific, and godly in it. This is a "wheat and weeds"[31] approach to things: affirming, yet shrewdly discerning; gentle, yet wisely sifting; in short, hospitable.

The hospitable methodology I have been describing expresses the attitudinal stance of the sacramental imagination exercised in this post-modern age. Its first instinct is to seek what unites, according to the mentality that "those who are not against us are with us." It is a predis-position of love toward all created realities—human creations too—a kind of "second naïveté" awareness (recall Paul Ricoeur) that underlies the intelligent and critical embrace of the world and all its fields of inquiry that one finds in the Catholic intellectual tradition. It sees with open eyes—there is no wilful blinding of oneself in it—but not with a rejecting or closed heart.

The Catholic sacramental imagination finds much to embrace and welcome in postmodernity. Postmodernity is much more hospitable to religion than was its predecessor, modernity. Like the sacramental way of seeing, the postmodern way does not approach the world with the assumption that we can be neutral observers. Postmoderns and sacra-mental thinkers know that there is no neat separating of what is observed or beheld from those who observe or behold it.[32] "Postmoderns insist that we are not spectators who approach the world but rather partici-pants in what we seek to know."[33] Sacramental thinking is participative and self-involving also. It places—as do postmoderns—considerable emphasis on context(s) and on communities. Its "criterion" is the One whose story is at the centre of the Christian narrative; and it is a *com-munity's* story. True, it is seen as a *meta*narrative; and here postmoderns will raise questions. Nonetheless, Christians and postmoderns *can* talk—for we have seen that we share much. Indeed, the strength of the Catholic, sacramental tradition (understood as broadly as possible) is that, attitu-dinally, it is disposed to dialogue and engagement with everything be-cause it recognises that only that which is manifestly evil—a privation of good (*privatio boni*)—lies beyond the pale of creation-faith's affirmation that *all*, every created reality, be it "natural" or "cultural," is capable of being a bearer of transcendence precisely because, ultimately, it owes its

---

[31] Recall here the parable of the wheat and the weeds: Matt 13:24-30, 36-43.

[32] See Stanley J. Grenz, *A Primer on Postmodernism* (Grand Rapids, MI: William B. Eerdmans Publishing Co.), 52 (the example of Schrödinger's cat).

[33] Ibid., 53.

origin to the Transcendent One. So go! Be avid, *wild* "detectives of grace"! Look for God in all things! For, as the poet Gerard Manley Hopkins wrote,

> Christ plays in ten thousand places,
> Lovely in limbs, and lovely in eyes not his
> To the Father through the features of men's faces.[34]

---

[34] That is, "our" faces!

Part 2

A Long, Loving Look at the Real

Practice Makes Reception:
The Role of Contemplative Ritual
in Approaching Art[1]

Joanna E. Ziegler

In the midst of a demanding and often exhausting personal and professional life, I have one hope for my work: that teaching the practice of looking at art should have a central place in the creation of a meaningful spiritual life in the Catholic academy. It trains the beholder— indeed the emphasis is on the beholder—by its discipline and daily routine and by its continual and repetitive confrontation with a work of art, to be ready to "see" in the fullest way. It teaches humility by training students to be open to the work of art on its own terms, rather than approaching it as a mirror of their own will and desires; it teaches them to pay attention, not just as a cerebral activity, but as one that involves the entire body and senses. It teaches an approach to what Esther de Waal calls "mindfulness, an awareness," which turns the process "from a cerebral activity into a living response."[2] The practice of looking, as I propose to teach it, comes very close to introducing students to a form of contemplative practice, such as those identified with the great spiritual and mystical traditions of Christianity and Eastern religions such as Zen Buddhism.[3]

---

[1] This essay first appeared in *As Leaven in the World: Essays on Faith, Vocation, and the Intellectual Life*, ed. Thomas M. Landy (Franklin, WI: Sheed & Ward, 2001).

[2] Esther de Waal, *Seeking God: The Way of Saint Benedict* (Collegeville, MN: Liturgical Press, 1984), 43.

[3] Two institutions have helped to encourage these ideas: Collegium and the Center for Contemplative Mind in Society. The visits with the participating fellows changed my thinking about contemplation and its importance to education. I cannot thank

It is fitting to begin with a quotation from de Waal's splendid book on Benedictine spirituality, *Seeking God: The Way of Saint Benedict*.[4] She shows us how to find the Benedictine spirit in the contemporary world of housewives, academics, and office workers, people like ourselves, by teaching us how to live that spirit in our daily lives. The theory of Benedictine spirituality does not, indeed cannot, as de Waal insists, exist apart from how one is actually to live a Christian life: "I have one hope in writing this book and that is that it may serve as a first step to an encounter with the Benedictine way, for reading about it is no substitute for living it."[5] Although this is not an essay about Benedictine spirituality, I urge the reader to consider precisely this point: that the pursuit of a meaningful spiritual life is not the result of amassing erudition and theory but of learning how one is to lead that life in a routine daily way. Art gives us one way to learn to do this. In chapter 3, de Waal offers a good place from which to begin our own exploration. Although she talks about "listening," let us include—in our mind and for our purposes—the word "seeing":

> The very first word of the Rule is "listen." From the start the disciple's goal is to hear keenly and sensitively that Word of God which is not only message but event and encounter. . . . To listen closely, with every fibre of our being, at every moment of the day, is one of the most difficult things in the world, and yet it is essential if we mean to find the God whom we are seeking. If we stop listening to what we find hard to take then, as the Abbot of St Benoit-sur-Loire puts it in a striking phrase, "We're likely to pass God by without even noticing Him."[6]

This essay explores the ways in which viewing art—the practice, the very act itself, of viewing works of art—can be profoundly spiritual. I would call us away from thinking about art in the usual ways, as something to do for mere recreation or entertainment, in our leisure or spare time. Of course looking at art is entertaining. We like to visit museums

---

sufficiently Tom Landy for getting me "on my way" by accepting me to attend Collegium in 1996 and the Center, along with the Nathan Cummings Foundation, for supporting the development with Joe Lawrence (Department of Philosophy, College of the Holy Cross) of a course on this material in 1998.

[4] De Waal, *Seeking God*.
[5] Ibid., 12–13.
[6] De Waal, *Seeking God*, 42–43.

during vacations and attend concerts and plays in order to relax, to escape from the demands of our overly pressured lives. On the other hand, when the religious purpose of art is raised, immediately we think of art with a religious subject matter. The history of art, especially from the medieval, Renaissance, and Baroque periods, is rich with paintings and sculptures of biblical narratives of Mary and Jesus, saints, martyrs, popes, and sinners—the redeemers and the redeemed.

Catholics therefore presume that for their art to be spiritually enriching, it must be religious art about the figures, symbols, and stories of Christianity. This essay proposes, however, that there is another role for art, one that is neither entertaining nor didactic in the ways we have come to presume: beholding art is a practiced discipline and, as such, teaches us to see closely, "with every fibre of our being," as de Waal would have it. This goal—to see "keenly and sensitively"—is essential if we are to be ready for an encounter with things as they are rather than as we would have them. With daily practice, what really looking at art gives us—openness to whatever and however one defines "the transcendent," either as God or "the other"—becomes something more than a scholarly exercise in rhetoric; it becomes attainable in actuality.

The discipline of art history, at least at this moment, has little to offer the person intent upon probing the deeper truths that art might have to offer, for it is more interested in social and political issues than philosophical or spiritual ones. This is not to say that there are no resources in the history of the discipline, but they are fragmentary, isolated cases of scholars here and there trying to introduce a personally meaningful element into writing about art.[7] Since the nineteenth century, art history has been concerned with developing a "scientific" approach, in the early modern academic sense of the word, which would ensure a place within the established hierarchy of disciplines in the academy. The earliest practitioners of art history were dedicated, therefore, to developing methods with a claim to objectivity through fact gathering and dependable documentary study. My goal is to promote an enlightened experience of art, too, but by using less objectifying means than current academic practice sanctions. My emphasis first is on today's viewers,

---

[7] I am relying in this paragraph on the work of Kathryn Brush, who has been researching the formative years of art history. In her first book, she was especially interested in the splitting apart of personal versus objective writing styles. In addition to her many articles, see *The Shaping of Art History: Wilhelm Voege, Adolph Goldschmidt, and the Study of Medieval Art* (Cambridge: Cambridge University Press, 1996).

who can find ourselves on deeply intimate terms with works of art, without becoming scholars or academics. If prepared through practice, viewers can experience works of art as immediate experiences, things to be penetrated with their entire being rather than objects of intellectual stimulation that are preserved in theories and reclaimed through books with very specialized access, at best. To approach art with a desire to grasp it fully is to approach it with reverence for what is divine in human creation and with the conviction that it has the power to lift us above the mundane and make us aware of the mystery and wonder of the human spirit. To do so is demanding; it requires discipline, practice, and preparedness.

It might be appropriate to examine some of the religious uses of art in the past: why have people really looked at art? This is an interesting and complex topic in its own right, very well studied and documented, and of interest to us primarily insofar as it helps us understand how it differs from the present project. Most curious is the church's position on images, its anxiety and recurrent attempts to prevent the laity from engaging in what it perceived as idol worship.

This was especially problematic in the later Middle Ages, when religious images were readily available in churches, on street corners, in graveyards, in the home—even to the person of humblest means.[8] It was a time of intense piety, and images shaped the religious imagination as much as preaching did. In fact, preachers adopted many of their narrative anecdotes for sermons from available statuary and painting.[9] In many ways, the Church's attitude toward religious imagery confirms the power not only of imagery itself but repetitious looking, which, after all, is integral to idol worship as an activity.

The spiritual value of looking at art, however, ought not be limited to religious imagery. Other periods and styles of art can be profoundly transforming, too. Things today, for example, are vastly different from the way they were in the Middle Ages. Art has been secularized, to use a favorite art historical term, which means the subject matter seldom is concerned with religious themes. Also, there are many new formats and techniques that were not available to artists of earlier times: photography,

---

[8] Joanna E. Ziegler, *Sculpture of Compassion: The Pieta and the Beguines in the Southern Low Countries, c.1300–c.1600* (Brussels and Rome: 1992).

[9] The classic history of the migration from image to word is in Franciscan preaching, particularly the recipes they used called *exempla*. One may consult various works by Caroline Walker Bynum, Walter Simons, and Jean-Claude Schmitt on this topic.

lithographic printing, installation, silkscreen, video, and so on. Yet art without religious subject matter can be as much about creation and offer as many opportunities for spiritual transformation as can strictly religious works of art. I should make it clear that for the time being, I use the word "art" to mean the art of museums—the paintings, sculpture, and drawings of the past. We will—and should—extend that meaning to include other art forms, such as music, dance, singing, and acting. When we learn to open our eyes, minds, and hearts to the life of the human spirit in art—indeed, when that is our fundamental reason for viewing art—the categories and terminology that specialists use to distinguish one art form from another, or the implications about importance or value which they draw from such distinctions, quickly become immaterial. As de Waal shows her readers the way "from the monastery to the kitchen," I similarly encourage the present reader to make the practice of looking at art a lived experience—as much for the housewife as for the scholar.

Some Moments in the History of Looking at Images

Although it is beyond the scope of this essay to provide more than a brief look at the role of religious images in Western civilization, history offers crucial evidence of the power of looking as a religious activity, as well as insight into our own views—dare I say prejudices—on the value of art as a religious experience today.

In the history of Christianity, there have been two periods when the response to the worship of religious images was violent in the extreme: in Byzantium between 726 and 842, and in Western Europe during the sixteenth century.[10] In both periods, the conflict over religious images was tantamount to civil warfare. On the one side, the iconoclasts attacked the veneration of images as "idolatry" and, on the other, the iconophiles literally wept with anguish over the desecration of sacred sites and imagery. In the latter period, the Reformation, churches were sacked and burned; sculptures were beheaded, urinated on, and thrown into rivers; altars were overturned; and consecrated hosts were fed to animals. The accounts from both periods of the destruction reveal the sadness and horror of watching as nearly everything considered materially holy was

---

[10] There were other iconoclastic movements during the French and Russian Revolutions. Western Europe lost for a second time many of its religious artifacts during the Napoleonic Occupations.

literally cast down, trodden upon, and otherwise desecrated. The consequences of the Reformation are still with us, much more tangibly than those of the earlier Byzantine Iconoclasm. After all, Protestant attitudes toward imagery, which draw the line between material and spiritual worship, have defined one of the central differences between Protestants and Catholics.[11]

Although since Vatican II in the 1960s the church has downplayed the external objects of devotion—the material imagery and church ornaments—newer Catholic churches nonetheless reflect a tradition of imagery, in banners and stained glass, which Protestantism has scorned since the sixteenth century. What these periods of violent destruction of images reveal is how deeply affective images could be, positively as well as negatively. One is not moved to destroy sculptures and paintings without having witnessed their effect on people.[12] As art historian David Freedberg describes in his monumental study, *The Power of Images*, "People have smashed images for political reasons and for theological ones; they have destroyed works which have roused their ire or their shame; they have done so spontaneously or because they have been directed to do so. The motives for such acts have been and continues to be endlessly discussed, naturally enough; but in every case we must assume that it is the image—whether to a greater or lesser degree—that arouses the iconoclast to such ire."[13] Freedberg insists that "the power of images is much greater than is generally admitted."[14] This is important. On some basic level, religious images have been deemed dangerous because they appear to steer the believer away from a cerebral, fully spiritual, and immaterial knowledge of God and toward a sense that the material thing itself, that is, the painting or sculpture, is somehow interchangeable—if not identical—with what is represented. We have a powerful reminder of this in the mighty wrath of Moses, incurred when he saw his people worshipping a graven image as though the image itself was divine.

Even in our own time, religious images such as Michelangelo's *Pieta* in St. Peter's Basilica in Rome still arouse anger and violence as well

---

[11] Carlos M. N. Eire, *War against the Idols: The Reformation of Worship from Erasmus to Calvin* (Cambridge: Cambridge University Press, 1986).

[12] Consult the brilliant though much-neglected short essay by David Freedberg, *Iconoclasts and Their Motives* (Maarssen: 1985).

[13] David Freedberg, *The Power of Images: Studies in the History and Theory of Response* (Chicago: University of Chicago Press, 1989), 10–11.

[14] Ibid., 429.

as—perhaps even because of—displays of intense piety and affection. Ironically, Michelangelo himself found excessive devotion to religious images to be extremely distasteful.[15] Current attitudes toward religious art bear some imprint of this past ambivalence and conflict. There is a view, perhaps a fear, that religious imagery can occupy the believer with an artificial presence rather than with a genuinely spiritual response. Church furnishings and decoration became noticeably spare in the wake of Vatican II, after which there evolved two, almost mutually exclusive, generations of believers: the older clinging to their statuary, calendars, and household pictures of Jesus, Mary, and the saints—the younger finding such images anachronistic, unnecessary, even somewhat ludicrous. Most of my current students at the College of the Holy Cross, for instance, claim that they have never prayed to a statue.

The academic disciplines, on the other hand, are fascinated by the isolated continuation of traditional devotion to images. The field of anthropology, for example, has produced numerous studies on Italian feast days (such as those centered on effigies of Saint Anthony), practices of ritual, and image devotion among the native Americans in the Southwest. The academic study and individual enclaves of active image devotion, particularly in Hispanic cultures, stand apart from the attitude of most practicing Catholics in America and Europe (albeit not the oldest generation), who generally find any form of devotion to imagery excessive and even ridiculous.

Yet the irony is that people still generally believe that for art to be spiritually efficacious, it must portray or reflect religious subject matter. There is a clear separation of religious from secular art in the minds of most people fostering spiritual purposes. Liturgical art guilds today, for example, are dedicated to promoting artists, but the art produced must be religious in nature, either in function (liturgical vestments, for example) or subject matter (portrayals of Christ and the Holy Family, and so on). Even folk music, introduced as part of the Catholic liturgy in the 1960s, makes reference in its lyrics to the sacred nature of things and experience. Study groups at local churches sponsor talks and workshops on the history of religious art and music. Although the changes in forms and attitudes in the second half of this century from devotional art of the past have been radical to say the least, what has not changed is the belief that for art to be useful in a spiritual way, it needs to communicate

---

[15] Joanna Ziegler, "Michelangelo and the Medieval *Pieta*: Sculpture of Devotion or the Art of Sculpture?" *Gesta* vol. 34, no. 1 (1995): 28–36.

and narrate Christian themes, motifs, and persons. In other words, religious art has undergone significant changes in the twentieth century, with one fundamental exception: for art to serve a religious purpose, it still must be concerned with religious subject matter.

Contemplation and Looking

Throughout the history of Christian art, there have been times when the activity of art—making it and looking at it—has been viewed as a serious and worthy spiritual activity in its own right. In the fourteenth and fifteenth centuries, nuns and beguines were involved in art-making practices that constituted a form of prayer: making was praying. The beguines, lay holy women who lived a communal religious life, provide a fascinating example of the identification of detailed manual work with prayer.[16] As a way of grasping what we are about to explore, it is not at all inappropriate, I believe, to call to mind the modern image of the beguines as thoroughly rapt in the activity of making lace, for which they were renowned. Early-twentieth-century beguines often were photographed bent over their little lace looms, heads hung as hands carried out the exquisitely detailed work of creating the ornamental patterns of the lace. The modern tourist industry in fact equates the religious life of the beguines with the manual labor that produced their famous manufactured product, lace. Day in and day out, the beguines' world looks inward on the combined activities of work and prayer, often merging as though they are one. These modern icons of lace-making beguines are signposts, guides into the past. They reveal a tradition in the beguines' life of a merging, an identity, of close, repetitious manual labor and prayer life.

Since earliest times, beguines were engaged in the cloth-making industry—spinning, carding, dying, and weaving wool. They also cleaned, scrubbing floors and washing laundry, and gardened. They baked and counted hosts for the liturgy. Their days were dedicated mostly to this sort of repetitious manual labor. It seems appropriate, then, that when beguines began to make art, it was the art of handicraft.

---

[16] I first introduced the spiritual nature of the relationship between the beguines and their manual labor in *Sculpture of Compassion: The Pieta and the Beguines in the Southern Low Countries, c.1300–c.1600* (Brussels and Rome: The Belgian Historical Institute of Rome, 1992).

The first creations for which they become known were so-called enclosed gardens, which were little worlds populated by religious figurines, in lavish artificial settings, and framed with glass.[17] The beguines made all parts themselves. For them, the discipline and concentration required for making the gardens was a form of religious activity, a form of prayer, if you will. Like the chanting of the holy hours of the day (prime, terce, sext, and so on), the making of these highly detailed shrines was itself a daily ritual realized, however, in manual rather than vocal form.

Art historian Jeffrey Hamburger raises a similar issue in his book, *Nuns as Artists*.[18] Hamburger studies twelve drawings produced around 1500 at the convent of St. Walburg—near Eichstätt in Franconia, which now is part of Bavaria, Germany—seeking to understand them within the devotional practices of the nuns who made and used them. He believes the drawings—with their unusual iconography and childlike drawing style—to be the work of a single, anonymous nun. Although engaging in its own right, Hamburger's study offers some points that directly relate to the concerns of this essay.

In the first place, he contends that the nuns' devotions were enacted through their eyes: "As defined by the drawings, to look is to love, and to love is to look";[19] "Sight itself becomes the subject of the image."[20] The drawings have unusual images, such as those titled "The Heart on the Cross" or "The Heart as a House," whereby the nuns were drawn through the wound of Christ's heart to the soul "nesting" there, "like a bird . . . in the clefts of the rock, in the hollow places of the wall."[21] This devotion to Christ's heart is what Hamburger calls the "wounding look of love."[22] Looking, then, is praying, according to Hamburger.

For these nuns, the goal of mystical devotion was to unite with Christ and feel his love. As we learn, some incredibly imaginative nun fashioned that love into images of Christ's own heart, which literally could be penetrated, entered, and felt sensuously just by looking. This goes far beyond our customary understanding of devotional practices that involve contemplating images or symbols of Christ. In Hamburger's view, passionate

---

[17] Joanna Ziegler, "Beguines," *Dictionary of Art*, vol. 3 (New York: Grove's Dictionaries, 1996), 502–5.

[18] Jeffrey F. Hamburger, *Nuns as Artists: The Visual Culture of a Medieval Convent* (Berkeley, Los Angeles, London: University of California Press, 1997).

[19] Ibid., 129.

[20] Ibid., 130.

[21] Ibid., 116, 166, and 219.

[22] Ibid., 128.

looking is a devotional end in itself. Looking is praying. Hamburger argues that, "In the handiwork of nuns, the two meanings [of *operor,* "to keep busy" and "to be engaged in worship"] converged: work itself was a form of worship."[23] In keeping with the Benedictine ideal of *ora et labora* (prayer and work), religious women throughout the Middle Ages were instructed to lead a life of pious work and prayer—"laboring like the Virgin with her spindle and thread."[24] Although Hamburger only hints at the true nature of this activity, he understands that repetitive work like weaving, calligraphy, and drawing—what we moderns now call "art"—is grounded in the body, encoded as eye-hand skills. Making is therefore intimately intertwined with seeing and feeling: hand, eyes, and heart as the vehicles and the ends of prayer. There is a lesson to be drawn from these medieval examples: a link exists between spirituality and the physical body; that perhaps the way to reach the divine is achieved not only by moving beyond the body but also by deepening the experience of the body through daily, concentrated, disciplined physical activity. Might there not be intrinsic value in work, defined this way then, not as a reference to ourselves (as self-promotion or self-gratification) but as a way to create a time for contemplation and a body that is ready for the physical demands of contemplation? Nuns and beguines were motivated by their superiors and conditioned by the religious culture of the time to pursue work as a form of prayer. How, then, can we achieve, within the nature of our largely secular reality, some of the same integration? Let us consider some thoughts on accomplishing this goal.

Ora et Labora: Practice and Contemplation Today

Should we wish to deepen our spiritual lives, we must find dependable, workable forms of such practice, as well as times when we can prepare the body to work with the eyes and the heart—as did the nuns and beguines in earlier times. Our means will differ from theirs, of course. Our culture differs; our daily routines and habits differ; and our expectations and reasons for pursuing spiritual matters differ. Even if religion is important to us, the context in which we live is a largely secular one. I contend, however, that learning to make and look at art is wholly appropriate to our present culture. This is achieved by heightening the skills of looking and listening, which can only be gained through

---

[23] Ziegler, *Sculpture of Compassion*, 95–113; Hamburger, *Nuns as Artists*, 184.
[24] Hamburger, *Nuns as Artists*, 186.

discipline, rigor, and daily routine. Beholders eventually assume some identity with the art and ultimately the artist.

Although young people like to believe creativity is a possession—either you have it or you don't—creativity actually is a product, built on a foundation of practice. The very essence of practice is habit and daily routine. The dancer, for instance, must exercise daily and in a dependable, repeatable pattern. Ballet class always begins with the dancers doing simple arm and leg movements at the barre, then movements on the floor, and finally rehearsing strenuous choreography involving the entire studio space. Every ballet dancer knows this sequence by heart—in body as well as mind. Certain movements become entirely inscribed in the body—for example, specific arm positions—so that they no longer need to be consciously recalled when learning choreography or when actually giving a performance.

Routine practice gives rise to creative expression: it is not identical with it, but is its prerequisite. Artistry is when technique is so encoded in the body that pure freedom from technique can be achieved. For artist and audience—which is the point I wish to emphasize—the fullest experience of an art form comes with practice. Like the pianist practicing her scales, so too must beholders practice, if they are to penetrate the deeper meaning of creative expression.

Where contemplation enters this picture is that the discipline of daily, habitualized repetitive activity, encoded in the body, is a form of contemplative practice. Asian practices of yogic meditation and the martial arts have long been recognized as demanding daily repetition of prescribed physical activity. Western art also affords this possibility of providing the practical discipline that underlies the contemplative act—for artist as well as audience.

To introduce students to the theory and practice of these ideas, I require them to visit the local museum, the Worcester Art Museum, on a weekly basis. (Ideally, daily visits would be preferable but are not possible for college students.) It has been an effective and wonderful assignment, one which students often have resisted at first but embraced by the end—one of the best signs that practice works. Students were asked to choose a painting by one of three artists: Thomas Gainsborough (English, eighteenth-century portraitist and landscape painter), Claude Monet (the French Impressionist), or Robert Motherwell (American Abstract Expressionist). None of these pictures, by the way, has a religious subject matter. The students were required to write one paper a week on the same painting for the entire semester—thirteen weeks, thirteen papers in all—each essentially the same, but reworked, refined, and rewritten. Students were asked not to consult any outside reading, even including the wall text provided by the Museum. Instead, I asked them to describe, as simply and directly as they could, "what they see," what is on the canvas, in a maximum of five typed pages. Notes and paper had to be turned in every week, and the students—in addition to other classroom work—returned to the Museum to repeat the assignment the following week.

The students were resistant at first, anxious over whether they would be able to find anything to write about, especially thirteen times in succession. Also, the notion of a repetitive activity other than sports or body-building (examples of great value in this context, by the way, for their nature as daily routine leading to "performance") was downright unattractive. The results, however, have been remarkable. The essays transformed tangibly from personalized, almost narcissistic, responses to descriptions firmly grounded in the picture. Descriptions evolved from being fraught with willful interpretation, indeed selfishness (students actually expressed hostility at being made to go the Museum once a week), to revealing some truth about the painting on its own terms. Most importantly, students developed a personal relationship with what became known as "my" work of art. It was a work they knew by heart, could describe from memory—brushstroke, color change, and subtlety of surface texture. Through repeated, habitual, and direct experience (not working from slides or photographs but confronting the real work of art), students were transformed from superficial spectators, dependent on written texts for their knowledge, into skilled, disciplined beholders with a genuine claim to a deep and intimate knowledge of a single work of art—and they knew it. Moreover, they learned that with practice, any work of art could be accessible to them on its own terms.

This assignment bears the essential ingredients for becoming a practiced beholder of any art form—be it music, dance, acting, or the visual arts. In the first place, the activity is a part of daily life. Students came to depend on the time in the Museum as the one routine in their harried lives they could count on. Many of them described it as "my time in the week when I get to be alone: just me and my painting." Looking at "their" work of art became a habit. It was a habit not only because it occurred weekly but because there was a repeated pattern to the activity, which I prescribed: taking a cab at the same time each week, entering the same door of the museum, sitting in the same place, looking at the same object, indeed returning time and again to one place. Interestingly, this resonates with at least one form of instruction in prayer: Ignatius of Loyola, founder of the Jesuits, instructed his followers to return to the same place at the same time every day as an aid to prayer and preparation to hear the word of God.[25]

At the heart of the contemplative activity lies repetition, for that is what frees the mind. With daily practice, the whole being and the whole person become ready to look and to listen. As my students experienced, full awareness of the object of their attention was possible only when looking had become habitual routine rather than demanding drudgery. Similar to other forms of genuine contemplative activity, looking also demands concentration, the result of routine physical discipline. To be ready—to be open—arises first from practice.

Although an assignment given to college students, this practice has a message for teaching us a range of ways to strengthen our inner lives. Becoming a practiced beholder of art is actually a wide-ranging exercise, which can become a vital part of spiritual experience because, above all else, it teaches us how to cultivate concentrated awareness by repetition and physical ritual. Although, as I indicated, I focused on looking at paintings in museums, the pattern of activity is applicable to other art forms. Learn one work well and experience it routinely. Pick a Beethoven piano sonata, for example, and learn it by heart. Play the same song again and again, until every line and every nuance is second nature. Then begin to listen to other performances, learning those equally well by heart. Do this every day, at the same time and in the same place. You will come to know, in the deepest sense, a work of incomparable creativity—as well as at least one of the performances that has brought this work into being. This is nothing short of a contemplative activity, which has opened you to the full expressive power of a work of art.

Learning one work of art well is demanding. It requires discipline and practice, as well as a commitment to developing a long-term routine. Every art form makes essentially the same demands upon its practitioners. Audiences should approach art with the same spirit if they wish to enter fully into the creative wonder. The same fundamental principle holds true in the performing arts. Performance is the result of rigorously encoded physical and mental habits. Singers and musicians begin their study, as well as their practice sessions, with the most repetitive activity

[25] I wish to thank Brian Linnane, SJ, and Jim Hayes, SJ, for this insight. Father Linnane led a mini-retreat at Collegium in 1996, where he outlined the idea of repetition as a preparation for prayer, that it offers something dependable and reliable when we often are not in our moods and emotions. Father Hayes taught a class in *The Art of Contemplation* seminar in 1998, covering many of the issues of prayer and practice.

imaginable: scales. Individual works are committed to memory by hours of daily repetition; they become inscribed in the mind and body of the performer.

Many actors do the same, although audiences are less prepared to understand the nature of creativity in theater than in almost any other art form. Acting is so much a product of the marketplace, with its celebration of superficial values of stardom, that the power and beauty of the art form are all but completely obscured. Yet acting is an art form, too, whose artistry is the result of practice and discipline. That genius of the theater, Konstatin Stanislavski, developed a system for teaching acting that was grounded in the principles of physical repetition and routine activity. Actors are taught to come into contact with their emotions through repeated physical actions. By disciplining one's body, the emotions could be channeled. Audiences have little knowledge of such practices. Yet, returning to the same performance over and over will reveal their effectiveness.

It is essential to understand that this is not as simple as recognizing that "practice makes perfect." We enter the full artistry of the actor's art only by repeated viewing and greater awareness of the foundation in repeated, encoded, physical action. This entails, as well, a transformation in our own practices and habits.

Conclusion

Habitualized practice is a foundation for what we earlier called "mindfulness." It gives beholders access to works of art as genuine embodiments of the human spirit. I emphasize, however, that what I mean by this is that daily practice can teach us to enter into a work of art as a thing in its own right. It teaches us to leave our will behind and approach objects on their own terms. There are two wonderful lessons in this that unite in a single idea: the search for truth requires discipline and habit and it is attainable in things outside ourselves. This is a contemplative practice. The development of concentrated awareness—"mindfulness"— is essential if we mean to find the spiritual life we are seeking. It involves the whole person—mind, heart, and body—which for centuries has been the vital sign of meaningful spiritual experiences.

Concentrated awareness must be learned, however. My goal is to teach students that art offers the unique opportunity for experiencing the great paradox of creativity: it is simultaneously a function of extreme rigor and practice and the manifestation of true freedom. There is something genuinely spiritual in this paradox, for contemplative ritual teaches artist and beholder alike about stability and fidelity to one thing. Perseverance and steadfastness promise readiness—and only with readiness can the freedom to transcend the activity and journey to the utterly spectacular realm of creativity become reality.[26] "Let your heart take courage, yea, wait for the Lord" (Ps 50).

> *"Love the art in yourself, not yourself in the art."* (Stanislaviski)

---

[26] As always, I thank Joe Vecchione for his unwavering interest in my work and his willingness to discuss it on what must seem endless occasions. I thank him for his editing, as well, which is always the paragon of sensitivity.

Radical Transcendence:
Teaching Environmental Literature
at a Catholic University

Kimberly P. Bowers

I have been teaching a course titled "Literature and the Natural Environment" for the past three years at the University of Saint Francis in Fort Wayne, Indiana. When I first began teaching it, I taught it in a way that it might be taught at any university. I used an anthology that consisted of a number of interesting readings (poetry and prose, fiction and nonfiction) about the importance of taking care of the earth. Aside from discussing two essays devoted to Christian responses to global warming, the class did not engage in any exercises or discussions that were particularly spiritual. While this approach was working fine, I was interested in making the course more Catholic, and specifically, more Franciscan. Since I am not Catholic, I was unsure of the best way to do that. I had a sense that meditation practices would enhance the course, but my secular education kept raising doubts in the back of my mind, making me skeptical of my best instincts. Some environmental literature scholars I have encountered eschew "touchy feely" practices in environmental literature and suggest that devotional practices can thwart political activism and critical thinking.[1] Despite these doubts, I sensed that devotion, activism,

---

[1] For instance, see Stacy Alaimo, "The Trouble with Texts; or, Green Cultural Studies in Texas," in *Teaching North American Environmental Literatures*, ed. Frederick O. Waage, Mark Long, and Laird Christensen (New York: Modern Language Association, 2008), 369–70. While Alaimo's primary concern in this essay is not with discussing spiritually themed texts or devotional practices, her suspicion of their utility in an environmental literature class is clear. Despite this suspicion, I should also note that the

and critical thinking were related, and, in fact, might enhance one another. After participating in a Franciscan reading group at USF, attending Collegium, and reading a variety of nature writers, I became much more convinced that meditative exercises could help my students fall (more) in love with the natural world and strengthen their commitment to caring for the earth and one another. This past year, I integrated meditative exercises and readings that complemented them into my environmental literature classes and have been very pleased with the results.

Before I discuss the exercises and readings I use in class, I want to say a little bit about why I initially thought meditative exercises could help an environmental literature course. One of the goals for such a course is to help students become more aware of the environmental problems facing our natural world. While students can read a number of essays attesting to such problems, the threat of environmental devastation can seem so overwhelming that students become depressed and feel helpless. Recognizing that warnings of wrath and destruction have not encouraged all citizens to become more environmentally conscious, the poet Mary Oliver suggests that if we experience the pleasures of the natural world, we will be more likely to care for it. She writes, "What we feel is making our lives richer and more meaningful, we cherish. And what we cherish, we will defend."[2] Unfortunately, many people do not have enough of a relationship with the natural world to experience its beauty so that they want to defend it. Noting that "we cannot love what we have not noticed,"[3] Oliver believes poets can help readers become more aware of the natural world and its possibilities for pleasure; they can help readers notice and fall in love with the beauty of the natural world.

Poets can certainly help draw attention to the natural world; however, noticing the world's natural beauty (even within a poem that celebrates it) is a skill that many people have not cultivated. The fast-paced contemporary world most of us live in has dulled some of our senses and decreased our attention span. In "The Walling of Awareness," activist and author Jerry Mander writes about a camping trip he took with his children. On the first day of the trip, they were all very bored and did not experience the pleasures of being outside. Mander writes, "We were

---

assignments Alaimo writes about in her essay, combined with the ones suggested in this one, would make for an interesting course.

[2] Mary Oliver, foreword to *Poetry Comes Up Where It Can: An Anthology*, ed. Brian Swann (Salt Lake City: University of Utah Press, 2000), xiii.

[3] Ibid., xiv.

all so attuned to events coming along at urban speed in large, prominent packages that our bodies and minds could not attune to the smaller, more subtle events of a forest."[4] Over the next three days, however, Mander and his children slowed down and began noticing the quieter details they had missed on their first day: the sound of leaves crunching beneath one's feet, the joy of skipping stones in a stream, and the pleasure of watching forest animals engage in their daily routines. Mander's family was able to stay in this environment for three more days, experiencing a growth of awareness and a restoration of senses that had been dulled by a contemporary, urban life.[5]

Mander's family's first-day camping experience is one with which my students relate. Many of my students lead very busy lives. In a freewriting exercise I assign at the beginning of the semester,[6] many of them report feeling stressed and disconnected from the natural world and each other. Some of them admit that they feel addicted to their cell phones and Facebook, occasionally making real-world encounters more strained for them than virtual ones. One of my students related a particularly telling incident that spoke to that problem. She said that she worked as a nanny over the summer and had the opportunity to play outside with the children (whom she adored) every day. But she said she found it a real challenge to enjoy playing with them without her cell phone nearby. She found herself more inclined to text her friends than to play with the children. She expressed that this inclination did not feel good to her, but she also did not feel like she could resist it. As she relayed this story to the class, many of us nodded in agreement. We understood this compulsion, this disconnection from the natural world. As an environmental literature teacher, and simply as someone who is concerned about environmental problems, I worried that this kind of disconnection from the natural world affects the way we treat it. Why care for an earth we aren't engaged with?

---

[4] Jerry Mander, "The Walling of Awareness," in *Literature and the Environment: A Reader of Nature and Culture*, ed. Lorraine Anderson, Scott Slovic, and John P. O'Grady (New York: Addison-Wesley Educational Publishers, 1999), 210. "The Walling of Awareness" is also a chapter in Mander's book, *Four Arguments for the Elimination of Television* (New York: William Morrow & Company, 1978).

[5] Ibid.

[6] The prompt I used for this exercise is simply, "How connected do you feel to the natural world?" Prior to giving them this prompt, my students and I usually discuss the ways our society has distracted us from nature. Technology and busy schedules are usually at the top of the list.

Unable to take my classes camping, and aware that camping trips last only a short while, I sought to implement an exercise that my students could practice in everyday suburban life, an exercise that would cultivate their abilities to pay attention and be present in the natural world. From my own personal experiences, I knew that meditation could serve this purpose. I have been practicing yoga for several years, and meditation is a part of my daily practice. It has calmed my anxiety, reconnected me with my emotions, and made me more attentive. The anxiety, inattention, and emotional detachment I have experienced in the past (and sometimes still experience, though to a lesser degree) at least partially spring from the fast-paced world in which we live. Despite my own positive experiences with meditation, I felt nervous about integrating it into my course. I worried that it was too new-agey, too "touchy feely" for a Catholic university.

It can be daunting to lead meditation for a group of twenty-five students who mainly fall into the eighteen to twenty-two age range and are sometimes skeptical about this "tree hugging" course they're required to take.[7] I knew that many would find the practice peculiar (to put it kindly) so I explained (and still explain each time I teach this course) that we were going to sit quietly *with our eyes closed* for five minutes at the beginning of each class to quiet our minds and prepare for the class itself.[8] I also tell them that caring for the environment requires mindfulness and that meditation can enhance our ability to be mindful. Despite this explanation, my instructions are still met with eye rolls and heavy sighs. They are also met with interest, and—from time to time—delight. Over the course of the semester, however, many of the eye rollers and sighers come to appreciate the practice. When about midway through the semester I dare suggest that we should skip the meditation for the day because of the intensity of our workload, I am always met with protests. "*Please*," one student objected, "this is my only quiet time all day!" The

---

[7] All undergraduate students at USF are required to take one environmentally themed general education course. Literature and the Natural Environment is one of a handful of options they have.

[8] Because it is a challenge to clear our minds of thoughts, I suggest that my students count their breath. I also tell them that they can alter their breath to affect their state of mind. If they find they are excited and are having difficulty settling down, I suggest that they exhale for a longer time period than they inhale. If, on the other hand, they are tired and need more energy, I suggest that they increase the time during which they are inhaling. I have encountered this practice of focusing on the breath in a number of different meditation classes and books.

practice stands, of course, and I never regret it. Most, if not all, of what I have planned to cover gets covered. Whatever is left behind will wait until another day.

While this practice is very rewarding, it is also a challenge to conduct. The first semester I initiated it, I thought I could sit in silence with my students, eyes closed. After a few days, I suspected this was probably foolish of me, and I began periodically opening my eyes to watch the students. Sure enough, a couple of students were texting, and one or two were quietly rereading the assignment for our class, or one for another class. I met their eyes, and they returned to the meditation. I explain after our meditation time is up that the exercise is part of their participation in class. Failing to practice it will result in a lower participation grade. While I do not like having to enforce the meditation this way, I have found that it is necessary, and I have to explain the practice and its importance a few times during the early part of the semester. Over time, students become more and more comfortable with it. While some never learn to love the meditation practice, others have told me after the semester has ended that they have integrated it into their daily lives. They appreciate the way meditation helps them quiet their minds and gives them a greater sense of peace.

I got the idea for the second meditative assignment I conduct from two sources.

The Franciscan reading group I was a part of at USF read Ilia Delio, Keith Douglass Warner, and Pamela Wood's *Care for Creation: A Franciscan Spirituality of the Earth*. The chapter entitled "Franciscan Contemplation" really stood out to me. Here the authors argue that prayer and contemplation play an important role in our efforts to care for the earth. Further, they ask how Christians can possibly love Christ and, at the same time, treat the earth with immense disrespect. One conclusion they come to is that our hearts and minds have become disconnected. Many Christians believe in God intellectually, but they have lost a physical and emotional connection to Christ; they do not feel God's presence in the natural world. Delio and others suggest that this disconnection can be healed through prayer and contemplation. Contemplation, for Saint Francis and Saint Clare, occurred after gazing on the crucifix. After seeing God through that image, they were able to see God in all things, in all aspects of creation. For Francis, time spent in nature enhanced his relationship with God.[9] The authors describe Francis' process of contemplation, writing,

---

[9] Ilia Delio, Keith Douglass Warner, and Pamela Wood, *Care for Creation: A Franciscan Spirituality of the Earth* (Cincinnati: St. Anthony Messenger Press, 2008), chap. 8.

"As Francis' heart opened to the overflowing goodness of God, he began to 'see' God's goodness incarnate—Christ—in every aspect of creation. Everything spoke to Francis of the infinite love of God. Trees, worms, flowers by the side of the road, all were for him saints gazing up into the face of God. Creation became the place to find God and, in finding God, Francis realized his intimate relationship to all of creation as 'brother.' He discovered himself to be a member of the large, diverse family of creation."[10] When a person recognizes a connection between one's self and other "aspects of creation," that person will be more inclined to care for those other members of creation. Saint Francis' recognition spoke volumes to me, and I longed for my students to experience something similar.

Of course, not all of my students are Christian. While some of them have spent time reflecting on Christ's presence in their lives, others have not. While it did not seem my role as a teacher of environmental literature to ask students to focus on the presence of Christ in their lives, I did think that I could ask them to focus on creation, hoping that as they gazed upon it, they would feel a connection to the natural world, which, for many, might be a window for experiencing God. For those who do not believe in God, I trusted they would still find a connection to the natural world and that feeling this connection might inspire them to better care for it.

Although I have not assigned chapters from *Care for Creation* to my students, I have assigned a second text that inspired the second meditative assignment I use in class. Terry Tempest Williams' *Finding Beauty in a Broken World* speaks to many of my goals in Literature and the Natural Environment.[11] As the book's title suggests, it recognizes many of the environmental challenges the world is facing while still emphasizing the world's beauty. While the book is composed of three different sections, the second section of the book helped me solidify my idea for incorporating a second meditative assignment in class.[12]

In this section of *Finding Beauty in a Broken World*, Williams recounts her experiences working with scientist John Hoogland in his efforts to

[10] Ibid., 129.

[11] Terry Tempest Williams, *Finding Beauty in a Broken World* (New York: Pantheon Books, 2008).

[12] I should note that the book is not formally divided up into three sections, but one can divide the book up that way, according to Williams' locale. In what I call the first section of the book, Williams is learning how to make mosaics in Ravenna, Italy. In the second part of the book, she is in Bryce Canyon National Park, and in the third part, she is in Rwanda.

study and care for prairie dogs in Bryce Canyon National Park. Hoogland has been studying the endangered species for years, trying to find ways to prevent their extinction. While some of Williams' work with Hoogland involves physical labor, like trapping the prairie dogs in order to tag them and take their blood, most of her work involves observing them from a tower twenty feet above the ground. For two weeks, Williams spends practically twelve hours a day simply observing the prairie dogs. At first she is fairly restless, a bit irritated, and uncertain about how she is going to make it through the duration of the project. She learns, however, to shift her vision, to pay attention to the details of not just the prairie dogs' lives, but the lives of other animals and the landscape that they all share.[13]

She learns to adjust her rhythm and slow down (when necessary) in this life of observation. She naps at midday—when the prairie dogs do as well—and holds her breath when the black-chinned hummingbird's wings "fan [her] face." She notes the pleasures of rising just before the sun and going to bed not long after it has set. "The closure of each day," she writes, "is a benediction of light." As she has slowed down, paid attention to, and fallen in love with her initially unfamiliar surroundings, she notes, "It is a gift to be outside and settle into the rhythms of this place. When do we have the opportunity to simply observe one square acre of nature for two weeks without disturbance? To be outside and settle into the native rhythms is to witness a unity of time and space." This unity of time and space seems to bring her peace, but it is not an experience that comes easily. "Each day," she writes, "is a discipline."[14] The schedule Williams maintains throughout her day and the careful recording of the prairie dogs require discipline and strength. At the same time, they allow her to slow down, to feel the grace that is present in everyday life that often goes unnoticed.

These observations, and the rewards that come with them, affect Williams' reflections on her life outside this two-week project. She thinks of her brother, Steve, dying from lymphoma, who found peace walking a labyrinth at a cancer retreat. She writes to Steve, "the days can be long, but that is my problem. I think of what you wrote from *Commonweal*, 'Sit still and look for what is looking for you.'" And then asking him about his experience, she writes, "Educate me. So that I may be more humbly

---

[13] Williams, *Finding Beauty*, 91–204.
[14] Ibid., 107, 137, 114, 120.

present with you as your loving sister."[15] This ability to be "humbly present" seems to be connected with Williams' ability to sit still and watch, an ability she cultivates while working with the prairie dogs.

Of course, not all is peaceful presence during prairie dog observation. The prairie dogs are often under a great deal of stress. They live in a land of predators, some human, some not. And they undergo the stress of being captured and having their blood taken. And Williams herself undergoes a related stress, that of blood taker, catcher, and waiter, hoping desperately that all the dogs will be marked and survive. They are all, Williams writes, "Sentient beings living in a charged world."[16]

Still, Williams finds that sharing these stressful moments with the prairie dogs draws her closer to them. She notes that to spend time with the prairie dogs, to watch them daily and to calm them when she traps them and then takes their blood as gently and lovingly as one can—"is to open the door to empathy and cross a new threshold of shared existence." This door toward empathy is absolutely crucial to walk through if humans are going to be able to protect endangered species. Williams writes, "A species in peril will most likely survive now only if we allow it to, if our imaginations can enter into the soul of the animal and we pull back on our own needs and desires to accommodate theirs. What other species require of us is our attention. Otherwise, we are entering a narrative of disappearing intelligences."[17]

As I read Williams the summer before I taught the text, I wondered how I might help my students open this door of empathy. How might I help them learn to be more present and compassionate toward another species when they have such difficulty giving attention to one another? I knew the meditation at the beginning of class would help, but I wanted something more. So I created an assignment I hoped would give them an opportunity to experience, if not what Saint Francis and Saint Clare experienced, then at least a taste of what Williams did.

This assignment asks students to sit quietly in nature for fifteen minutes a week over a period of ten weeks. Ideally, they are to pick the same spot, but if they are unable to do that for one reason or another, they can choose a different spot as needed. Each week, after spending time in nature, they are to type up a page about their experience. I tell them they can write about the experience itself and/or thoughts that they had

---

[15] Ibid., 110.
[16] Ibid., 119.
[17] Ibid., 105, 203.

during the experience that are related to our class's subject. The pages should be collected together as an environmental journal. Additionally, I ask them to make some sort of visual record of their meditation spot(s). The students turn the journals and visual records in at the end of the semester; they also share some of their writing and their images with the class in a five-minute presentation.

This assignment has been immensely successful. While some of the students dread it initially, many of them come to enjoy it over the course of the semester. More importantly, many students find that the project does bind them to nature and helps them to see nature's beauty; some of these students also attest to experiencing God's love during their projects. Their journals speak to these results and the value of the assignment as a whole. One student, an atheist, attested to the perfection he saw while watching his spot in a cemetery near campus. He wrote, "Light pours into the graveyard and drenches everything in sight. The snow melts. The grass peaks up from its slumber. The trees that mingle with one another are rejoicing. They know soon this sun will give them life. It is their mother. At this moment in time everything seems perfect. *Life* is perfect." Recognizing the beauty, the perfection of God's creation, became a way for this student to experience peace, even if he didn't identify that peace as God's. He also recognized the connection between elements of nature and saw that life, despite all of its problems—some of which he recognized in his paper—is good. Such a recognition enhances one's love for life, one's compassion and desire to care for the earth.

Another student, this one Catholic, ended each reflection of her journal with a prayer to God. She also spent a significant portion of her journal discussing metaphors she found between the natural world and her relationship with God. Spending time outside after a blizzard, she writes, "The snow is untouched. I look at this and I can see the life that I have ahead of me. It is untouched. There are no tracks to follow. The snow covers the ground so I see no path. This path is for God and me to create." She speaks further of trust and thanks God for "unconditional love that never leaves." Fulfilling my greatest hope for the assignment, she writes in her final prayer to God, "Break our hearts for what breaks your heart [. . . .] Fill us with your spirit as we seek to make a difference in the community[. . . . H]elp us to[. . .] be the servants and stewards of creation that you have called each of us to be."

Other students have shared stories that spoke to the ways their connection to the land deepened as they spent time in nature. One student who was particularly defensive about being in the class for at least the first half of the semester became quite captivated with a family of rabbits who lived underneath a bush in the space he was observing. During his presentation, he shared how he became protective of the rabbits over the course of the semester, wanting to protect them from the neighborhood cats and any other harm that came their way. Seeing this student tell this story and watching his transformation over the semester touched me on a deep level. The project and the course had clearly left an impact on him.

The students' visual projects are just as rewarding to see as their journals are to read (perhaps more so). These projects give the artists in class a chance to shine, and they give all the students an opportunity to engage with their projects in a different way. The diversity of projects is always a delight to see. Many students take pictures or film their spots; however, others have created different kinds of art projects that reflect their experiences: drawings, collages, and even wooden panels covered in cloth and embroidered with flowers. Two students worked together to create a film; one focused on the film's visuals, and the other on writing and recording a musical sound track to go along with it. (This last project has encouraged me to expand the possibilities of the assignment: perhaps all records need not be visual.) Whatever the project, most of the students' works show a deeper connection to nature, more care for the world, and an appreciation for God's work.

Of course, the students' own projects helped them to understand Terry Tempest Williams' work better, and reading her work helped them understand the value of their own assignment to sit in nature. In an essay I assign on Williams' book and other readings we do in the course, one student reflected on the importance of spending time in nature. He wrote, "Nature and the land can be used as tools for one's own spiritual growth. Nature is isolating and beautiful. By removing ourselves from the modern world and the mind-cluttering attractions it [im]poses upon us, we are forced to think. We are allowed to sit in silence with no automobile noises in our ears or factory chemicals in our lungs; the earth and the trees become living beings just as we are ourselves. Sometimes when our lives are juxtaposed with the life of the land, it causes a reevaluation of the self." While this student was writing about Williams' time with the prairie dogs, I could not help but think he was also thinking about his own time in nature. Without the assignment to sit outdoors, Williams' observations would have been easier to dismiss.

Other texts stand out as particularly useful for environmental literature and would also work well in other courses at Catholic institutions.

One such text is Alicia Ostriker's poem "Daffodils."[18] Like Williams' book, this poem looks at some of the atrocities in our world while emphasizing the beauty. The first stanza of the poem captures this juxtaposition well:

> The day the war against Iraq begins
> I'm photographing the yellow daffodils
> With their outstretched arms and ruffled cups
> Blowing in the wind of Jesus Green.[19]

Throughout the rest of the poem, Ostriker vacillates between the idyllic beauty of the pastoral scene she inhabits and the "cruel" dark world of war and "stupidity."[20] She acknowledges that her position of privilege, the one that allows her to appreciate beauty, also allows her to "taste pain" and suggests that it is the poet's job to look for the beauty in spite of the darkness. She writes, "[. . .] life is hard / But better than the alternatives / The no and the nothing [. . .]"[21] and ends the poem asking her readers to "defend" the beauty of the natural world, "the day we see the daffodils[.]"[22] The poem speaks to the importance of defending the beauty of our lives in the midst of destruction; it refuses to put the natural world beneath the world of war.

My students all seem to love this poem. One student who did not enjoy much of environmental literature claimed that this poem gave him hope and offered him a new perspective on life. He said he often felt depressed by all the trouble in the world and had never considered Ostriker's point that our world, rife with problems, is certainly better than no world at all. The beauty in it must be defended—even if it feels like an uphill battle, a task too great for a single human being.

While the problems of our world do seem to call for collective rather than individual action, some peace activists and spiritual leaders have emphasized the important role the individual can play in creating a more beautiful world. In the foreword to Thich Nhat Hanh's *Peace Is Every*

---

[18] Alicia Ostriker, "Daffodils," in *No Heaven* (Pittsburgh: University of Pittsburgh Press, 2005), 126.

[19] Ibid., lines 1–4.

[20] Ibid. Line 22 reads "The cruel wars are good the stupidity is good."

[21] Ibid., line 21, lines 25–27.

[22] Ibid. The last four lines of the poem read "[. . .]Don't you think / It is our business to defend it / Even the day our masters start a war? To defend the day we see the daffodils?"

Step, the Dalai Lama argues that individual "internal transformation" is "the only way" to "bring about world peace."[23] While some activists might balk at this suggestion, the Dalai Lama reasons that "[p]eace must first be developed within an individual."[24] Hanh recognizes this as well; in *Peace Is Every Step*, he illustrates how meditative practices, specifically focusing on the breath, can help a person cultivate peace in everyday life. He contends that without peace in our own lives we are unable to bring peace into the world.[25]

Of course, as a professor, I hope that my students will take the skills they learn in my class out into the world. If they can develop a greater sense of tranquility within themselves, perhaps they can share that with others and help to create a more peaceful world. Teaching Williams' *Finding Beauty in a Broken World* offers the students an example of how inner tranquility can impact both personal and global relationships. As I mentioned earlier, the stillness Williams cultivates as she observes prairie dogs affects her relationships with others. She learns to give her brother Steve the attention he deserves as she asks him to educate her about what he is feeling as he moves closer to death.[26] Later in the book, Williams goes to Rwanda with a group of artists who are creating a memorial for those who died in the genocide. During her time in Rwanda, she bonds with a number of people and learns much from them.[27] Reading these excerpts from the book, my students and I discussed how important it is to really listen to others and give them our full attention. The ability to do so is a skill that seems to be diminishing in our fast-paced world.

Reflecting on my class's discussion, I had to laugh, somewhat sheepishly, as I realized I was teaching a group of twenty-five students who did not know each other well. Some of them were friends, but most of them were not. Many of them did not know each others' names at the midpoint in the semester. How could I teach the importance of community in a community that was not very cohesive? Recognizing this problem, I suggested we cancel class for a day and just talk to each other, learn from one another, and get to know each other better. We went

[23] His Holiness the Dalai Lama, foreword to *Peace Is Every Step*, by Thich Nhat Hanh (New York: Bantam Books, 1991), vii.
[24] Ibid.
[25] Thich Nhat Hanh, *Peace Is Every Step*, 99–100.
[26] Williams, *Finding Beauty*, 110.
[27] Ibid., 223–387.

around the class, sharing whatever we wanted to about ourselves: something unusual or ideas that were important to us.[28] At first the discussion was a bit awkward and forced, but as the students and I relaxed and began joking with one another, it quickly evolved into something heartfelt and genuine. It also radically changed the dynamic of the course. While many of the students in my classes gel really well together, at times—and this is especially true for general education courses—the students just don't seem to bond or connect with one another as easily. Taking the time to shape this community in the middle of the semester created a bond between us we had been previously missing. The class, which had been a bit bumpy for a bit, went much more smoothly for the rest of the semester. Giving each other our presence in this way midway through the semester positively impacted the rest of the course in a dramatic way.

While the meditation practices and readings that are assigned with them have deepened my students' connections to the natural world and each other, I am still looking for ways to take this work further. Later this year, I am planning on incorporating service learning projects into the course, a move that will extend my students' connection to their more immediate environments in the larger Fort Wayne community. This move will also reinforce the connection between meditative practices and community service.

As I continue to shape Literature and the Natural Environment, I feel deeply grateful for all the opportunities given at a Catholic university. Without my experiences in the Franciscan reading group at USF, I might still be hesitating, imagining that the course would benefit from meditative practices but feeling uncertain about how to integrate them. I might still be held back by my own secular education, fearing that being explicit about the sacramentality of the natural world and the personal might somehow diminish the intellectual rigor of the course. Such hesitation would have kept my students and me from experiencing something deeper, from recognizing the connection between stillness and caring for the earth and one another.

Meditative practices have enhanced my course and drawn my students and me closer together. They have made us closer as a community and more concerned about our connections with one another. They have

---

[28] I usually have these kinds of conversations on the first day of each semester; however, I had begun this particular course by asking students about their environmental interests.

made us better listeners and helped us experience the beauty in creation. In a fast-paced, chaotic, and sometimes violent world, sitting in silence can be a radical act. Catholic education allows us that opportunity.

You Are Here:
Engagement, Spirituality, and Slow Teaching

Anita Houck

During my first year as a professor, I was saved by Grice. I'd been pretty happy with how my classes had gone until the course evaluations told me that many of my students weren't: the books were too hard; the workload was too heavy for a general-education course; I kept telling them they were wrong; and, above all, I insisted that it was important to care about grammar in a class that was definitely not in the English Department. In the soul-searching that followed, the work of linguistic philosopher Paul Grice—distilled, at first, by James L. Ratcliff—gave me some insight into the gap between my students' perceptions and mine.[1] The heart of understanding what Grice called "cooperative discourse," as Ratcliff put it, is that "participants see discourse occurring *according to the aims of their own interactions*."[2] In other words, people tend to judge

---

[1] Grice's Principle of Cooperative Discourse—"Make your conversational contribution such as is required, at the stage at which it occurs, by the accepted purpose or direction of the talk exchange in which you are engaged"—rests on assumptions that describe well effective teaching and learning: "our talk exchanges . . . are characteristically, at least, cooperative efforts; and each participant recognizes in them, to some extent, a common purpose or set of purposes, or at least a mutually accepted direction." Paul Grice, "Logic and Conversation," in *Studies in the Way of Words* (Cambridge, MA: Harvard, 1989), 26. My thanks to Dr. M. Catherine Gruber for generously sharing her perspectives on Grice.

[2] James L. Ratcliff, "What Works in General Education: What the Research Tells Us," paper presented at the Association of American Colleges and Universities conference "Best Practices in General Education and Its Assessment: Bridging Theory and Practice," Atlanta, Georgia, February 22–24, 2001. The emphasis is Ratcliff's.

a conversation based on how well it accomplishes the goals they brought to the conversation in the first place. Before long, I'd translated Grice's maxim into my own: if a student comes into the classroom expecting *a*, and I come into the classroom planning to teach *b*, the student isn't likely to be delighted that I'm opening to her the exciting new world of *b*; she's much more likely to think that I'm trying to do *a*, and doing it badly.

Researcher Barbara Walvoord, writing specifically about teaching religious studies and theology, has called this expectation gap "the great divide." Walvoord's surveys found that, while faculty and students in these courses agree in valuing "factual knowledge" and "understanding other religions," faculty consider "critical thinking" a more important goal than students do. Meanwhile, students in these courses also rate very highly a goal faculty generally don't: to "develop their own spiritual and religious lives."[3] A good deal of recent evidence suggests that this discrepancy exists throughout the college curriculum, as students frequently come to their classes expecting to reflect on their spiritual lives and questions of meaning.[4] As it turns out, encouraging students to meet goals that are often classified as "spiritual"[5]—for instance, examining their experiences and assumptions, knowing themselves more deeply, and forming values that will help them move with integrity into the wider world—can help students meet more traditionally academic goals as well. In fact, the best conversations in my classes seemed to incorporate both approaches, as students connected scholarly knowledge and self-knowledge. I first noticed the pattern toward the end of that revelatory first semester, and I sketched it in a handout entitled, with appropriate tentativeness, "Circle of theological reflection according to

---

[3] Barbara E. Walvoord, *Teaching and Learning in College Introductory Religion Courses* (Malden, MA: Blackwell, 2008), 6, 15–18.

[4] For a helpful overview, see Allison Pingree, "Teaching, Learning, and Spirituality in the College Classroom," *Essays on Teaching Excellence: Toward the Best in the Academy* 19, no. 6 (2007–8), The Professional & Organizational Development Network in Higher Education, accessed October 10, 2013, http://podnetwork.org/publications/2007 -2008-essays/.

[5] The definition of spirituality is notoriously fluid and often ambiguous, as Pingree's discussion shows; ibid. Scholars in the academic field of spirituality, however, insist that it requires the practitioner to engage his or her own beliefs in a process of "self-implication." The classic discussion is Sandra M. Schneiders's in "The Study of Christian Spirituality: Contours and Dynamics of a Discipline," *Christian Spirituality Bulletin* 6, no. 1 (Spring 1998): 1–12; the essay is reprinted in *Minding the Spirit: The Study of Christian Spirituality*, ed. Elizabeth A. Dreyer and Mark S. Burrows (Baltimore: Johns Hopkins University Press, 2004), 5–24.

RLST 213, Fall 2001: A DRAFT." Ever since, I've been observing, tweaking, and teaching the circle as a way to help students engage new academic material while also encouraging students' self-knowledge.[6]

Being explicit about students' self-reflection may daunt the faint of heart or rushed of syllabus, and indeed, walking through the circle can take up a good part of an early class. Teaching the practice of hermeneutic engagement, though, has its rewards: it provides language to discuss the process of learning, a familiar method for entering unfamiliar texts and ideas, a gentle way to respond to misunderstanding, a reliable structure to facilitate students' work outside of class, a model for integrating what's sometimes called "head knowledge" and "heart knowledge," and even a humane tool for assessment. Used in all these ways, references to "the circle" become habitual in my classes, a shared shorthand for the practice of slowing down our judgments so that we honor our own reactions but don't confuse them with understanding or final evaluations.

At the end of my courses, students now often report that the circle helped them master the content of the discipline and think critically about it: the circle "helped me understand and learn about religions other than my own" and "narrowed down a knowledge-packed course."[7] In addition, some note that the circle helps them reflect on how they learn: "This [the circle] was challenging because it forced me to look at what I knew before and then I had to see where my idiolocator [starting point] ended up after each religion. I enjoyed it though because I kind of used it as a tool to see how much I had learned." I make the point that the circle isn't limited to work in religious studies or theology, and students agree that they use it beyond the classroom: one wrote, "I love [it]

---

[6] Like most other details, the title of the circle itself has changed, first from "the circle of theological reflection" to "the circle of theological reflection or praxis" and now, since I teach almost only religious studies rather than theology courses, to "the hermeneutic circle." The credits listed in the diagram also appear on the handout I give to my classes. They acknowledge the influence of the students at Saint Mary's College, Notre Dame, Indiana, who enrolled in Experiencing God, one of several courses that meet our two-course general education requirement, the first time I taught it; Thomas Groome's work on catechetical praxis, for instance, in *Sharing Faith: A Comprehensive Approach to Religious Education and Pastoral Ministry; The Way of Shared Praxis* (San Francisco: HarperSanFrancisco, 1991); the discussion of empathetic and critical approaches in Gary L. Comstock with C. Wayne Mayhall, *Religious Autobiographies*, 2nd ed. (Belmont, CA: Wadsworth, 2004), viii–ix, 13–19; and Patricia O'Connell Killen's insightful suggestions—particularly on the ordering of steps 2 and 3—in the 2003–2004 Colloquy for Pre-tenure Faculty at the Wabash Center for Teaching and Learning in Theology and Religion.

[7] Comments from students are quoted from course evaluation forms.

The Circle of Theological Reflection or Praxis, or the Hermeneutic Circle
(with thanks to Fall 2000's RLST 213 class, Thomas Groome, Gary L. Comstock, and Patricia O'Connell Killen)

new idiolocator

X

(1) You are here (the idiolocator)
What do I believe? What do I do?

(6) Decisions on what you've learned
Do I want to change my beliefs or actions?

(2) First response to the other
What are my initial feelings, questions, and thoughts?*

(5) Reflection on what you've learned
How does this encounter challenge or confirm my own beliefs or ideas, my culture, my tools for understanding?

(3) Critical reflection on your response
What do my responses teach me about myself?

(4) Understanding the other*

(4b) Second (and later) step: Understanding from the outside (using critical reason, your own perspective and knowledge; etic)
What do I learn from looking through my own eyes at the other's worldview? What can I see that the other sees differently or doesn't see?

(4a) First (and later) step: Understanding from the inside (trying to see through the other's eyes, active listening; emic)
How does the other see the world? What does the other see that I don't see? What do I learn from seeing as the other sees?

* If your initial reactions are positive (I agree with or like the other's view), you may learn more if you emphasize the *second* step in understanding, using the outsider's perspective.

* If your initial reactions are negative (I disagree with or don't like the other's view), you may learn more if you emphasize the first step in understanding, looking at the experience from the insider's perspective.

because it is not only useful in a religious context but also in other life situations," while another wrote that the "balance of teaching religion as an academic discipline integrated with our own experiences taught me about myself & others." Though not all students find it helpful (more on that later), some make it a habit of mind and heart. It has surely become that for their teacher.

The circle begins with an X labeled "You are here (the idiolocator)," borrowing the official name for one of those helpful, similarly marked dots or arrows on a map. The idiolocator comprises everything we bring to an encounter, consciously or not: assumptions, past experiences, questions, emotions. A non-cartographic equivalent is the metaphor of lenses through which we see the world. Drawing attention to the idiolocator is important, both because our starting points define what we'll see and what we'll miss, and because each person's perspective can contribute in a unique way to the conversation ahead. Asking students to articulate this starting point can be helpful, especially if it's likely students are coming to the topic with misinformation; "What have you heard about Islam?" almost invariably precedes our study of that religion.

Most often, though, our class sessions leave the idiolocator tacit and don't enter the circle until we encounter something specific—a chapter, a movie, a chant—that introduces an "other." The word "other" is an admittedly imperfect attempt at a broad, neutral term for whatever we encounter, whether a religion, a novel, a newspaper story, or a person met at a party. A person's initial response to an other (step 2 in the circle) is usually at least as emotional as intellectual: Tibetan throat-singing sounds creepy, like a horror movie; I like this character because I can relate to her; hey, doesn't that guy look like Draco Malfoy? The last, to be honest, is the example they now hear first. Over the years, I've come up with examples to show that the circle really is at work in many interactions. As a result, the current popularity of Harry Potter in my college has made Draco a helpful comrade in introducing the circle. Students seem to easily imagine two friends, whom a recent class named Stacy and Judy. They hear that Judy is a passionate Potterite, a spiritual daughter of Gryffindor, and immediately have a partial sense of her idiolocator. They can then imagine her going to a party where Stacy introduces her to a friend—recently named Chad—who looks for all the world like Tom Felton, the actor who portrays Draco in the films. What might Judy's first-contact response be when she meets this other, the spitting image of Harry's classmate and nemesis at Hogwarts?

The example isn't perfect, and it will be obsolete before too long, but it has some points in its favor. First, it brings in humor. Humor, particularly self-deprecating humor and inside jokes (as the saga of Judy and Chad becomes), has been shown to relieve stress and enhance memory in the classroom.[8] Second, the example provides a more-or-less neutral parallel to the many other prejudices we carry. Students can see Judy's Dracophobia without rushing to condemn her, and before long they can

---

[8] Probably the most prolific writer on the subject is Ronald A. Berk, whose books include *Humor as an Instructional Defibrillator: Evidence-Based Techniques in Teaching and Assessment* (Sterling, VA: Stylus Publishing, 2002). Avner Ziv summarizes studies on humor and teaching through 1988 in "Teaching and Learning with Humor: Experiment and Replication," *Journal of Experimental Education* 57, no. 1 (Fall 1988): 7.

see parallels to their own biases, some of which are not as innocuous. Students sometimes make this connection in evaluating the circle: "The circle helped me see my first prejudices about a religion and how I developed into understanding the different terms and stories"; "I have learned that I was judgmental toward Islam and sometimes other religions. I have also learned how important it is not to make generalizations about entire religions or groups of people." Finally, neuroscientific research suggests that people are reluctant to change their minds—that is, to learn—when faced with facts and logical argument. In a popular overview of this research, Chris Mooney observes, "We apply fight-or-flight reflexes not only to predators, but to data itself." Echoing students' concern for personal growth, he writes, "We have other important goals besides accuracy—including identity affirmation and protecting one's sense of self—and often those make us highly resistant to changing our beliefs when the facts say we should." What can lead people to change their minds, he finds, is a presentation that begins in shared values[9]—in terms of our earlier Gricean maxim, a sign of a shared *a* and *b*. An example like Dracophobia can do this work: not everyone is a fan of J. K. Rowling, but everyone knows someone who is, and most students would agree it's good to meet people and make friends, and bad to dismiss other people out of prejudice.

To emphasize the value in attending to first responses, it is worth making three points explicit to students. First, the first response is where we begin an encounter, not where we end it. All of us can be tempted to react to something and immediately think we've made sense of it: we now have an opinion and can act on that basis. Instead, the circle emphasizes the "first" in our first reactions to the other. To rest in an initial impression would mean not learning, not growing—an outcome neither students nor teachers find satisfying.

Second, the only criterion for a good first response is honesty. As I can all too readily illustrate from personal experience, often we aren't proud of our responses; they can reveal prejudices we'd rather not admit, rather not have. But if we aren't honest about them, the rest of the circle won't work. Honesty is essential to our intellectual goals because we can't see clearly until we know how our lenses are shaped; it's also essential to our spiritual goals, since, once we're willing to see biases in ourselves,

---

[9] Chris Mooney, "The Science of Why We Don't Believe Science: How Our Brains Fool Us on Climate, Creationism, and the Vaccine-Autism Link," *Mother Jones* (May/June 2011), accessed October 10, 2013, http://motherjones.com/politics/2011/03/denial-science-chris-mooney.

we have the freedom to choose whether to nurture them or to work toward changing them. Maybe Judy can't help gasping and recoiling when she first meets Chad, but once she observes her reaction, she can decide whether to persist in the assumptions that motivated her response, or to question and revise them. Honesty, and the safety that allows it, are crucial if students are to learn about themselves and be open to learning about an other. In Mooney's words, "If you want someone to accept new evidence, make sure to present it to them in a context that doesn't trigger a defensive, emotional reaction."[10] Accordingly, it's important to commend honesty in first responses, even—perhaps particularly—when the teacher disagrees with the responses themselves.

Third, a first response teaches us less about what we're encountering than about ourselves. One reason a class needn't explicitly discuss idiolocators on most topics is that our first responses do so much to reveal them, including aspects of them we may not have been able to articulate before. Donald L. Finkel echoes a tradition at least as old as Plato when he writes that "we often do not know what we think [or, he could add, feel] until we hear what we say. We are too close to the thoughts inside our own head to get any distance, and our unvoiced ideas are often too fuzzy and indistinct to be readily grasped. Putting our thoughts into words both forces them to take on a more distinct shape *and* allows us to become acquainted with them."[11]

Because our reactions reveal more about ourselves than about the other, the circle moves from noting first responses (2) to reflecting on what those responses tell us about ourselves (3). Perhaps Judy's burst of revulsion on meeting Chad will show her that she's internalized the Potter saga a bit more deeply than she realized. Similarly, when my first-year students encounter, early in the semester, a street play depicting the mischievous child-god Krishna, their sometimes-vehement responses tend to say more about how they feel about children or lying, or how attached they are to a certain vision of the divine in their own tradition, than about their nascent understanding of Hinduism. Sometimes students can benefit from some structure as they process their responses and gain insight into themselves. For instance, another tool used early in my courses, as in many religious-studies courses, is a set of elements of religion; in my case, these are (roughly) the transcendent, beliefs, ritual, ethics, and community. I propose to students that people, often without

---

[10] Mooney, "Science."

[11] Donald L. Finkel, *Teaching with Your Mouth Shut* (Portsmouth, NH: Heinemann/Boynton/Cook, 2000), 88.

knowing it, tend to believe one or the other of these is most important, and I invite them to use their responses to Krishna to see whether my hypothesis is right. Sure enough, the students who feel most disconcerted by the tricksterly toddler god tend to prioritize ethics in their understanding of religion, while those enamored of him put more value on the transcendent or on myth's ability to express beliefs. I encourage them to use this expanded awareness of their idiolocators as they analyze their reactions to future texts. Students sometimes comment that they make this kind of analysis a habit; as one evaluated the circle, "Loved it! I analyze my first contact responses all the time now." Similarly, once students in a second-year course on religious experience identify themselves as more healthy-minded or sick-souled, they frequently report having a better understanding of their relationships with friends and roommates.

The next steps, 4a and 4b, move from focusing on self-understanding to focusing on understanding the other. Like many models—the hermeneutic of charity and the hermeneutic of suspicion, Gary L. Comstock's "empathic" and "critical" approaches,[12] Peter Elbow's believing and doubting[13]—the circle defines understanding as a process in two movements, here called "understanding from the inside" and "understanding from the outside." Two quotations appear on class handouts to express the attitude of engagement that characterizes this two-part approach: Arvind Sharma's claim that "Both the insider and the outsider see the truth, but genuine understanding may be said to arise at the point of their intersection,"[14] and the insight of Sal Della Bella and Denise Bedard Ruiz, participants in the Catholic Common Ground Initiative, that "The overarching question should be, 'What do others see, that I cannot yet see?'"[15] Understanding, in other words, grows in the conversation between student and what is studied, first in taking on the perspective of the other (4a) and then in examining that perspective with informed critical awareness (4b).

[12] Comstock, *Religious Autobiographies*. For many students, the word "critical," used by Comstock and many others to describe this kind of reasoning, connotes fault-finding rather than reasoned critique. After semesters spent trying to rehabilitate the word, I surrendered and adopted the metaphors of "inside" and "outside."

[13] John C. Bean, *Engaging Ideas: The Professor's Guide to Integrating Writing, Critical Thinking, and Active Learning in the Classroom* (San Francisco: Jossey-Bass, 2001), 142–43.

[14] Arvind Sharma, e-mail message quoted in Amy M. Braverman, "The Interpretation of Gods," *University of Chicago Magazine* 97, no. 2 (December 2004): 36.

[15] Sal Della Bella and Denise Bedard Ruiz, "Archdiocese Teaches Effective Dialogue," *Initiative Report* 8, no. 3 (December 2004): 5.

Understanding from the inside (4a) is always the first movement in understanding, and one to which we need to return repeatedly. It recalls David Gitomer's insistence that anything we study deserves not only our respect but also our sympathetic engagement: "one who studies the religion of another has an obligation to explain what there is about that religion that makes it so compelling that someone would choose it."[16] Gaining an accurate and sympathetic understanding of the other typically entails a good deal of work: with the help of authoritative sources, we set ourselves to master new vocabulary, situate in history, research context, decipher allusions, and try to grasp concepts through which the world may look quite different than it did before we started. Until we learn the grammar of this new world, we're likely to remain befuddled— or, worse, to settle unwittingly into the assumption that others see the world as we do but just use different-sounding words to describe it.

Fully understanding the other must begin with, and continually return to, this insider stance and the sources that inform it. But understanding also includes standing outside. In this second movement of understanding (4b), we try to see what the other might not see, making comparisons, probing with questions, drawing out implications, and perceiving connections and seeming inconsistencies. With the sound information gained in 4a, and with the humility of honest beginners, we can move toward making informed judgments about what we've learned. Given our own ethical stances, what questions would we ask about a god who lies, prefers butter to enlightenment, and grows up to lure milkmaids from their husbands' sides by the sound of his flute? How convincing is Diana L. Eck's comparison of the tastes of Krishna to the faces of Christ?[17] Once she rallies the patience to hear him out, how might Judy evaluate Chad's logic when he disparages J. K. Rowling's work in favor of J. R. R. Tolkien's?

In these first four steps of the circle, students experience the disequilibrium that comes from encountering something new. Faith Adiele describes this movement well in *Meeting Faith: An Inward Odyssey*, a memoir I've used in introductory classes and quoted on syllabi: "I want

---

[16] David L. Gitomer, " 'Tell Me One Thing, Krishna . . .': A Personal Reflection on Catholic Faith and Religious Pluralism," in *As Leaven in the World: Catholic Perspectives on Faith, Vocation, and the Intellectual Life*, ed. Thomas M. Landy (Franklin, WI: Sheed & Ward, 2001), 70.

[17] Diana L. Eck, *Encountering God: A Spiritual Journey from Bozeman to Banaras* (Boston: Beacon, 2003), 97–101.

to speak for the importance of risk and movement, of going outside yourself and your comfort zone. I want to champion the lessons of failure and seduce you into traveling the world to find home. I want you to imagine the unimaginable and use literature to embrace a life different from your own. And I want you to question."[18] In the last two steps of the circle, students ask how their new understanding of themselves and the other will affect how they see the world (5) and how they'll live their lives (6). This movement parallels Finkel's model of good teaching, summarized as "providing experience, provoking reflection": "the environment a teacher designs should prompt two different kinds of outcomes, each in its proper time. First, it should yield a potentially instructive experience, one that provokes thinking because it causes some disequilibrium. Second, it should allow for thinking about that experience, reflection that aims to fathom its meaning. If successful, the reflective effort will result in an increase in intelligence (however small): It will yield more fruitful habits of response. These new habits, in turn, enable the pupil to have new and more meaningful experiences from the same environment."[19] Finkel's description recalls the rhythm of the Rite of Christian Initiation of Adults (RCIA). In that process, sacramental initiation is followed by a period of mystagogia, in which the initiates reflect on their experience in light of Scripture and Christian theology. Similarly, in steps 5 and 6, students reflect on their encounter with the other, evaluate their beliefs and actions in light of it, and step into new idiolocators.

In what's no doubt something of a mixed message, I tell students that steps 5 and 6 are crucially important to their education—and that they'll generally have to happen in the 9,930 minutes every week during which we don't gather as a class (which include the 300-plus minutes of my office hours). In a reverent nod to Grice, I'm honest that we'll devote most of our time together to the two steps of understanding (4a and 4b) rather than to the integrative work that follows it. My goals, after all, like those of most faculty Walvoord surveyed, fall largely into the categories of knowledge of religions and development of critical-thinking skills. But classes in many institutions and disciplines may have learning goals that require ample discussion of integration. Clooney, for instance, writes eloquently of practicing in the classroom "the process of re-creating our

---

[18] Faith Adiele, *Meeting Faith: The Forest Journals of a Black Buddhist Nun* (New York: Norton, 2004), 295.

[19] Finkel, *Teaching with Your Mouth Shut*, 152.

religious selves,"[20] of enabling students "to see God within our own religious tradition or across religious boundaries."[21] Similarly, Gitomer observes that "to teach a non-Christian tradition at arm's length is to say that God's love does not have the power to come to us, to illumine us, and to ignite us"; he seeks a fuller engagement, an approach that "is not the kind that allows you to see only what you came to find, but the kind that changes you."[22]

While I don't devote much class time to the reflection of steps 5 and 6, we discuss it in our early lessons on Dracophobia and, in some courses, observe it in memoirs like Adiele's and Diana L. Eck's *Encountering God: A Spiritual Journey from Bozeman to Banaras*. Students then practice these steps in a short project that narrates a complete turn around the circle. They attend (and, often, participate in) a religious event from a tradition not their own and not Christian, frequently one explicitly open to outsiders—for instance, a group visit to a synagogue for Saturday services or a local weekly Zen gathering to which all are welcome. After the event, their assignment is to recount their experience by using the circle. Most semesters, I've required an essay that walks through each step of the circle, starting with an honest account of their idiolocator—for instance, what they knew about the tradition, how they felt about attending—and then describing the event along with their responses to it. Most essays have been admirably honest about fears and misconceptions, and the best have been concrete and self-aware as they described the experience.

One especially thoughtful essay grew out of considerable disequilibrium, even discomfort, and took impressive advantage of the occasion to reflect on it. Tabitha, as I'll call her, wrote that she was "taught about many religions in [pre-college] school but always with the underlying idea that these other religions were against God." As a result, her account of Zen sitting interweaves descriptions of her surroundings with descriptions of her conflicted emotions, creating a vivid dialogue: "There is an epic battle of ideals commencing in my head: Western religion vs. Eastern religion or good vs. evil. But why should this battle take place? I was openly welcomed by the leader of the meditation."

Her account eventually comes to a powerful expression of integration: "I have a new experience under my belt that is beneficial to my emo-

[20] Francis X. Clooney, SJ, *Hindu Wisdom for All God's Children* (Maryknoll, NY: Orbis, 1998), 16.

[21] Ibid., 62.

[22] Gitomer, " 'Tell Me One Thing, Krishna,' " 70.

tional and physical well-being. This is my first conclusion. The second conclusion centers on my original worldview that I brought into the meditation room. I know that the core of Christianity is peace. I attained peace within myself by meditating. I did not pray for peace. Peace came through an action that is not a part of my regular ingrained religious practice. How could this be against God?" Most impressively, Tabitha comes to these insights not only by being open to the new experience—for instance, appreciating the welcome she received—but also by turning to her own tradition, in particular by reflecting on Jesus' acceptance of those his society rejected. Her engagement demonstrates the circle at its best, a movement that Clooney describes well: "No encounter with the 'other,' even with a religion very different from my own, can be fruitful unless I also explore my own self, figuring out who I truly already am, from the beginning. When I encounter religious traditions different from my own, I am not taking up an entirely new topic; I am still exploring myself, too. When I know another religion, I know myself anew, differently, more deeply."[23]

Despite such successful essays, I confess some discomfort in imposing a fixed, retrospective structure—an essay built step-by-step on the circle—on what can be, as it was for Tabitha, a profound and even prayerful experience. Moreover, in merely practical terms, the essays don't always seem especially effective in helping students practice the circle and learn from their experiences. Some essays, for instance, don't clearly apply each part of the circle, so they don't consistently allow me to see how well (to borrow language from Bloom's cognitive taxonomy[24]) the students understand the circle and can apply it to new situations. Second, many essays sound quite similar, even formulaic, when they arrive at steps 5 and 6: the authors affirm their own religious commitments, even saying the experience made them "stronger" in their faith, while also acknowledging that they appreciate what they've experienced and would like to learn more about the tradition they encountered. Such integrative responses may well be honest enough, and they may be adequate for a young adult's brief encounter with a new tradition. Like any

---

[23] Clooney, *Hindu Wisdom*, 4.

[24] A helpful image of the traditional and revised versions of Benjamin Bloom's famous cognitive taxonomy—along with links to further information—can be found at Richard C. Overbaugh and Lynn Schultz, "Bloom's Taxonomy," Old Dominion University, accessed October 10, 2013, http://ww2.odu.edu/educ/roverbau/Bloom/blooms_taxonomy.htm.

stiff conclusion paragraph, though, they suggest that the authors may be fulfilling a rhetorical structure more than probing their unique perspectives; the authors may not yet have made their experiences fully their own.

In response to both my nagging conscience and these gaps in the essays, I've recently adjusted the format of the project. Students now use the circle to record detailed notes on each step of the circle, but they may use a genre of their choice (letters and blogs are common) to reflect more fully on what they learned from their experience. This format gives me more explicit evidence of how well they understand and can apply the circle; it also allows for more creativity, more space, and perhaps more integrity as students process their experiences. As a result, my assessment is sounder, my conscience clearer, and the students' written work less formulaic. However, it seems likely that, without—and perhaps even with—deeper changes in the assignment and course, profound integration like Tabitha's will remain exceptional.

Though I continue to ponder (and sometimes fret about) the assignment, even students required to write the most structured essays have regularly evaluated the out-of-class project as one of the best parts of the course, and those who comment explicitly on the essay say that using the circle helps them clarify their experience. For one, "This [the circle] was most helpful while participating in the out-of-class experience. The circle of theological reflection helped me understand and learn about religions other than my own. . . . even enjoyed writing the essay." For another, the circle structure "just made me think about it [the experience] intellectually and assign words to feelings." A third wrote, "I liked using the circle as a way to reflect on a new experience or encounter with a new religion like we did in our out-of-class experience paper. I think it is a method that we often use subconsciously, and now that I have learned about it in class, I take the time to really reflect on situations that I come upon."

As I mentioned earlier, the circle doesn't impress every student, and that last comment hints at the usual objection. In each class of twenty, two or three students are likely to report disliking or being unimpressed by the circle, most often because they see it as obvious. It's an objection I'd find it difficult to contradict. The circle is, after all, something I observed, not something I created. It's an attempt to articulate a process that seemed to happen fairly naturally in my classes and that, I suspect, happens fairly naturally for many of us when we have to make sense of something new. The only time I suspect the process is not natural, in fact, is when we're panicking; because, while the circle may be intuitive or even obvious, it's also insistently slow. It aims to make us observe our thoughts and feelings, preventing initial reactions from taking the place of learning. As a result, working attentively through each step takes time and effort. But doing so can reward us with not only a better understanding of others, but a better knowledge of ourselves. One evaluation showed the student's admirably circular growth in engaging the circle itself: "At first the circle seemed kind of silly. However, it made me acknowledge how my past experiences have shaped my beliefs and how new experienced [sic] continue to shape them."

Like any relationship, the relationship between teacher and student is lived in two directions: the partners' looking together at the world around them, and—less frequently, if the relationship is healthy—the partners' looking at each other. Primarily, then, the process of teaching and learning means that the students and I explore together whatever it is we're studying. As a teacher, though, I also need to look at the other incarnate in the students around me. As I do that, the circle becomes not only a structure I try to explore with my students, but a habit I try to nurture in myself. It's not uncommon, for instance, for students to enter into conversation with a text by expressing their unedited, and usually unsubstantiated, opinions: "I really liked this book"; "This writer doesn't make any sense." By identifying different steps in the learning process, the circle has helped me to see such comments not as failures of, but as early steps in, the process of learning. If a student does a particularly good job of articulating her reaction, I can even commend her for getting the second step of the circle down especially well. Then, just as naturally, I can invite her to investigate the preferences that shaped her response (3) and, next, to work on understanding the text on its own terms (4a). Among other things, then, the circle provides a shared, fairly neutral language for responding to students, as well as an organic tool for what we've come to know (for good or ill) as assessment of student learning.

Of course, as Finkel points out, listening to students is often a "humbling experience."[25] Sometimes, as with Tabitha's essay, I'm humbled by the profundity of their learning. More often, though, as Finkel predicts, I'm humbled because they seem to have learned less than I hoped. "For obvious reasons," he writes, "many teachers would prefer to be spared exposure to this evidence. But if they take their intellectual goals seriously, and if their goals pertain to what the students are *learning*, and not simply to what they themselves are *teaching*, then they will be grateful

---

[25] Finkel, *Teaching with Your Mouth Shut*, 105.

for this insider's view of their students' understanding."[26] To get that insider's view, I often have to remind myself of a central lesson of the circle: just as it insists that we slow down as we engage a text or religion, so it insists that I slow down as I listen to and respond to my students. Slow teaching means being vigilant not to speak out of my own immediate reactions (2) to what students say, or to critique their views (4b) before I've worked to understand what's behind their words (4a). As a teacher, I usually have the power to speak before I listen. To truly teach, however, I need to slow down, pay attention, and speak to students where they are. I have to acknowledge that the *a*'s they bring into our classroom have as much influence on our shared conversations as my *b*. The Committee on Developments in the Science of Learning, summarizing recent educational research, comes to a similar conclusion: "There is a good deal of evidence that learning is enhanced when teachers pay attention to the knowledge and beliefs that learners bring to a learning task, use this knowledge as a starting point for new instruction, and monitor students' changing conceptions as instructions proceed."[27] If we can find out where our students are in their learning, we can usually meet them there and point the way ahead. Providing a map from any other location isn't likely to help them much.

As a commitment to meet an other—indeed, "another"—honestly, the circle invites what we might call conversion: by being honest in our responses and open in our listening, we seek to replace our prejudices with something much nearer the truth. Anyone who makes that commitment in faith is under the reign of what Richard McBrien has called the "*sacramental principle*": "Everything is, in principle, capable of embodying and communicating the divine."[28] As is true of liturgical sacraments—the RCIA, invoked above, provides the norm in this regard—slow teaching and learning are formative processes that require a gradually deepening willingness to see and to change. Like a sacrament, the circle provides a structured way in to something we can experience but only

---

[26] Ibid.

[27] Committee on Developments in the Science of Learning, *How People Learn: Brain, Mind, Experience, and School*, exp. ed. (Washington, DC: National Academy Press, 2000), 11.

[28] Quoted in Susan A. Ross, *Extravagant Affections: A Feminist Sacramental Theology* (New York: Continuum, 1998), 34. See also Dennis C. Smolarski, *Sacred Mysteries: Sacramental Principles and Liturgical Practice* (Mahwah, NJ: Paulist, 1994), 158: "Surely, we all need to become more and more aware of God's presence, to see day-to-day objects and events as gifts from God."

partly know—in this case, the endless, elusive mysteries of the classroom: the texts we study, the venerable traditions we try to understand, the company of each other.

As a model of engagement, the circle promises that learning about an other will also teach us about ourselves and point us toward better ways of being in the world. As a model for teaching, it promises no less. After all, I, like my students, hope for more from a course than just "understanding other religions." Just as they may come into our shared classroom expecting both scholarly learning and spiritual growth, so I come to class hoping not only to become a more skilled teacher and student of my discipline but also to become a better human being. The circle helps remind me that the way I teach is a large part of the person I am. Following it gives me innumerable opportunities, bidden and unbidden, to grow in attention, knowledge, and generosity. If teaching is a vocation, after all, it is in the day-to-day conversations with students that teachers are shaped, not just as professionals but as persons.[29]

[29] I would like to thank the Wabash Center for Teaching and Learning in Theology and Religion, which supported my early work on this circle in its 2003–2004 Colloquy for Pre-tenure Faculty.

Pauses

Peter Alonzi

We professors lead our students through the established concepts of our fields and grapple with their loose ends. Throughout these tours, we look into our students' eyes. We look to sense when to press on, when to repeat, and when to retreat and start again. All of this is good.

But there are times to pause. Pause to behold, as Gerard Manley Hopkins uses the term in the closing of his poem "Hurrahing in Harvest":

> These things, these things were here and but the beholder
>   Wanting; which two when they once meet,
> The heart rears wings bold and bolder
>   And hurls for him, O half hurls earth for him off under his feet.[1]

There are times in my economics course when pausing to behold allows me to share with students my sense of the presence of God in economics. There is neither neglect of my academic area's concepts or principles, nor stinting from the discipline's rigor. Rather, at crucial moments, when the presence of God is there to behold, right there in the middle of what the course is doing, we pause. Without the pause, the class skitters along the surface and the opportunity to behold evaporates.

When teaching Principles of Microeconomics I take several pauses. They are brief. But they are there, not skipped in the crushing hustle and

---

[1] Gerard Manley Hopkins, "Hurrahing in Harvest," accessed October 10, 2013, http://www.bartleby.com/122/14.html.

bustle of covering the material. They are there so the students can behold, or not. It is their choice. The pauses open wedges in class time providing opportunities to behold.

Principles of Microeconomics might seem an unlikely subject area for beholding the presence of God. But I think not, as the following examples are intended to reveal. More than reveal, perhaps they provide examples that will encourage the discovering and sharing of "pauseable" moments in other courses. The remainder of this essay sets out eight ways of creating pauses. The first part orients and assures the reader that the course truly is a conventional economics course. The next parts focus on a specific section of the course—each part relates that section's particular pause.

The Principles of Microeconomics Course

The course begins by identifying the fact of economic life—scarcity—and proceeds to explore how humans use markets to deal with scarcity by addressing three essential questions:

1. How does a market work at its best?

2. How does a market system work at its best?

3. How does a market system fail to work at its best?

In addressing the first question the student learns: nine pillars of perfect competition, the law of demand, the law of supply, the interaction of demand and supply, the role of price signals, and elasticity. In addressing the second question the student goes behind the law of demand to examine household decisions rooted in utility maximization, goes behind the law of supply to examine the business firm's decisions rooted in profit maximization, and studies the coordination of these independent, voluntary, decentralized decisions guided by the price and profit signals of Adam Smith's invisible hand. In addressing the third question, the student examines four situations problematic for a market system: monopoly, externalities, public goods, and asymmetric information. Each situation lacks one or more of the pillars needed for perfect competition. Without the pristine environment of perfect competition, the market system's price and profit signals misdirect buyers and sellers. Consequently the market system fails to work at its best.

Addressing these three questions, the exploration utilizes seven principles economists have identified over the past two centuries:

1. Opportunity Cost

2. Cost Benefit Comparison at the Margin

3. Substitution

4. Comparative Advantage

5. Increasing Opportunity Cost

6. Equilibrium

7. Efficiency

Within the economics course just described is the presence of God. As the students grapple to understand the concepts, principles, and questions of economics, God is there to behold if we but pause. Each of the following sections relates such a pause.

Opening the Course

At the very beginning there is an opportunity. My course begins with a prayer.

> Thank you for
> the sun that warms us,
> the air that inspires us,
> the rain that refreshes us, and
> the earth that feeds us and is our home.
> No human has made these,
> they are Your gift to us.

So at the very beginning of the economics course, we pause to realize the true nature of sun, air, rain, and earth. Too often we offhandedly refer to these gifts as natural resources and then get busy with the important stuff of building. Upon the base of natural resources we first build the explanation of how market price signals guide human endeavors to rework the gifts into the good things that will meet our needs and fill our wants. Second, we get those good things distributed. So much time is devoted to building and learning this economic apparatus of markets, price signals, decision-making, production, and distribution that unless context is provided, students take natural resources for granted. The natural resources are just there from the beginning. While taking the resources for granted is a convenient assumption,[2] it is most important to remember that natural resources are not just there. They are gifts. So at the very beginning of the course we pause. We call natural resources by their true name—gift—when we say thank you to the creator.[3]

Nine Pillars

A market is a complex human institution. To greatly simplify the explanation of its workings, the market is placed in a pristine environment. Just as scientists use the pristine environment of their laboratories, economists begin by considering markets in their pristine environment of perfect competition. The assumptions, or pillars,[4] of perfect competition spell out the acronym LIKE PATH$. They are:

Lots of buyers and sellers

Independent buyers and sellers

Knowledgeable buyers and sellers

Easy exit and entry

Property rights are well defined and enforceable

Able adults in action (making the decisions)

Transactions costs are zero

Homogeneous product

$ Dollar income and wealth as currently distributed

[2] But when we forget what we assume, much is lost. Just put forward slashes in the word assume and you see that when we forget our assumptions we make an ass/u/me; that is we make an ass of you and me.

[3] There is a little bit more to the prayer than related above. What is not part of the prayer and what we do not say is Amen. I tell the students that without a concluding Amen, the whole course is a prayer and that they can say the big Amen after the final exam.

[4] In my experience students relate to the concept of pillars more readily than assumptions. Assumptions are abstract whereas pillars are a physical object that supports important structures.

These pillars eliminate everyday frictions, imperfections, bumps, and warts and so place the market in a "pristine" environment. In this pristine environment, the forces of demand, supply, and price signals emerge most clearly, and the coordinating role of price signals work at their best.

CV After stating the nine pillars, but before delving into the exploration of demand, supply, and price signals, I pause. We reflect on the meaning of the pillars—especially the sixth: able adults in action. While most economists explicitly include pillars one through four and eight, not many mention my sixth pillar. But it is an essential component. When made explicit, it provides an opportunity to pause.

Assuming all those participating in the market place are able adults making decisions, I raise two questions. First, who is unable? More specifically, who is left out of the decision-making part of the market play? Those left out include the elderly who have become feeble of mind; children who are less powerful than the physically stronger and more worldly adults; the mentally ill; and those incapacitated by poor health, injury, or war. There are exceptions in each of these categories, of course: Warren Buffett, the Olsen twins, Stephen Hawking. These aside, the key point concerning those left out is posed in the second question: what is the responsibility of the able, those "left in," to care for those who are left out? In raising this question one glimpses the creator. For it is in facing this question we hear the invitational test and measure of any society: how it treats its less fortunate. We sense the truth offered in Luke 12:48: "When a man has had a great deal given him, a great deal will be demanded of him."[5] We begin to sense the common good, and with it, the presence of God.

Utility Maximization

When the course turns from the first question of how a market works to the second question of how a market system works, it goes behind the laws of demand and supply. It explores why those laws are. Behind and underlying the law of demand is utility maximization rooted in the "Rational Economic Person" paradigm.[6]

---

[5] Luke 12:48 in *The Jerusalem Bible* (Garden City, NY: Doubleday & Company Inc., 1966).

[6] Over the last fifteen years much research has been devoted to a complementary but different approach than the Rational Economic Person paradigm called Behavioral Economics.

In the Rational Economic Person paradigm, economists explore how people make consumption decisions not only about food, clothing, and shelter, but also transportation, entertainment, and each of the things we consume in life. Which of these goods and services will a person choose to buy? What quantity of each good will a person choose to buy? Several factors are essential in this paradigm's exploration of a person's consumption decision: the person's income level, the price of each of the many good things the person can choose between, and the person's preference ordering between those good things. In the context of these three key factors, economists assume that the person chooses the bundle of goods that provides the person with the most satisfaction. Since the word economists use for satisfaction is utility, they call this choosing of the best bundle the Utility Maximization problem.

CV The Utility Maximization problem has many technical intricacies such as marginal utility (MU), the law of diminishing marginal utility, and the rules for identifying the utility maximizing combination of goods. One representation of this rule is that the marginal utility of good X (i.e., MU_x) per dollar spent on good X (i.e., P_x) must equal the marginal utility of good Y (i.e., MU_y) per dollar spent on good Y (i.e., P_y). This is expressed in equation form as $\frac{MU_x}{P_x} = \frac{MU_y}{P_y}$. This rule can be understood intuitively once one grasps that the ratio $\frac{MU}{P}$ is just the bang (marginal utility) for the buck (the price). The rule says one has the right amount of each good (i.e., the utility maximizing amount of each good) if the bang for the buck spent on X is the same as the bang for the buck spent on Y. If there is an inequality (i.e., wedge of opportunity) rather than an equal sign between the two bangs for the buck, one can increase one's utility by taking a dollar out of the money spent on the good with the lower bang for the buck (the lower side of the wedge) and spending it on the good with the higher bang for the buck (the higher side).[7]

Once all this technical stuff is done, it is again time to pause. What does it mean to choose the bundle of good things that provides the person

---

[7] Suppose the MU_x is 14, the price of X is $2, the MU_y is 12, and the price of Y is $3. Then forming the ratios one has a bang for the buck spent on X of 7 and a bang for the buck on Y of 4. Comparing these one has:
$\frac{14}{\$2} = \frac{7}{\$1} = \frac{MU_x}{P_x} > \frac{MU_y}{P_y} = \frac{4}{\$1} = \frac{12}{\$3}$. By reallocating one's fixed budget, taking one dollar from the amount spent on Y and spending that one dollar on X, one gives up 4 units of satisfaction by having less Y but gains 7 units of satisfaction by having more X. This substitution produces a net gain of 3 = (7-4). The assumption is you can buy a dollar's worth of each good, that is, the goods are divisible not lumpy.

with the most satisfaction? Seems like the answer to this question would be "duh." But more pointedly, the question is, what is at the center of the person's preference ordering?

Without pausing and raising this question, the consumer's decision problem lacks context. The student is left in a void, without perspective. In the void, the student wallows. Often the default image is Mr. Scrooge: the miserly, myopic, narrow "Economic Person" who decides heartlessly by comparing costs and benefits. God is squeezed out, unneeded and unmentioned. And most devastatingly, we don't know that we don't know that God has been squeezed out.

But in the pause, we remember the gifts . . . the sun that warms us, the air that inspires us, the rain that refreshes us, the earth that feeds us and is our home. As we realize and accept that no human has made these, we contemplate their origin. These gifts, as Michael Himes reminds us, are not from Zeus, a noun.[8] Rather, they come from the verb Himes calls Love.

CV This Love transforms the anthropology of the Economic Person Paradigm. No longer is the "Economic Person" a Zeus-ian wannabe who, as the beginning and the end, decides on the basis of me alone. Rather, the "Economic Person" is one who knows he or she is a creature emerging at birth from the source and remerging at death with the source. This Economic Person, in his or her temporal parenthesis of thirty or sixty or ninety years, is a temporary caretaker, a steward of the resources entrusted by the source, the Love.

Profit Maximization

CV When the course turns from the first question of how a market works to the second question of how a market system works, it also goes behind a second law: the law of supply. Here the course explores why the law of supply exists. One major assumption underlying the law of supply at the principles level is that the firm's goal is profit maximization.

Profit maximization's description has many technical parts and takes a week or more to develop. The first part is the definition of profit: total revenue less total cost. The quest is to apply the cost-benefit principle to

---

[8] Michael J. Himes, "Finding God in All Things: A Sacramental Worldview and Its Effects" in *As Leaven in the World*, ed. Thomas M. Landy, 91–103 (Franklin, WI: Sheed & Ward, 2001).

the firm's profit maximizing production decision. This application requires identifying marginal cost (i.e., MC) and marginal revenue. Focusing first on the costs, the story starts with the notion of marginal product and Mother Nature's law of diminishing returns. The diminishing marginal product results in a U-shaped marginal cost curve. Lastly, revenues are investigated. In the pristine environment of perfect competition, the seller's marginal benefit of selling another unit of the good is just the price per each unit. The assembly of all these technical parts in the comparison of marginal benefit to marginal hurt yields the decision rule for the competitive firm: the profit maximizing quantity of production is the one at which the Price is equal to Marginal Cost. Restated in equation form: set quantity where $P = MC$. After engaging this weeklong technical derivation, the student is apt to sigh, "Is that all there is: set Q^* where $P = MC$?"

So it is most important at the beginning of the journey into profit maximization, at its very start, to pause and reflect upon what profit maximization means. Most students grasp that profit is total revenue less total cost. Consequently they think they understand profit maximization: make profits as big as they can be. But without pausing, the student might corrupt profit maximization into the mere miserly accumulation of more. Students miss God's presence. They miss God's call for businesspeople to be effective stewards of the resources entrusted to humanity by God.

CV Thus at the very beginning of the development of the competitive firm's decision problem, I relate to students what a sacramental orientation toward profit maximization might mean. Since profit is total revenue less total cost, there are two ways to raise profits: raise revenues or cut costs. Revenues can be raised by manipulating price upward. But given the nine pillars of perfect competition, a firm cannot manipulate price. Since there are "lots of independent buyers and sellers" via pillars number one and two, each buyer and each seller is so small no buyer, no seller can affect price. Price manipulation—that is, raising price above the market determined price—is ruled out by the pristine environment, the definition of perfect competition.[9] On the other hand, one can raise profits by lowering costs. One can seek to lower costs or avoid production

---

[9] Of course in the real world, in which perfect competition does not occur, there are tempting opportunities to manipulate price. These temptations emphasize the need for integrity, the inner moral compass. Once again a pause here reveals the importance of sensing the presence of God.

costs by stealing resources, abusing employees, and in general breaking the law. Repeatedly stressing the quest to maximize profits might give the student the mistaken notion that stealing, abusing, and breaking the law are encouraged if they result in lower costs. One should not assume that all students understand that profit maximization to economists means to operate within the law.

CV Since the competitive firm cannot manipulate price and does not break the law to lower cost, there is but one way the firm can maximize profit. It must use resources efficiently rather than wastefully and frivolously. Looking at the real world, we see many instances of wasteful use of resources. On the executive level there is the executive who orders the company's maintenance people to work on his or her own home when the executive's employment contract does not include such services as a part of the executive's compensation package. Students in my class readily offer other examples. But it is not only on the executive level that waste can occur. There are the three p's—phone, photocopier, and PC—of seemingly innocuous waste. Employees can use (abuse) the company's phone, photocopier, or personal computer for personal rather than company business. This shifting raises corporate costs and so lowers profit. Each "p" is small when one person does it. But just as the drip, drip, drip fills the bucket, cumulatively the profit drain can be large. In short, the company must avoid the all too human tendency to let costs drift higher through wasteful, frivolous use of resources.

CV Gathering this reflection into a focused point, profit maximization is transformed. No longer is profit maximization the miserly, greed-is-good, accumulation-regardless-of-all-else in which anything goes. It becomes the high calling to all those in business, from the most senior executive to employees doing the most menial tasks: profit maximization means being an effective steward of the resources entrusted to you.

Thus, at the beginning, before delving into the long technical treatment of profit maximization, I plant the seed in the minds of students that profit maximization means effective stewardship. And at the end of the long technical treatment of this topic I again recall this perspective.

The School Motto

CV By now you probably are asking yourself, "What is that *CV* sprinkled throughout this essay? Is it a printing error that slipped past the copy editors? Does the author intend it to mean 105 in Roman numerals?"

This is another moment to pause.

The first thing I write on the board at the very start of each class session is *CV*. I write it in the top left-hand corner of the board. Similarly I have sprinkled it throughout this chapter. It is not a typo. In most courses, eventually a student asks, "What is that *CV* you always put on the board but never talk about?" Then I pause and share with the class why it is important.

CV is the abbreviation of Dominican University's—my university's—motto: *Caritas et Veritas*. It is the foundation and touchstone for who Dominican University is, what it does, and why it does what it does. In class, when the first student asks, I take the opportunity to unpack the meaning of *CV*.

Caritas is Latin for love in the sense of love as limitless self-giving. In his first epistle (1 John 4:16), John writes: "God is love and those who abide in love abide in God, and God abides in them." So *Caritas* is one way to resonate with, to dwell with, the Divine. *Veritas* is the Latin word for truth. In John's Gospel (14:6), he quotes Jesus saying, "I am the way, the truth, and the life. No one comes to the Father except through me." So *Veritas* is another way to resonate with, to be with, the Divine.

CV is not the easy path of either/or—either *Caritas* or *Veritas*. The motto calls the entire university community—students, staff, faculty, administration, alumni, trustees, benefactors, and friends—to do both/and—both *Caritas* and *Veritas*; both love and truth.

You can encourage a similar pause. Put the abbreviation of your school's motto on the board first thing, every class, and wait for the question. When it comes, unpack for the students what your school's motto means to you and how it might guide them. And if the question never comes, you have a natural midterm bonus question. Asking on the midterm "What does *CV* mean?" always encourages at least one student to ask the question when we go over the exam. And we can pause to behold.

Closing Gifts

The course is nearly over and everyone wants the last class session to be short. But after wrapping up the course with concluding remarks, I take one last pause. On its face it has nothing to do with the course, but it is to me a crucial, centering part of the course. In that pause I share with my students three gifts I have received in my life: the goal, the means for reaching the goal, and the milestones along the way revealing progress toward the goal.

The first gift is the goal. It was given to me by my college president, Monsignor Eugene Lyons. "Gentlemen," he thundered at freshman assembly, "be happy, be holy, and be effective. Not two out of three. All three!" That was it, the whole assembly talk. Since that day these three goals have served as my North Star. Looking up and beyond the current trials and triumphs keeps me balanced and pointed in the right direction.

The second gift is the means for reaching the goal and was given to me by Sir Winston Churchill. In a post–World War Two commencement address to the lads at the school he himself attended, Sir Winston told the students: "Never, Never, Never give up." That was the whole commencement speech! Never giving up is the second gift I offer.

The third gift is the set of milestones along the way that reassure one that all the effort and energy of never, never, never giving up truly is bringing one to the goal of happy, holy, and effective. This third gift was given to me by British Jesuit Father Bernard Basset. He said, "Pray." But more than merely saying "pray," he taught me how to pray. He said that to pray, one need not be on one's knees on the stone floor in the church in the cold with the lingering incense playing havoc with one's asthma. One can be flat on one's back in bed. Father Basset said there are three things one needs to do: recognize that one is in the presence of God; ask for God's help; and have a conversation with God. My conversations have gone through three stages so far, and it is in the third stage that I realized that in prayer, one finds the milestones.

In the first stage, for the first several years of doing what Father Basset suggested, I let God know everything that God missed: my twin sons are so challenging that they are driving me nuts; my wife is so thoughtless when cooking as she dirties every pot and utensil in the kitchen and leaves the cleaning to me. From there my list of complaints went on and on and on.

The second stage happened when I realized that being all-powerful, God is omniscient. In realizing God's omniscience, two insights struck me: God knew all the stuff I was complaining about. And I realized that God gave me free will to choose. God waited until I chose to turn toward God and opened myself to God's presence.

It was then that I chose to say: "Thank you." Thank you for my twins. They are great, energetic guys who are making a difference in the world, a difference that started by evoking from me loving responses that made me a happier, holier, and more effective person. Thank you for my wife. She truly loves me; all of me: my strengths and also my foibles. And I get to eat all those great meals. Thank you for the ability to read. I can talk to Aristotle or Mick Jagger. Thank you for Mozart and the Beatles.

Father Basset had said that prayer is a conversation. Up to then I was doing all the talking; I finally shut up and listened. I didn't hear anything with my ears. But in the quiet of turning toward God and opening just a small wedge of myself, God came in. I felt a resonance deep within. I recorded no data. But I knew when I was being holy and effective but unhappy and would adjust. I could tell when I was happy and effective but not holy. So again I would adjust. And I would know when I was happy, holy, and effective. I had discovered that the milestones are in the mindfulness of prayer.

This long way around is the pause. It concludes with my encouraging the students to pray often, pray daily. Pray when they are happy or sad. Just pray. For when one prays, one opens the little wedge in one's life circle through which God enters.[10]

I close this last pause by letting students know that I prayed for them before they were my students. I prayed for them since they became my students. And I will pray for them every day after we are no longer in class together. My prayer for them is that they be happy, holy, and effective.

Conclusion

In *The Idea of a University*, Blessed John Henry Cardinal Newman points out that in the university it is easy to mistake the part for the whole.[11]

---

[10] Prayer is powerful! For as Mother Theresa reminds us peace is an inside job that radiates from within one to the world, and it begins with prayer:

> The fruit of silence is prayer,
> The fruit of prayer is faith,
> The fruit of faith is love,
> The fruit of love is service,
> The fruit of service is peace.

[11] John Henry Cardinal Newman, *The Idea of a University* (London: Longmans, Green & Co., 1891), 96–98. This rather long excerpt, especially the highlighted ending, is offered to give full treatment of the short summary statement made in the text. "And now to sum up . . . hostility [toward theology by other sciences] . . . is coincident with an evident deflection or exorbitance is sure to take place, almost from necessity. . . . if Theology be not present to defend its own boundaries and to hinder the encroachment . . . And this occupation is proved to be a usurpation by this circumstance, that these foreign sciences will assume certain principles as true, and act upon

When the theology—and the Theos—is left out of a university, the other disciplines fill in the vacuum. With the vacuum eliminated, the remaining disciplines do not perceive what is missing because there are no gaps from their viewpoint. Perhaps an analogy makes this clearer. Consider the university as a beautifully circular pie. Newman is pointing out that if a wedge—call it Theos—is removed from the pie, the remaining disciplines do not stand still and leave the vacated space empty. They do not mourn the complementary piece that is missing. Instead they fill the empty space, closing it, by expanding. Indeed, the other disciplines might be squeezing the Theos out in response either to accreditation requirements or donor dollars. But since the disciplines still have the same amount of stuff as they expand into the wedge left by the ejection of the Theos, their outer perimeter moves inward, closer to the center. In this process of filling the Theos's wedge space, a circle is reestablished. A whole seems present. But without the Theos, the whole that is reestablished is smaller and not "the whole which included the Theos." For without the Theos, the new circle's radius is shorter and so its area is smaller. The new circle without the Theos fits completely within the original circle that included the Theos. The new circle is but a part of the whole original circle.

The pauses taken in my Principles of Microeconomics class that are presented here are my way of refusing to settle for just the part, as I had for so long. These pauses are my way of opening the students to the whole that includes the presence of God in all things, including economics. Without neglecting or turning from the concepts and principles of economics—indeed, while engaging them rigorously—we realize the presence of God right in the middle of the course. We realize God's presence because we pause to behold. If we fail to pause, the class skitters

---

them, which they neither have authority to lay down themselves . . . the first point, which I undertook to maintain . . . whereas it is the very profession of a University to teach all sciences, on this account it cannot exclude Theology without being untrue to its profession. Next I have said that, all sciences being connected together, and having bearings one on another, it is impossible to teach them all thoroughly, unless they all are taken into account, and Theology among them. Moreover, I have insisted on the important influence, which Theology in matter of fact does and must exercise over a great variety of sciences, completing and correcting them; so that, granting it to be a real science occupied upon truth, *it cannot be omitted without great prejudice to the teaching of the rest. And lastly, I have urged that supposing Theology be not taught, its province will not simply be neglected, but will actually be usurped by other sciences which will teach, without warrant, conclusions of their own in a subject-matter which needs its own proper principles for its due formation and disposition"* (emphasis added).

along the surface, confuses the part for the whole, and misses the opportunity to realize God's presence.

The pauses—the opening prayer, the meaning of competition's pillar of able adults in action, utility maximization as stewardship for the common good, profit maximization as the high calling for businesspersons to make decisions that provision the community without wasting resources, the challenging call of the school's motto, and the closing gifts revealing the power of prayer—are brief. But they are steadfast. They are not sacrificed to the crushing hustle and bustle of covering the material. They provide context for the students, opportunities for beholding.

My hope is that these examples encourage readers to find pause-worthy moments in their own courses and to take the time to pause and behold.

Bibliography

Alonzi, Peter. "The Economics/Business—*Caritas et Veritas* Connection: Bah Humbug or Authentic?" *Proceedings of the 2010 Caritas Veritas Symposium*. Edited by Mary Payntor, 85–86. River Forest, IL: Dominican University, 2010.

Buber, Martin. *I and Thou*. Touchstone Edition. New York: Simon & Schuster, 1996.

Himes, Michael J. "Finding God in All Things: A Sacramental Worldview and Its Effects." In *As Leaven in the World*. Edited by Thomas M. Landy. Franklin, WI. Sheed & Ward, 2001.

Hopkins, Gerard Manley. "Hurrahing in Harvest." http://www.bartleby.com /122/14.html. Accessed October 10, 2013.

The Jerusalem Bible. Garden City, NY: Doubleday & Company, Inc., 1966.

Newman, John Cardinal Henry. *The Idea of a University*. London: Longmans, Green, & Co., 1891.

Part 3

Word and Sacrament

Rhetorics of Silence:
A Pedagogy of Contemplation,
Empathy, and Action

Melissa A. Goldthwaite

The gift of an attentive life is the ability to recognize patterns and find our way toward unity built on empathy. Empathy becomes the path that leads us from the margins to the center of concern. . . . Finding beauty in a broken world . . . is the work of daring contemplation that inspires action.

—Terry Tempest Williams, *Finding Beauty in a Broken World*

I'll begin this essay the way I opened one of my classes when I taught a course called Rhetorics of Silence: Communication and Contemplative Practices, by inviting you to reflect on, to be attentive to, the complexity of silence in your own life.

- First, consider a time when you experienced a negative silence: perhaps someone gave you "the silent treatment" or silenced you, or perhaps you silenced yourself when you wished to speak. How did this silence feel in your body? What were its effects?

- Next, consider a time when you chose silence for a particular purpose: perhaps to protest an injustice or to give someone else space. Remember the details surrounding that experience, what you did and why, what the effects of that silent action were.

- Now, consider a specific time in which you experienced a positive silence: perhaps when a person comforted you with a gentle touch but spoke no words, or when you were alone in a quiet place and felt safe and at peace. Bring yourself back to that time and place.

In the autumn of 2009 and again in 2011, I taught a graduate course that considered all these forms of silence and others; I did so with the belief that attentiveness and contemplation can inspire empathy and lead to positive action. In the process of examining the complex rhetorical relationships among silence, speech, and writing, my students and I focused on the multiple ways people both deliver and receive silence in intentional (and sometimes unintentional) ways, and considered the rhetorical and even bodily effects of these silences. As the opening demonstrates, we considered a range of practices involving silence: the potentially destructive practices of silencing oneself or others, the potentially empowering effects of choosing to be silent for a particular purpose, and the calming and potentially healing effects of meditative, contemplative, and empathetic silences.

The reading for the course included selections from rhetoric and composition scholars such as George Kalamaras, Cheryl Glenn's *Unspoken: A Rhetoric of Silence*, Krista Ratcliffe's *Rhetorical Listening*, Jacqueline Jones Royster's "When the First Voice You Hear Is Not Your Own," and Pat Belanoff; novelists, nonfiction writers, and poets such as Audre Lorde, Azar Nafisi, Tillie Olsen, Shusako Endo, Sandra Steingraber, and Jane Hirshfield; and also selections from those who take a more philosophical approach, such as Robert Sardello, Max Picard, Thomas Merton, John Cage, and Arthur Zajonc. Through a mix of reading, discussion, writing, and contemplative practices, I sought to help students pay attention to the multiple ways silences communicate (and sometimes inhibit communication), so that they could be not only more intentional about their own uses of silence but also more mindful of the ways they incorporate contemplative silences into their own lives.

In terms of assignments, students wrote weekly reading response papers, kept a journal, and did an extended final project of their choice—from short stories that included silence as a central theme, to an analysis of the many silences surrounding autism; from a study of a group of cloistered nuns, to a project about Quakers.

I began each class period with a contemplative practice, and asked my students to reserve fifteen minutes a day for silence and journaling about that time of silence. It's these two elements—classroom contemplative practices and students journaling about their daily silences—that I wish to focus on in this essay, for it is these elements that I believe helped create deeper receptivity to the material we discussed.

Practice and Reception: Background Silence

Ever since the 2004 publication of Cheryl Glenn's *Unspoken: A Rhetoric of Silence*, I have incorporated a unit on silence in my graduate course, "Rhetoric Then and Now," a required course for all students in Saint Joseph University's Masters in Writing Studies program. In addition to selections from Glenn's *Unspoken*, students read Audre Lorde's "The Transformation of Silence into Language and Action," as well as sections from Krista Ratcliffe's *Rhetorical Listening*. We also examine particular uses of silence as protest—organized daylong vows of silence to protest everything from LGBT discrimination to the conflict in Iraq to abortion. And we talk about silent retreats. We *talk* and write about silence, but until a few years ago, I had not fully considered the importance of incorporating into the class the kinds of contemplative silences that create space for a new kind of openness and receptivity, an openness and receptivity that can be life changing yet also feel risky.

As a writer, I spend a lot of time in silence. Perhaps because I need silence so much—by vocation and temperament—it affects me deeply. To open oneself, to be receptive, is risky. When I enact my morning ritual during the summer months I am holed up alone in rural New Hampshire, I open myself in a fairly controlled environment and begin to pay attention to what is around me and what is within (neither of these completely controlled, but with a lot of time alone, that's not a problem). To open oneself in a classroom full of others, however, can feel far more risky.

I felt this risk, this sense of danger, a few years ago when I was placed in the role of student rather than teacher. As a teacher, I have long been providing opportunities for silence and quiet in the classroom, often through guided in-class writings. Even when I do the writing with students, however, I am not fully open to the experience. I am watching the clock (for if I don't, the entire class period could go by without my notice), watching students to see who seems bored, who needs not to be interrupted. It's always difficult to know when to end the silence because some people need more time than others. I sometimes offer those who are finished something else and ask those who need more time to keep writing. I know and tinker with this ritual, and ones like it. But I wasn't fully prepared for the effect other ritual silences would have on me as a participant.

At Collegium, a weeklong, summer colloquy in which participants were invited to consider the topic of faith and intellectual life, the days were packed and patterned, scheduled from seven thirty in the morning until ten at night. Between different lectures, outings, and services, the stable event of each day was one or two small-group discussion meet-ings—eight or nine professors from different disciplines and a leader gathered in the same room for an hour or two to talk about common readings and lectures. What could have been, in other situations, a high-spirited matching of academic wits or an agonistic battle of ideas was in this situation a calm and quiet exchange of differing positions. We joked about being "the quiet group," and I'm not sure everyone thought that was a good thing.

Certainly every group, every class, has its own personality—a mixing and melding of people with different talents, experiences, backgrounds, and temperaments—seemingly beyond the leader's control. Surely that was part of it. But there was more. In many ways, this "quiet group" was created, sustained, challenged, and perplexed by ritual silence.

Jody Ziegler, author of "Practice Makes Reception: The Role of Con-templative Ritual in Approaching Art," also included in this volume, helped create that silence. She had placed a collection of objects at the center of the large seminar table: a glass of water holding one pink rose; a teapot filled with sand; a handmade ceramic tea bowl; a bell; and a candle. The candle drew me in. I often light one when I write or when seeking quiet intimacy in other situations. When Jody lit the candle, talked briefly about the significance of each object on the table, and invited us into a moment of silence, something opened inside of me; a calm descended more deeply with each rising and falling breath. She repeated the ritual lighting of the candle and space for silence at each group meeting.

Jody invited us to bring something to open our time together, and throughout the week, participants brought everything from Ravel's *Pavane pour une infante défunte,* played from a cell phone, to a reading from Saint Augustine, to a reading from *Tao Te Ching.* I read an Anne Sexton poem; someone else read a verse from the Bible.

We were invited, too, to bring our own objects to the table. On the second day, I brought in a one-inch carved bear fetish, which I've carried for over ten years but until that moment had never placed on a public table (literally or figuratively). When asked to say something about its significance, I could only muster three words—solitude, strength, protec-tion—instead of expanding on the fuller symbolic meaning, that solitude helps transform passion to wisdom, that hibernation allows for gathering strength and the integration of new experiences, and that there is healing and protection in introspection. Never mind the personal stories I could have told. Another day, a participant placed a newly purchased Bible—a soft blue leather cover, embossed—at the center and told the story of its significance.

Because we had no forewarning of this invitation to bring in a personal object, no one was rushing to the store the night before, trying to find something to impress or overthinking what object would best represent his or her self. We had what we carried with us, whatever held—until that point of sharing—private meaning. As I saw my own fetish sitting among other people's objects, I thought about an in-class writing I do in poetry workshops. I bring in a collection of items from my office (photographs, magnets, a small sculpture, a painting, anything that seems evocative and portable) and ask the students to write a poem somehow suggested by the object but filtered through their own imagination and experience. I also tell them that they have the option of choosing their own inspiration, something they carry with them—a piece of jewelry, a keychain, lip gloss, a scar, a tattoo. I had always seen it as a "successful classroom exercise" and felt gratified when students volunteered to read their poems aloud after ten or fifteen minutes of writing. What I hadn't fully realized, though, is how vulnerable students might be in this sharing—or even in choosing not to share, in remaining silent, for even what we fail to say has effects.

At Collegium, I felt both the deep positive and calming effects of ritual silence, but I also felt a sense of risk, a sense that I was opening myself to other people, new ideas, ones I wasn't sure I was ready to accept. My defenses were down, and I felt vulnerable.

Weeks after this complicated experience of silence at Collegium, I was moved to reflect on it and its effects in a poem, a villanelle with its repeating lines to heighten the sense of ritual.

On the Danger and Necessity of Silence

To invite quiet and all that it affords,
she lights a candle, yet that faint scent of pear
is far more dangerous than the spar of words, even swords.

She offers cool water, a rose in full bloom, a gesture towards
life and beauty—all the fruit we can bear—
to invite quiet and all that it affords.

A candle, water, rose, a teapot filled with sand: these cords
bind us as a group. All symbolic, but this, I swear,
is far more dangerous than the spar of words, even swords.

The rose asks us to open but not wilt, to let go of our hoards
of books, of knowledge, even for a second, and *be* there
to invite quiet and all that it affords.

We know the shield and armor of learning, words
as weapon, but the sound of a bell lingering in the air
is far more dangerous than the spar of words, even swords.

There is more in that silence than a thousand blackboards
can contain but no way to access what's behind a tear or a stare.
To invite quiet and all that it affords
is far more dangerous than the spar of words, even swords.

The sense of "danger" I focused on in writing this poem was meant to be taken, at least in part, as ironic, since silence is often linked to weakness and emptiness. My experience has taught me that silences for the most part are neither weak nor empty; rather, they are powerful and full, worthy of attention.

Through study, experience, and reflection, I have come to believe classroom contemplative practices have the potential to create openness in students—openness to themselves and the ways their lives and experiences shape their learning; openness to their classmates, to understanding how another's perspective might differ yet not necessarily be "wrong"; and an intellectual openness, an attitude that allows students to explore new ideas and to reflect on those ideas rather than simply react to them. Although students might feel a sense of vulnerability and risk in being open, I believe it's this sense of openness that allows for true learning. It is the doorway to a sacramental worldview.

Opening Silences, Silent Openings

It was important to me, from the very first day of class, to open with a contemplative practice, one that would create a context for discussing a particular issue or reading, yet one that would also allow us to center, to let go of the rush of the workday and frustration of the commute, to set aside our daily preoccupations for two or three hours.

Sometimes, I would simply begin class with a couple minutes of silence, a centering silence. Another practice I used, which I learned from my yoga classes, was beginning class by asking students to silently set an intention—perhaps to listen better or to speak or to learn something new, or maybe even just to stay awake. At the end of class, in another period of silence, I asked students to return to the intention they had set.

Other practices, such as exploring metaphors, were meant to reveal students' associations with and feelings about silence. Late in the semester, I opened class with this practice:

> Metaphors allow us to see abstractions like silence in a more concrete way. Poet Jane Hirshfield, for example, figures an "unheard, unspoken" thought as *"Runt-of-the-litter thought, [. . .] unable to get to the tit."*
>
> On a piece of paper, answer the following question with a sensory image (it can be a couple words—"a rock"—or a phrase—"a snow-covered field at dawn"): *What is silence?*

After the students created their metaphors, we went around the seminar table, each student reading his or her image and then asking the question, "What is silence?" before the next person responded. This practice in metaphor allowed us to recognize the range of associations individuals have with silence: that it can be sturdy like a rock used as a foundation, or destructive like a rock thrown at a person or through a window. It can be peaceful, like a quiet morning in a field alone, or cold like a frozen stare.

Oftentimes I would give students more direction, perhaps a writing prompt or a guided exercise such as a version of "Listening Out" that I learned from Mirabai Bush at the 2009 Contemplative Curriculum Development Summer Session. Here's an adaptation for the present context:

> If you're comfortable doing so, close your eyes. Listen to yourself, to your own body. Hear the sound of your own breathing.
>
> Now listen a little further out, perhaps to the person nearest to you in your home, office, or wherever you're reading this essay. Become aware of that person's presence. Is she uncrossing and re-crossing her legs, clearing his throat, putting pen to the page?
>
> Listen out further.
>
> Can you hear sounds beyond this room? Outside the door? Outside the window? Through the thin walls? What life is there? How far can you extend your listening? What do you hear?

When I did this practice with my students, we were reading Krista Ratcliffe's *Rhetorical Listening*. I used this physical practice as a metaphor for the work of rhetorical listening, just as I did the next week when I began class by having students write out one of the ways in which they are privileged on one sheet of paper and one of the ways they are non-privileged on another. Ratcliffe proposes laying one's privileges and nonprivileges alongside each other. Students did this and then simply went around the table and read these without commentary. They listened to one another, seeing and hearing in a physical way that no one person is either completely privileged or without privilege. It's one thing to know intellectually that each person has a life marked by privilege and nonprivilege, but silence to reflect first on one's own life and then silence for listening to others without the expectation for verbal response can create receptivity and a context for more informed, more empathetic, conversation.

Tying the opening contemplative exercise to the reading was an important way for me to help students see connections between our intellectual/academic conversations and their own lives. One week we read Alice Mattison's "Silence and Storytelling," about how writers, usually women, censor themselves, sometimes by not writing at all and other times by using stylistic or formal features that introduce ineffectual silences into their work. I opened that class by asking students to call to mind the things they had chosen not to write about: to consider whether those silences were good silences or harmful silences, to question whether such silences were the result of self-censorship, censorship by others, kindness, trust, discretion, or something else. I asked them to acknowledge the place of that silence in their writing life, to make a decision whether to break that silence or to continue keeping it. Using silence as a space for reflection allows students to consider the complexity of silence and to make decisions about how they wish to incorporate silence into their lives. It also provides space to consider negative or ambiguous silences and to seek to eradicate the negative ones. This practice encourages taking action in one's own life.

One of my goals, through these contemplative openings was to help students reflect on the fullness of silence in their lives—even the ways silence can reveal other sounds. Composer John Cage drew attention to environmental sounds, especially in his 1952 composition "4'33'," four minutes and thirty-three seconds of silence in which to hear the "music" of one's surroundings. When we read John Cage's "Experimental Music," I played a song by independent singer/songwriter Amy Martin. The song is called "Gentle as the Moon," and it incorporates sounds of nature in the background and a long period of silence in which the music is absent but in which those natural sounds can be heard. Her gentle refrain in this song is the words, "I vow nonviolence to everything," a message reinforced by leaving space for the sounds beyond her own voice or her own making.

All of these opening practices were meant to deepen students' engagement with the texts and one another and to help students to make connections between what we were reading and their own lives and experiences. Such practices helped make students more fully present in class and helped facilitate conversation because they had time to reflect, to think, and to experience the power of silence.

Reflecting on Silence

"... listen to the voice of the wind / and the ceaseless message that forms itself out of silence."

—Rilke, from *The Duino Elegies*

In addition to participating in contemplative openings, students in my course spent fifteen minutes a day in silence and wrote journals reflecting on the experience. When I introduced these assignments on the first night of class, students seemed unconcerned. They seemed far more concerned about practical matters such as how much reading they'd have to do, what the response papers should look like, and how on earth a graduate course in rhetoric—a discipline devoted to speech and being heard—could be devoted to silence. "I can't force you to do it; I'm not grading you on it," I said, when asking them to find this place of silence in their own lives. "I won't know if you choose not to do it, but I invite you to try." What I found is that students, despite the difficulty many found with the assignment, not only tried it, but also wrote in their journals about developing sensory awareness and deepening intuition, about finding a space for reflection and calm, grieving and comfort.

When I asked students whether they would be comfortable allowing me to quote from their journals and class materials, all responded positively, signing a form allowing me to use their words and real names. I explained it was conventional to create pseudonyms when quoting students (and gave them the option of creating their own pseudonym), yet I also described my discomfort with such a practice because I believe such elision silences students; like scholars, these students deserve recognition for their ideas and words. Every student elected to have his or her real name used. I include my students' words and names in this section as a way of honoring their experience and powers of reflection—and to break a conventional academic silencing that often ignores students' desire to be heard and valued.

Perhaps the most prominent theme in students' responses to this assignment was the difficulty of finding one's way into silence. The students in this class were in different stages of their graduate program in writing studies. Some were twenty-two-year-olds who had come straight from undergraduate programs; others—like a fifty-something-year-old administrative professional who was writing her thesis on contemplative nuns—were taking their last course. Some were parents; many had full-time jobs in addition to being a student. Except for two students who said they did yoga, none professed any regular experience with contemplative practices. They all claimed busy lives, balancing many responsibilities.

One student, Amy Lewis, who worked as an adjunct professor at three schools, said that she desired silence, yet she found herself wanting to check e-mail or play with her phone when she attempted fifteen minutes of silence. She writes, "I think I am someone who has no idea of what true silence means. . . . I am rarely silent in a reflective sense, still, or at peace, and this is something I hope to work on in this class."

Others described trying to create meditative environments or to attempt meditative practices. Michael Banks wrote of buying a fountain on clearance at Target to help create a meditative environment. Unfortunately, to him, it sounded like a running toilet. He concludes that "you cannot market and sell peace and quiet. Those things will never be on clearance." Laronnda Thompson describes a difficulty many people have in beginning a meditation practice; she writes, "I tried some basic meditative practices, inhale, exhale, inhale, exhale . . . I tried to listen to my heartbeat, and not to think of anything except my heartbeat. After a few minutes I managed it . . . however my thoughts still drifted to every abrupt temporarily unidentifiable sound that occurred. The house creaked, pipes rumbled, next-door neighbors ran up and down the stairs, and the refrigerator clicked on and off; there are no quiet places in my house!" Aaron Van Gossen, too, noted the ways in which his silence was not very silent: he noticed the sound of the clock and the planes landing at a nearby airport, but mostly he noticed the noise of his own thoughts.

Likewise, Stacy Schreiber in an early entry reflected on the difficulty of sitting in silence for fifteen minutes; she listed every noise she heard, from the snoring of her dogs to her neighbor yelling at his dog, from a noisy car muffler to the rattling ceiling fan. These noises annoyed her;

she wanted, instead, the noisiness of her "normal" life—the television, music, or talking—that would drown out these sounds. Yet in a later entry, Stacy pondered gentle silences: her nineteen-month-old son sitting on the kitchen floor, "thumbing through his books fully engaged" or Stacy holding him "after he has taken a bath and is all cozy in his pajamas." She continues, "Silence is when he puts his head on my shoulder and pats my back. Silence is laying my little boy down and kissing him one more time before closing the door for the night." This movement from experiencing silence as "annoying" to recognizing its value shows a development many students in my class experienced.

Through reflection, students learned to interpret and reinterpret the place of silence in their lives. Ken Brown, a student who works construction, described falling asleep five days in a row when trying to practice his daily silence. At first he felt a sense of guilt for not staying awake. Yet he came to recognize how difficult it usually was for him to sleep. He came to depend on the time set aside for silence, not only to calm himself, but to reflect on the ways he wanted to use silence positively at work and in his relationships.

This kind of reflection, which often allowed students to connect the theoretical issues of the class readings to their personal experiences, was another theme that came up in student journals and class discussions. Nicole Katze, who said she was having a hard time finding fifteen minutes a day to be silent, finally found that time by running without her iPod. She found she used that time for reflection. "I began thinking about things—memories or conversations, and, yes, silences in my life—that I may have been ignoring." She found questions rising, "How often do I silence others? Am I actively silencing someone now? What is at stake when I silence someone? Am I too silent? Do I play an active, speaking role in my own life? In the lives of others? What about the people around me? Do they?" These were questions she explored not only in the rhythmic quiet of her daily runs but also in the rhythmic tapping of the keys when she wrote. I believe contemplating these kinds of questions, the very questions Nicole Katze was asking, is foundational to developing empathy and to taking action in positive ways.

Another theme I noted in students' responses to their practices of daily silence was a developing of sensory awareness, which often led to deepening intuition and heightened description in their writing. Margaret Ryan-Atkinson writes, "The house is quiet, so much so that I hear one of the turtles on the back porch as he plunges from his perch into the seemingly always-dirty water. I wonder how often those turtles do that a day. I wouldn't know. I wouldn't even notice because the sound would be muffled by telephones, televisions, dinner table conversation." Here, Margaret pays attention to the kinds of silences to which John Cage drew attention in his writing and experimental compositions. She extends her awareness to other forms of life, to the value of their lives and ways of living.

Another student, Colleen DeFruscio, describes her experience of eating in silence at a restaurant: "Without being engaged in a conversation or plugged into an iPod or immersed in a book, I noticed my food was louder. Yes, the sounds of chewing, crunching, slurping, and sipping— but also the tastes, the smells grew louder. The soup tasted even better, the salad even worse. I consciously went through the sensations of each veggie or meat or dressing I was consuming." She also became more aware of others, explaining,

> In my silence I observed, absorbed, and learned. I began paying attention to the emphasis, the inflections in the people's voices, the gestures and facial expressions that lent more meaning to their words. I was able to infer the tones, the topics, and feelings of the conversations around me, even those I couldn't quite hear. I could guess at the nature of the relationship, the intimacy level, and attitudes toward one another of tablemates.

She goes on to write, "I was amazed to realize how much we give away in our silent cues—and how much we can pick up when we silently listen and observe. We tell so much of our story in our silence, even to strangers eavesdropping from tables far away." This kind of close observation creates an important awareness of others, an awareness that can deepen one's understanding of both self and others.

This same student observed some of her fifteen-minute silences while driving in her car and became more fully aware of her surroundings— "the whirring and clunking of the engines around me, the music seeping through the sealed windows of cars nearby and the rush of speeding drivers in the left lane as I sat at a red light." She also noticed the noise inside her, saying, "At first this silence bothered me. . . . My mind was going in five different directions, which is one of the reasons . . . I sometimes use the radio—to distract my busy brain." She came, however, over the course of the semester, to use this silent time to organize her thoughts and develop calm, the same kind of calm she experiences doing yoga. "As I get into the routine," she writes, "and start to move my body and my breath purposefully, my mind is quieted. I become so focused on the present—on the moves and the rhythm of my breathing—that all stress is lifted from my mind and I am open. I feel present and free and appreciative of the stillness around me. . . . There is an inner silence that I experience that is not the result of suppression of thought or anything like that, but of simple existing without any distraction."

Acknowledging the noises around her and inside her, without adding to that noise in order to create a distraction, was a significant step for Colleen toward using silence as a means of developing focus and calm. She was able to draw upon such reserves when facing a time of grief.

Perhaps the most surprising theme to me—and I'm not sure why it was surprising because I have experienced the same thing in my own meditative practice—was students' focus on the ways silence provided a space for grieving and comfort. Upon hearing the news of a family member's death, Colleen spent some time in silence to reflect on her loved-one's life and death (something she hadn't done before when loved ones had died). She writes, "In the stillness I was able to see his face, hear his voice, smell his familiar pungent cologne, and I was comforted in a way that talking about it right away or being immediately consoled by family and friends would not have allowed."

Another student, Kristen Adams, described the importance of silent comfort in a time of loss and grief. She writes, "Today, my silence resulted in memories. . . . Sitting on my desk chair in my room, I worked on quieting my mind, and as I tried focusing on my breathing, I slowly became aware of the ring I was twirling around my right ring finger." Kristen goes on to describe the cross cutout, how this was her Mimi's ring, how Mimi had passed away six months before. She described the way her roommate held her in silence as she grieved the night of her grandmother's death and used her journal entry to consider the emotions that arose in her silent practice.

Kristen describes a similar moment, when she lost her grandfather, how her mother knelt beside her and cradled her the way she had when she was a child; she explains, "We stayed like this for a few minutes; me sobbing into her wool sweater, clinging to her, while her silent tears dripped onto the top of my head." Those who have experienced such empathetic silences understand the comfort of such wordless actions.

Perhaps the reason this focus on grief and comfort surprised me when I read my students' journal entries is because it hadn't come up in classroom discussions. They'd been very open in class, talking about silencing themselves and others, about being silenced, about the creative possibilities that arise in times of silence. But grief, no one had really talked about grief. And this classroom silence reminded me that there are things that students will write in journals that they will not readily speak about in class, that writing can provide an open space.

Both the contemplative classroom practices and the assignments students completed outside of class worked together to create an awareness of and an appreciation for the role that contemplative silences can play, not only in their communicative practices (and the ways they evaluate the practices of others) but also in living more empathetic lives, doing the work of what Terry Tempest Williams calls "daring contemplation that inspires action"[1] on behalf of and in solidarity with others.

Conclusion: A Silence for Listening

> *"The ever-present movement of the currents of Silence takes us into the world as dramatic performance, where it weaves polarities, opposites, and contradictions together in its active motion. When we perceive the world through Silence, the world reveals the utterly particular in tension with the deepest meaning of things around us."*
>
> —Robert Sardello, from *Silence*

In "The Fruit of Silence," poet Marilyn Nelson describes her understanding of contemplative pedagogy: "to teach not technique, but attitude"; she continues, "I ask my students to explore several ways of listening for, and listening to, silence. I hope they will develop a contemplative attitude, and learn how to hear silence."[2] Many of the readings in the course I taught dealt directly with contemplative silences. They considered practices of emptying, listening, awareness, and reflection. We discussed those readings at length and in fairly intellectual ways, yet I believe it was the practice of contemplative silence, both in class and outside of class, that allowed true learning to take place.

What I told my students about their practice of silence is to pay attention. I said, "Be attentive to what your own body tells you about silence: listen to the lip bit bloody, the pounding heart, the tight jaw of self-silencing; feel the comfort of human touch, the rhythm of your own breath, the freedom of not having to say a word."

---

[1] Terry Tempest Williams, *Finding Beauty in a Broken World* (New York: Pantheon, 2008).

[2] Marilyn Nelson, "The Fruit of Silence," http://contemplativemind.org/resources/nelson-fruit-of-silence.pdf; accessed February 4, 2012.

I believe, as Kathleen Dean Moore has written in "Silence Like Scouring Sand," that "Silence is not the absence of sounds, but a way of living in the world—an intentional awareness, an expression of gratitude, to make of one's own ears, one's own body, a sounding board that resonates in its hollow places with the vibrations of the world."[3] It's about listening: listening to yourself, to your friends, to your teachers, to the environment, and listening even to those with whom you might not agree. It's about finding a space and place of openness in which you can honestly assess the complicated silences: the necessity of a foundation of trust in relationships yet the weighty burden of being sworn to secrecy; the right to privacy that nudges against political and personal needs to speak up, or the pressure to speak that can sometimes be an unhealthy, even dangerous, demand for exposure and other times be the key to freedom.

What I asked my students, in short, was to find the openness and space in their own hearts and minds and lives to do the important work of examining complex silences: the kinds that harm, those that heal, and those so complicated that they require time and space to understand and sort through. And I offered contemplative silence as a possible means for doing this work—work that is both academic and personal, perhaps spiritual and yet certainly mundane: always full of possibility.

Bibliography

Hirshfield, Jane. *Given Sugar, Given Salt*. New York: Harper Collins, 2001.

Moore, Kathleen Dean. "Silence Like Scouring Sand." *Orion*. November/December 2008.

Nelson, Marilyn. "The Fruit of Silence." http://www.contemplativemind.org /resources/nelson-fruit-of-silence.pdf. Accessed February 4, 2012.

Rilke, Rainer Maria. *Duino Elegies*. London: Hogarth Press, 1939.

Sardello, Robert J. *Silence*. Benson, NC: Goldenstone Press, 2006.

Williams, Terry Tempest. *Finding Beauty in a Broken World*. New York: Pantheon, 2008.

[3] Kathleen Dean Moore, "Silence Like Scouring Sand," *Orion* (November/December 2008): 69.

Stumbling toward Grace:
Meditations on Communion and
Community in the Writing Classroom

Ann E. Green

*Knowing of any sort is relational, animated by a desire to come
into deeper community with what we know. . . .*
*Knowing is a human way to seek relationships and, in the process,
to have encounters and exchanges that will inevitably alter us.
And its deepest reaches, knowing is always communal.*

—Parker Palmer, *The Courage to Teach*

*Relationship: connection: kinship: family: love: the movement from
an abstract and emotionless awareness that there are needy people out
there to the give-and-take—tender, quarrelsome, jokey, impassioned—
of siblings crowded together under the roof of Mary's house.*

—Nancy Mairs, *Ordinary Time: Cycles in Marriage, Faith, and Renewal*

Mary, a student who has studied with me previously and who is currently taking my "Beyond Black and White" class comes to my office on
her birthday. Her nephew has been in the neonatal intensive care unit
at a local hospital, and she has been shuttling back and forth between
her sister's home, the hospital, school, work, and an internship.

Mary had previously broken down in my office over all of this. Plus,
she was sure that with the baby in the hospital, her mom would forget
her birthday. On her birthday, another faculty member and I get her a
cake, and we all cut it and eat it in my office. It's a chocolate cake I get

from the local Amish: double chocolate. Her mom did remember her birthday, but she's happy that we remembered it, too. She completes her degree at Saint Joseph's and goes on to a yearlong volunteering program and eventually a master's degree in social work.

A former student, Sally, who has taught in urban Philadelphia schools for two years messages me on Facebook. We worked together in two courses, and I directed her yearlong honors thesis project, a memoir that traced her growth through her service-learning experiences. I wrote her recommendations for the teaching program she entered. She's touching base because she's in a residential treatment program to address her eating disorder. As a teacher in a special education classroom in Philadelphia, she encountered many students who had been sexually abused. Since she is also a sexual abuse survivor, this has contributed, in part, to her continued struggle with her own issues that resulted in her entering the treatment program. We plan to meet for coffee.

Vickie graduates after six tumultuous years at Saint Joseph's. Formerly homeless, she has mental health issues that impede her progress toward graduation. During one of her bad episodes, she calls our home in the middle of the night, and I stay on the phone with her until we can get her help. After this episode, I suggest that she take some time away from school until she is able to pursue her education. She is angry. During her last semester, she takes a class with me, in part, she says, to prove that she can do it. Her writing has beautiful images, but the sentence level structures are incredibly rough. We talk about smoothing these over. In the years since the middle of the night phone call, I have reflected a lot about the circumstances of Vickie's life and what has brought her to Saint Joseph's and how we have failed her. We have also helped her, of course, but this is not so simple.

As a cradle and cafeteria Catholic and a feminist, my understanding of the sacramental, of communion, is that it is about relationship. When other members of my family, not Catholic, ask about my personal relationship with Jesus Christ, I think about communion. My relationship with God is based in communion; not only in the literal sense of the Host but also in the communal, the community. If I am engaged in the Jesuit mantra of finding God in all things, the place where I find God in my daily work is in my students and my relationships with them and in the community we create in the writing classroom.

As a teacher of writing, relationships are crucial to the work I do. Writing at its most elemental is about connecting with a reader. While writing can be performance, argument, what Nancy Mairs calls the "male model of ceremonial combat based on the boast and the *flite*," in the feminist writing classroom, writing can be about building relationships with the reader, about making connections and creating meaning collectively (*Bone House* 1995, 177). This is the kind of writing that I teach.

When I teach a course like "Writing through Race, Class, and Gender," I am interested in creating a space where students can write across differences, where we can build communities and make connections. In *The Peaceable Classroom*, Mary Rose O'Reilley explores some of the foundational texts of "decentered" writing pedagogy, including Jerry Farber's essay, "The Student as Nigger." As O'Reilley points out, Farber's overarching point is simple: "*what* we are taught is not as important as the *method* by which we are taught" (1993, 67). As a teacher of writing, the method I employ is based in building relationships and creating community. But this requires finding ways around some of the typical constraints that limit our work within institutions that are often, as institutions are, inconsistent in their stated missions (in the case of my university, "a transformational commitment to social justice") and perhaps incapable (because they are institutions) of creating spaces for the "whole person."

What are the typical constraints that limit connection and the possibility of communion? Early in my career as a teaching assistant and then an adjunct faculty member, it was difficult building relationships that included advising and mentoring. And it was difficult for simple reasons. I didn't have an office where students could come to be advised, and I didn't teach upper-level courses that might be sequenced so a student could choose to deepen his or her understanding of social class or race by taking a second course with me. For the most part, I didn't know students beyond their first-year courses.

During my first semester as a teaching assistant, my evaluation by a well-meaning colleague suggested that I spent too much time conferencing with individual students and that this would not be practical once I taught multiple sections. Her comment pushed me directly into writing center work where I could spend time working one-on-one with writers, but it also frustrated me. Time, it seemed to me, was the one thing that a beginning teacher might have that a more experienced teacher would not. As an adjunct faculty member, however, I did have less time to spend conferencing with students. If, as Parker Palmer writes, "Good teaching is an act of hospitality," then the kinds of hospitality I was able to provide when my position was tentative and contingent was limited by the lack of institutional support and the amount of time I could spend (1998, 50).

In institutions increasingly relying on adjunct faculty members, we must be mindful of how material conditions limit the possibility of community and the communal. If we are tenure-track faculty members, this is another good reason to advocate for more tenure-track lines. If we are part-time faculty members, this is an acknowledgement that the communal may be different because of the material conditions that affect that work. Much of what I am able to do now is because I have those things that I lacked as an adjunct and a teaching assistant. I have an office. I have a long-term (tenured) commitment to an institution. I am able to teach new courses that I design that meet both my needs as a teacher and the needs of students, and I do not have to follow a core syllabus constructed by others. I am able to design assignments that create space for community, and I am able to spend time with students shaping these assignments in ways that engage with *cura personalis*. I have relationships with students, other faculty, and the institution itself that offer support and build community.

I mention these institutional supports and material conditions before returning to the specifics of my classroom because it is easy to emphasize the spiritual nature of our pedagogy without acknowledging the material conditions that constrain our work. As tenure becomes increasingly rare and faculty are more and more contingent (70 percent of faculty currently are contingent[1]), the ability to teach courses that enrich and enhance students spiritually as well as intellectually will be compromised. The more we are expected to define our work by "deliverables," "course objectives," and assessable data points, the less we will be able to model learning as magic, as an absorbing spiritual and intellectual process that does encompass, when it's working, the whole person, and that can in the process of building the communal, lead to grace. The best part of what I do does not fit on a rubric and cannot be assessed at the end of the semester. If, as Kolvenbach writes, "The real measure of our Jesuit universities lies in who our students become," then our assessment must consider the difficult to quantify long-term effects of our teaching (2000, 10). At some point, someone is going to ask us how we assess the sacramental, and I know of no clear instrument for quantifying grace.

As someone from a working-class background who teaches about privilege, I am, perhaps, overly suspicious of the institutional. Institutions, even those with social justice agendas, by their nature flatten,

---

[1] Audrey Williams June, "With Student Learning at Stake, Group Calls for Better Working Conditions for Adjuncts," *Chronicle of Higher Education* (July 31, 2012).

oppress, and lacquer over difference. Institutions desire a smooth surface, a well-oiled machine. The communal, by contrast, is messy. As Patricia Williams describes it, "Creating community . . . involves this most difficult work of negotiating real divisions, of considering boundaries before we go crashing through, and of pondering our differences before we can ever agree on the terms of our sameness . . ." (1997, 6). Relationships in community involve negotiating conflict. They take time. You cannot fill out a form to create a community. You cannot think that because you had a great community in your spring class that you will have a great community in your fall class. Each semester you must engage in this process of building community and creating a space for the communal. Sometimes fourteen weeks is not enough (and God love you if you teach quarters). While the end result is unpredictable and difficult to assess, what is important in both writing and community-building is the process.

So what does communion, the communal, community look like in the writing classroom? How do you create space for the communal within an institution that is, by its nature, and for a lack of a better term, institutional? It often begins, as actual communion does, with bread.

In the fall of 2010, I taught a new course called "Beyond Black and White: Exploring American Identities." The course was a faith/justice studies course as well as an English course, and it was small—fourteen students, all women. Ten of the students self-identified as white and four identified as either mixed race or Black. Two students identified as the children of immigrants (Haiti and Jamaica), and one student disclosed to me her status as an illegal immigrant. I had either advised or taught five of the students in the course before, and Vickie, the formerly homeless student I previously mentioned, was in the course as well. The course came from my own interest in exploring issues of race and class beyond the Black/white binary that my other classes, like "Reading and Writing the Civil Rights Movement," often explore, and as it developed, the literature we read focused on issues of immigration, race, and class. Elizabeth Ellsworth, in her foundational critique of critical pedagogy, argues that there must be time for knowing people outside of the classroom in order to develop trust for talking about difficult and challenging subjects like racism (1989, 316). Time to know one another outside of class needs to be built into the work of the semester. If I neglect this particular aspect of the class, the classroom community is not as strong. It's important to give the class a space to talk about what they might want to do together outside of class so that they own the event.

   Students are often resistant to outside-of-class bonding and community building. Even in a faith/justice course, where community is an important aspect of the minor, students proclaim their busyness. As Vickie wrote in her end-of-the-semester evaluation, "When I first got into the class and heard that there needed to be out-of-class activities I initially thought, 'I need to drop this class ASAP' because I knew this semester was going to be tough already." Always, when I explain that we need to find some time to spend together, either at an off-campus event or sharing a potluck, they explain to me why they can't do it. Always at this point, I am frustrated. Why, I think, do I want to spend time with students? "I am busy, too," I mutter under my breath. I'd rather spend time playing Angry Birds than spend time answering e-mails about this. Grumble, grumble. It is in this moment that I typically give the students time in class, when I have left the room, to come up with what they would like to do and when, and then to tell me about it. Pedagogically, if they design the activity, they own it. Spiritually, if this is all about a journey toward grace, no one can be on the sidelines. We all must participate in the trip.

   After about ten minutes, "Beyond Black and White" called me back in and told me that they had decided on a potluck with a theme of food from their cultural backgrounds, insofar as it was possible (string bean casserole made with cream of mushroom soup was eliminated). They agreed to my suggestion that we add a film to the mix, *The Life and Times of Harvey Milk*, as we were expecting a visit from San Francisco Jesuit Donal Godfrey who would speak about ministering to LGBTQ people, especially during the HIV/AIDS crisis. The documentary on Milk, I thought, would give everyone some background on San Francisco. A Jesuit friend who lives in a large university house let us use his living room and kitchen, so we had a great space for the fifteen of us to gather. Tom didn't have a DVD player, though, so one of the students said she'd bring hers. We'd meet on a Sunday night.

   The road toward the communal is not smooth. As soon as the class had come to their decision, the e-mails and wailing and gnashing of teeth began. Everyone had conflicts with that date. I was asked if it was okay to miss the potluck because of work or practice. Some people could only come for half an hour because they needed to have a meeting to prepare a retreat for an immersion experience. Mary's nephew was still in the hospital. She might need to miss to babysit her other nephew. Everyone except Mary got the same answer from me: It is important that you attend this outside-of-class event. "How does it 'count'?" many asked. "Is it an absence?" "It is important that you attend this outside-of-class event, but you must make your own decision." "Is it okay if I miss the potluck?" "It is important that you attend this outside-of-class event."

My answer to questions about missing the potluck was deliberately as neutral as I could make it. Attending an outside-of-class event cannot feel like punishment, and each individual student must make the best decision for herself. More importantly, in every class I teach, students have to be allowed the freedom to make their own decision and the freedom, if necessary, to fail. I can model a level of engagement and a kind of approach to writing and social justice, but what I am putting out there might not be what a particular student needs at that particular moment. We're striving for community, but we're also limited by our individual lives. If we're stumbling toward grace, no one can be dragged along.

I had family obligations, too, and I ended up driving three hours back from my parents' house with a cake my mother baked for the occasion (can't get more heritage based than that). Cake in tow, I showed up at Tom's house expecting that he and I would be eating a whole bunch of chocolate cake alone. To my surprise, every single person in the class arrived, explained why they brought what they brought (even if it was, "I was really busy so I brought chips and salsa," or, in more cases than mine, "my mother made this for me"). Everyone ate, and everyone stayed. Tom ate and watched the movie with us. Nothing at all memorable happened. We spent time together. We talked a little before and after the movie. Everyone loved my mother's chocolate cake.

Before the potluck, Vickie already had a series of absences that put her in danger of failing the class. Mary struggled to do her schoolwork while balancing her job, her internship, and caring for her sister's other child. The class had been a very quiet one. After the potluck, other students in the class asked about Mary's nephew, and Vickie came to class. When we read Edwidge Danticat's *The Dewbreaker* about torture in Haiti and immigration to the United States, Alice, a very quiet person, the child of Haitian immigrants, spoke about some of the Creole in the text. Nothing miraculous happened, and maybe Vickie would have come to class, Mary would have shared about her nephew, and Alice would have offered her insights without a potluck, but I don't think so. I think we broke bread together, and we came closer to grace.

In *The Long Loneliness*, Dorothy Day describes the anointing of a dying Catholic Worker by a mumbling priest. "[D]espite the lack of grace in the human sense," she writes, "Grace was there, souls were strengthened, hearts were lifted" (1952, 199). When we create communities in our classroom, we create the possibility for grace, no matter how imperfect and mumbling our attempts are. Day continues, "Ritual, how could we do without it?" (199). Our classrooms with smart technologies and bells and whistles on campuses that look like country clubs can be devoid of rituals that give hope. If we create spaces where students can integrate the spiritual, intellectual, emotional aspects of their lives by breaking bread together, we can foster in them the kind of "whole person" whom we too would like to encounter when we seek medical care, when we send our children to elementary school, and when we too need charity.

Later on that semester, when Mary's nephew was sicker and she cried in my office, I took Mary across campus to the local sandwich shop and bought her a pizza because she hadn't been eating. When you know your students, *cura personalis* extends to the corporal works of mercy, too, I guess. They are more apparent to me than the spiritual ones, so I try and meet those needs when I can.

But what, you're asking now, does this have to do with writing? It's fine that you teach these small classes and that you build this kind of community, but how does this change students' writing? If school writing is to writing as ketchup is to a vegetable, what I am trying to do in my writing classroom is give students authentic writing experiences, a really good vegetable, even a new vegetable. I hope that students are engaged in writing that they care about and are invested in. I hope that they may discover that they like kohlrabi or delicata squash and that they can prepare it to feed others as well as themselves. It is not, as Mary Rose O'Reilley characterizes it, "McSchool" (1998, 7). We're going to have the best of the food from the potluck: nutritious, homemade, substantive, maybe organic. By building relationships with students in the writing classroom, I am trying to model a process that applies for both writing and social justice work. If I want to teach justly, the way that the class is structured must be based in a process of engagement that recognizes the personal and establishes the communal, and the way that writing is assigned, too, must move from the personal toward the communal (O'Reilley 1993, 61).

But it is not only the social justice emphasis itself that is important. Social justice work is not possible without the relationships that I form with students in the writing classroom. In other words, as Kolvenbach writes:

> Adopting the point of view of those who suffer injustice, our profes-
> sors seek the truth and share their search and its results with our
> students. A legitimate question, even if it does not sound academic,
> is for each professor to ask, "When researching and teaching, where
> and with whom is my heart?" (2000, 12)

By creating assignments that ask students to consider "where and with
whom is my heart?" I want a deeper and more serious level of engagement and commitment than fourteen weeks and three hours. And if, as
Parker Palmer writes, "What we teach is who we are," I hope that students see that my heart is with them and with the poor (1998, 1).

In order to do this, what I must bring to the table are assignments that
are keyed to the students in the room. Thus, I might have a general idea
of what kinds of writing I will ask for, but the specific kind of assignment
I design comes from the students and the material, and the students'
reactions to the material. A good assignment both pushes students to
write and think differently while giving them the space to find their own
way. A good assignment gives students control in shaping their writing
and a chance to struggle with it, and it lets them connect their personal
experiences to the writing at hand. In other words, if we're building
relationships in the classroom because we're creating community, students also have relationships with their writing, and it's that process
where they engage in finding a good topic, drafting, and shaping an
essay, while sharing it with the class along the way, that creates space
for the writing to improve. Without the relationships we have with one
another in the classroom, writing may improve on a technical level, but
students are much more likely to stay with safe topics and familiar forms,
rather than to stretch into new territory.

In "Beyond Black and White," I had sequenced the assignments to
begin with a personal reflection on what it means to be "American" (or
to be living in America, for those who were not) moved to a "Boundary
Crossing" assignment that asked students to consider a point of view
that differed widely from their own, and finished by asking students to
use Catholic Social Teaching as a tool for analyzing literature. The first
assignment introduced students to each other, and they kept their writing to relatively safe topics. They did not yet know each other, and many
of them did not know me, so they stayed close to what they perceived
was safe. Although the assignment allowed for space for "coming out,"
no one wrote about sexuality as an aspect of identity. Because we didn't
know each other well, it was a good place to start. This kind of "low

stakes" writing helps establish the atmosphere in the classroom where a community can be built.

In the second assignment, I asked students to write from a perspective of someone who had lived a life that was extremely different from their own in order to imagine if we could connect across our common humanity. In response to this assignment, Angel wrote a lyrical short story imagining the pain of Rutgers' student Tyler Clementi as he decided to end his own life after his roommate used a webcam to spy on his sexual encounter with another man. As she took on the persona of Clementi and incorporated text messages, Facebook posts, and narration to explain his pain, she described her process as similar to the literary moves used by Toni Cade Bambara in her short story about social class called "The Lesson." Vickie decided to write about the women in her family and their experiences with education. In her work, she used repetition and a fragmented form like Michelle Cliff's *If I Could Write This in Fire* to explore her experience. In both pieces the writing was strong, invested. In their final self-reflections for the course, both students cited these papers as their strongest writing and discussed what they had learned from writing them.

Dorothy Day writes, "The only answer to this life, to the loneliness we are all bound to feel, is community" (1952, 243). For Day, community is essential for the sacraments and the sacramental. The corporeal and spiritual works of mercy are not possible without "the living together, working together, sharing together, loving God and loving our brother, and living close to him in community so we can show our love for Him" (243). Ideally, classrooms can be communities where we share grace. Dorothy Day is a touchstone for my teaching. While she does not write (for the most part) directly about the classroom, what she offers are visions of community and the communal that inspire compassion. While students' writing improves in my classroom, I am committed to fostering places for other kinds of growth and community. I know something has changed when graduates get in touch to talk about the work they've done in Jesuit Volunteer Corps or the Peace Corps. Or when they go into social work or education or law and tell you that they approach their work differently because they took writing courses that engaged with social justice work. Developing relationships and building community is a way of inciting the transcendent and creating a space for the possibility of grace.

At the beginning of this piece, I mentioned Sally, one of my former students who now teaches at a Philadelphia public school who contacted me to talk about her eating disorder. We keep in regular touch. She's been in recovery now for a year, and we have regular coffees and conversations about teaching together. The relationship has continued long past the classroom experiences and is evolving into a friendship. When we build communities in our classrooms, we are sometimes surprised by the gifts of grace that arrive at our doorstep.

Works Cited

Cliff, Michelle. 2008. *If I Could Write This in Fire*. Minneapolis: Minnesota UP.

Danticat, Edwidge. 2005. *The Dew Breaker*. New York: Vintage.

Day, Dorothy. 1952. *The Long Loneliness*. San Francisco: HarperCollins.

Ellsworth, Elizabeth. 1989. Why Doesn't This Feel Empowering?: Working through the Myths of Critical Pedagogy. *Harvard Educational Review*. 59.3: 297–324.

June, Audrey Williams. 2012. With Student Learning at Stake, Group Calls for Better Working Conditions for Adjuncts. *Chronicle of Higher Education*. June 31.

Kolvenbach, Reverend Peter-Hans. 2000. The Service of Faith and the Promotion of Justice in American Jesuit Higher Education.

Mairs, Nancy. 1993. *Ordinary Time: Cycles in Marriage, Faith, and Renewal*. Boston: Beacon Press.

———. 1995. *Remembering the Bone House*. Boston: Beacon Press.

O'Reilley, Mary Rose. 1993. *The Peaceable Classroom*. Portsmouth, NH: Boynton Cook.

———. 1998. *Radical Presence: Teaching as Contemplative Practice*. Portsmouth, NH: Boynton Cook.

Palmer, Parker. 1998. *The Courage to Teach: Exploring the Inner Landscape of a Teacher's Life*. San Francisco: Jossey-Bass.

Williams, Patricia. 1997. *Seeing a Color-Blind Future: The Paradox of Race*. New York: Farrar, Straus, and Giroux.

Looking into the Bible[1]

Michael Patella, OSB

Over twenty years ago, when I was a student in Rome, I spent won-derful Sunday afternoons walking through various neighborhoods in the city. The degree to which artwork covered nearly every door, façade, and window was astounding. Moreover, religious art was not confined to churches; it jumped out at the citizenry from every nook and cranny. I remember thinking back then that a person could learn a whole round of Christian devotions, if not theology, simply by walking the streets of Rome, and to be sure, seeing that city in action pretty much convinced me that such is what Romans have been doing for centuries. Further reflections on those Sunday afternoons had brought me to the conclusion that color, form, and beauty convey truth in a way that words and in-struction fail; they can speak Truth to those who are deaf to theological discourse.

This experience in Italy came back to me about four years ago when I was looking for a way to revamp my class, Introduction to the Biblical Tradition, one of two theology courses required of students at Saint John's University and the College of Saint Benedict. Teaching Sacred Scripture to undergraduates at this point in time has its many challenges. Our American culture has historical roots that are both deeply religious and soundly secular, which can create a pronounced cognitive disso-nance. There are those students who read and study the Bible with the

---

[1] Portions of this essay appear in *Word and Image: The Hermeneutics of* The Saint John's Bible (Collegeville, MN: Liturgical Press, 2013).

belief that everything one needs to know is contained solely in its pages. Opposite them are those students who retaliate against such notions and refuse to open a Bible's cover, let alone read it with any seriousness. Then there are those in the middle who may or may not have heard of the Bible, but in any case, have no feelings toward it one way or the other but are interested in finding out more about it.

Theology is a science embodying a wide array of disciplines, from linguistics to biology to philosophy. We fail our students and our mission if we do not excite them to see the glory of God in every corner of creation. Biblical studies has its own rich methodologies for deciphering and understanding a text, and it would be a tremendous disservice to our students if they never encountered them. There are the patristic fourfold ways of interpretation (literal, allegorical, moral, anagogical), the historical-critical method, narrative, and reader-response criticisms, to name a few.

Yet the object is to get the students into the text, not to dwell solely on the science of the text. Can one combine the experiential insight with the intellectual rigor? Yes. From my teaching experience, I have found that the historical-critical method excels in answering the questions posed by inquisitive yet skeptical minds, and if employed well, it can prompt those same minds to ask questions which challenge their skepticism. Simultaneously, historical-criticism can lead those students who fear losing everything they believe in to see the beauty and richness of Sacred Scripture within the complexities of the text.

Historical-Critical Method

If there are any polemics involved in studying Scripture, they will arise in the role the historical-critical method plays in interpreting the text. The deeply pious often see historical-criticism as a secularist reading of the inspired Word of God, and indeed, all too many of its adherents present it in such a way. In some cases, a professor or two may even find pleasure in watching faces of those in front of them as a number of students see their faith dissolving into ether. Ironically, the hardened postmodernists may rightfully criticize the arrogance of a methodology that purports to result in the totality of a passage's meaning without reference to any personal dynamic. Yet, because they cannot acknowledge the claims of a privileged text, the pious will not find allies among the deconstructionists. A big worry of mine is to end the semester with one-half the class dispirited and disappointed while the other half is simply bored.

In any Catholic educational institution, the goal for an introductory Scripture course, indeed a goal for any course, is to get the pious student to embrace critical scholarship enthusiastically for its ability to reflect God's greater glory, and to prod the postmodernist student into seeing a foundation for claims stemming from revelation. The way to accomplish this task, I believe, is to take a more organic approach.

One of the shortcomings of historical-criticism flairs up when exegetes present it as capable of answering all the questions a text may raise, instead of employing it as a methodology to arrive at a certain set of necessary answers. For example, historical-criticism cannot answer a question on why or how a certain biblical passage is used in a liturgical antiphon. Because it cannot, certain professors may feel that the respective passage has no place in the liturgy at all and, unfortunately, may say as much.

A more organic approach (and a more honest one) would be to admit the limits of historical-criticism by introducing the polyvalent nature of Scripture, the context of its use within the history of the living faith, and why certain writers and artists have interpreted it in such and such a way. Doing so breathes life, creativity, and excitement into the subject matter while showing a great deal of sensitivity and humility before the Word of God. Students coming from a variety of positions, from liberal to conservative, can understand and become enthusiastic by such an open approach. Examples from the component parts of historical-criticism make this point clearer.

Source Criticism

An element of biblical studies is answering the question, "Where did this story, psalm, parable, etc., come from?" Such a discussion will wrestle with the similarities Genesis has with Babylonian creation myths, how a particular psalm parallels an Egyptian poem, or the inconsistencies between Matthew and Mark. It would be easy for one to brush off Scripture as simply derivative of literature from civilizations greater and more glorious than ancient Israel and Palestine. The presentation of the material, however, can be done in such a way that rejoices in divine truth wherever it may be found, and shows how God uses human means to reveal God's self.

Literary and Textual Criticism

We view the New Testament as the Word of God. We see its revelatory nature within the gospels, and we stand upon the theology contained in it. The New Testament comes to us, however, in over seven thousand extant papyrus fragments, Greek manuscripts, and Latin lectionaries, and these written texts do not always agree with each other. In the face of all these variant readings, claims about gospel authenticity will not be very convincing to a class. A positive way through the material would be to get the students to see the great body of texts as the result of the early church's great enthusiasm for evangelization, an evangelization spurred by the Holy Spirit. It is a superb lesson, and a most enjoyable experience for both professor and pupil when one can read the words on the page and can see the truth beyond the fact. The terms, "Word of the Lord" or "Word of God" are greater than the sum of their consonants and vowels.

The Hermeneutical Stance

The Catholic Church today is, in many ways, still living under the shadow of the modernist controversy from about one hundred years ago, when people feared that critical research in the biblical sciences led one to abandon faith. This modernist dynamic manifests itself in strange ways within the classroom. While the students I have may not be, and certainly do not see themselves as, either rigid historical critics or strict biblical fundamentalists, the positions they take often reflect these particular biases. For example, a student with a historical-critical slant will seek scientific proof that the angel Gabriel actually appeared to Mary (Luke 1:26-38), whereas the student with fundamentalist proclivities will argue that the black ink on the white page is all the proof that is needed. In the end, neither argument is helpful in reaching an interpretation that can inform faith, for neither has anything to do with faith. Both students stand on the *same* side of the fence when they try to argue with each other, in that both seek empirical evidence in making their respective but opposed points.

In a reading of Scripture from the Catholic side of the fence, faith and reason walk hand in hand. Instead of looking for proof that the angel Gabriel actually appeared to Mary, my students here will study the nature of vision stories in the ancient world, focus on angelic appearance passages throughout the whole Bible, and concentrate on those verses mentioning Gabriel (there are only four: Daniel 8:16; 9:21; and Luke 1:19, 26), and draw conclusions from these. The findings will seek to establish the historical, social, and biblical context for Luke's description of Mary's mystical experience with the God of Israel.

By establishing the point of inquiry from this vantage point, it is much more difficult for my students to lose sight of fact that Sacred Scripture deals with divine revelation. As a teacher I can do justice to the rigor and insight of the historical-critical method, yet also enable the study of scripture to be a theological exercise, which is, by Saint Anselm's famous dictum, *faith seeking understanding*. From the students' perspective, it is a short leap to viewing the sacred text as the Word of God in human words. Such an open, dynamic, and faith-filled response should be the goal of those teaching Scripture and theology on a Catholic campus, but getting there is far easier to say than to do.

The empirical hermeneutic permeates so much of culture. Why and how we gauge our lives and experiences along this line goes beyond the subject of this essay. Suffice it to say that my students are not immune from it. An understanding of the biblical text that incorporates tradition, symbol, and history while holding to the literary nature of the Word is better experienced than explained. In planning my introductory class, my experience with the art of Rome came to mind, and alongside it, the completion of the first volumes of *The Saint John's Bible*. I saw there that art invites people to disarm themselves of their discomfort with things religious. Art seemed then to do a good job in opening people up to the mystery of salvation. I thought of using it to help my students open themselves up to the Bible's fuller meaning. Reaching for *The Saint John's Bible* seemed like the natural choice.

The Saint John's Bible

Fifteen years ago Saint John's University commissioned the Queen's calligrapher, Donald Jackson, to write by hand and on vellum the whole text of the Bible, complete with images. With input from theologians and scholars from Saint John's School of Theology•Seminary and other university departments, the completion of the last of seven volumes was celebrated in spring 2011. Because education within the Benedictine and Catholic character of the institution was a major reason for the undertaking, the theology department at Saint John's University and the College of Saint Benedict uses *The Saint John's Bible* for much of its required, introductory course, The Biblical Tradition. For my approach to the course, I adapt the monastic practice of *lectio divina*.

Lectio Divina

I am a Benedictine monk teaching in a Benedictine institution. In the monastic tradition, *lectio divina*, the slow, meditative practice of sacred reading, is part of the ethos we stress, particularly in our Scripture classes. A wordplay on this practice has had some of us develop *visio divina*, i.e., the slow, meditative gazing upon a biblical image. For my classes, I decided to employ *visio divina* by using the images from *The Saint John's Bible.*

One of the first classes on the biblical narrative I teach is, quite naturally, the creation account in Genesis. It certainly may make logical sense to begin the scriptural narrative with the first book of the Bible, but in terms of class management and course goals, dealing with Genesis at the start takes on paramount importance, because from the creation accounts in Genesis surface all the hot button issues, not only with regard to the study of Scripture, but also with upbringing, social class, and politics. The biblical studies classroom is not divorced from the polarized society in which we now find ourselves, and how the discussion goes these first few days of the semester will determine how students view the class, the professor, and each other going forward. In addition, how those in the classroom respond will determine how other students view them. I feel it is far better to deal with all the questions and issues above and below the surface at the get-go rather than let fears and suspicions simmer for several weeks before facing them. The rest of the semester will be more fruitful and enjoyable if I do.

The Process

Students are assigned to read and prepare Genesis 1–2 before class, including any questions about the text they may have. When class meets, I spend the first part going over their comments and questions and then switch to the presentation of images. So for Genesis, I choose two images from *The Saint John's Bible*, *Six Days of Creation* and *Adam and Eve*.

As the image is on the screen, a student reads from the corresponding text. After several moments of silence, I ask students what they see. I keep track of their responses, usually writing them on the board. With the image still on the screen, the students read the text to themselves quietly. Once we complete the section with the visuals, the floor is open for discussion. I go over the comments listed on the board by categorizing, comparing, and contrasting them. The result is that there is plenty of material from which to build discussion on source theory, historical-critical method, hermeneutics, and just about any discipline associated with biblical interpretation.

The *Six Days of Creation* image is laid out as six tall columns of varying height followed by a seventh in gold, the Lord's day of rest; each column represents a day as described in Genesis 1:1–2:3.[2]

> In the beginning when God created the heavens and the earth, the earth was a formless void and darkness covered the face of the deep, while a wind from God swept over the face of the waters. Then God said, "Let there be light"; and there was light. And God saw that the light was good; and God separated the light from the darkness. God called the light Day, and the darkness he called Night. And there was evening and there was morning, the first day. (Gen 1:1-5)

The image corresponding to these verses is a cacophonous set of dark swirls and ragged edges rising and falling. In the lower corner written in Hebrew is the phrase, *Tohu wa Bohu*—dark and formless void. The abstract images evoke chaos and foreboding, and the Hebrew reference grounds the image and the words into the life of real people, tying the whole account to its religious tradition.

> And God said, "Let there be a dome in the midst of the waters, and let it separate the waters from the waters." So God made the dome and separated the waters that were under the dome from the waters that were above the dome. And it was so. God called the dome Sky. And there was evening and there was morning, the second day. (Gen 1:6-8)

A deep, azure blue fills the bottom quarter of the second column, while gray half circles rise above it; there is a hint of blue at the top register as well. This image provides the opportunity for me to explain how the

---

[2] All biblical quotations are from the *New Revised Standard Version* Bible, Catholic Edition (National Council of the Churches of Christ in the United States of America: 1989, 1993).

ancients viewed the cosmos as an upside-down bowl under which we humans dwell, supported by earthen pillars and surrounded by water, the symbol of chaos. Theologically, the writer of Genesis wants us to know that the Lord God is responsible for good order, and the same Lord God protects creation from destruction.

> And God said, "Let the waters under the sky be gathered together into one place, and let the dry land appear." And it was so. God called the dry land Earth, and the waters that were gathered together he called Seas. And God saw that it was good. Then God said, "Let the earth put forth vegetation: plants yielding seed, and fruit trees of every kind on earth that bear fruit with the seed in it." And it was so. The earth brought forth vegetation: plants yielding seed of every kind, and trees of every kind bearing fruit with the seed in it. And God saw that it was good. And there was evening and there was morning, the third day. (Gen 1:9-13)

Using a satellite photograph of the Nile Delta as a template, the third column presents a view of rivers and streams running between large patches of green and brown. Grasses and flowers sprout from the lower register. The idea of setting water and land in their proper places certainly comes forth. A more important feature, however, is the fact that the photograph upon which the image is based is a contemporary snapshot of the ancient land of Egypt, and thus an integral part of biblical geography. It becomes a subtle way to introduce the timelessness of the biblical narrative along with the ongoing quality of creation. The students' preconceived notions of *Genesis* are challenged in a nonthreatening way.

> And God said, "Let there be lights in the dome of the sky to separate the day from the night; and let them be for signs and for seasons and for days and years, and let them be lights in the dome of the sky to give light upon the earth." And it was so. God made the two great lights—the greater light to rule the day and the lesser light to rule the night—and the stars. God set them in the dome of the sky to give light upon the earth, to rule over the day and over the night, and to separate the light from the darkness. And God saw that it was good. And there was evening and there was morning, the fourth day. (Gen 1:14-19)

This fourth column stands at the center of the page. Its purple hue is reminiscent of twilight or dawn, that shadowy border between night and day. A bright golden disc floats at the top, and a paler disc of the same size rests in the lower third. Visually connecting the two is a spangle of stars. Students can see a glaring inconsistency even before I voice it: If the sun and moon are not created until the fourth day, where did the light come from when God created it on the first day? There is no easy answer, which allows for all sorts of speculation, and that is a good thing, for students are now able to enter into the mythic poetry of the account. As a professor, I can use the opportunity to discuss the role of genre and form criticism in interpreting a reading.

> And God said, "Let the waters bring forth swarms of living creatures, and let birds fly above the earth across the dome of the sky." So God created the great sea monsters and every living creature that moves, of every kind, with which the waters swarm, and every winged bird of every kind. And God saw that it was good. God blessed them, saying, "Be fruitful and multiply and fill the waters in the seas, and let birds multiply on the earth." And there was evening and there was morning, the fifth day. (Gen 1:19-23)

The depiction in the fifth column is set on a sea blue background. Nondescript birds dart across the sky, and there is no mistaking the fish swimming in the sea, but here the artist introduces evolutionary theory. The drawings of the fish in the sea are based on fossil evidence; most of the species no longer exist. This image is a response to the requirements of the Committee on Illumination and Text, the group of scholars who gave the theological input to *The Saint John's Bible*. The Committee insisted that nothing in the Genesis artwork pit evolutionary science against theology, but rather depict the two fields as complementary. By visually combining scientific discovery within theological discourse, students can let their collective and individual guards down. The next panel accentuates the compatibility of the two branches of knowledge.

> And God said, "Let the earth bring forth living creatures of every kind: cattle and creeping things and wild animals of the earth of every kind." And it was so. God made the wild animals of the earth of every kind, and the cattle of every kind, and everything that creeps upon the ground of every kind. And God saw that it was good. Then God said, "Let us make humankind in our image, according to our likeness; and let them have dominion over the fish of the sea, and over the birds of the air, and over the cattle, and over all the wild animals of the earth, and over every creeping thing that creeps upon the earth." So God created humankind in his image, in the image of God he created them; male and female he created them.

> God blessed them, and God said to them, "Be fruitful and multiply,
> and fill the earth and subdue it; and have dominion over the fish of
> the sea and over the birds of the air and over every living thing that
> moves upon the earth." God said, "See, I have given you every plant
> yielding seed that is upon the face of all the earth, and every tree
> with seed in its fruit; you shall have them for food. And to every
> beast of the earth, and to every bird of the air, and to everything that
> creeps on the earth, everything that has the breath of life, I have
> given every green plant for food." And it was so. God saw every-
> thing that he had made, and indeed, it was very good. And there
> was evening and there was morning, the sixth day. (Gen 1:23-31)

A great deal of activity occupies the sixth column. The stars from the
fourth day, and the birds from the fifth spill over into the sixth. Human
figures appear to be hunting and gathering, and indeed, they are modeled
on cave wall sketches from 20,000 to 30,000 years ago. This prehistoric
dating continues the discussion on evolutionary theory, especially when
students are reminded that, according to the Bible, the earth is not even
six thousand years old.

> Thus the heavens and the earth were finished, and all their multi-
> tude. And on the seventh day God finished the work that he had
> done, and he rested on the seventh day from all the work that he
> had done. So God blessed the seventh day and hallowed it, because
> on it God rested from all the work that he had done in creation.
> (Gen 2:1-3)

A column of gold leaf completes the full page illumination of the first
creation story in Genesis. The Lord God rests on the seventh day; only
color transports the meaning to the reader. Unifying all seven columns
are a series of small gold squares progressing across the page from left
to right, with one square at day one and seven squares at day seven; the
hand of the Lord God is present at each moment of creation. In addition,
in the middle of the page is a rather large bird flying across days three
to five. That avian image reprises at various points in *The Saint John's
Bible,* connecting God's ongoing revelation to humankind through all
seven volumes.

An interesting development on the facing page of calligraphy always
catches the students' eyes. Despite a five-fold proofreading process, one
line of text was inadvertently left out. The scribe discreetly includes it
with a little note and arrow in the margin. History shows that this is a

common practice for correcting mistakes in the manuscript tradition, and it is a great aide for a professor to position himself or herself for a discussion on textual criticism.

For the creation story of Adam and Eve and the Fall (Gen 2:4–3:24), the artwork changes entirely, yet there are still visual references going back to the opening panel. In a lush depiction reminiscent of Paul Gauguin, we see a garden filled with colorful flora and fauna, complete with more cave paintings in the background and a rather large coral snake. On the facing page is a quarter section of Adam and Eve with segments of the same snake slithering between them; the colors are muted, and they are no longer in the garden.

Several things happen visually. Anyone comparing the images here to what he or she sees on the first page would have to conclude that we are opening another story, but it is a story that has some connection to what comes before, and indeed it does. It is a visual way to mark the two different creation accounts in Genesis.

Further questions

The first response this depiction of the creation story is generally along the lines most young people use to express themselves, "Cool!" "Awesome!" "Rocks!" come to mind. The foundation is laid, however, for the probing questions. What does the depiction communicate? Is the image faithful to what the text is saying? How have others represented creation? In fact, showing an image of Michelangelo's Sistine Chapel ceiling is very helpful here. As the discussion progresses, students are led to see that there are different ways to render the same essential story: God creates out of love, and creation is good.

Initiating students into the Scriptures in such fashion opens them up to asking other questions that serious study must tackle. Revisiting each of the elements of historical-criticism that I discussed earlier can show how.

Source Criticism

The respective images found in the seven columns have a variety of sources. The *Tohu wa Bohu* is the Hebrew at the basis of the English translation, *dark and formless void*, for example. The artist's use of satellite photographs, prehistoric cave drawings, and fossilized fish borrowed from prior sources give meaning to the story of creation. Students can see this and make the connection to the development of the parallel accounts in Scripture. When I then explain to students that Babylonian creation myths are a source for the biblical story, we can spend more time working on what the Genesis writer is trying to say with the changes made to the Babylonian account than on defending the proposition that much of the story came from Israel's national enemy.

Literary and Textual Criticism

Students can see the various layers of design that have gone into making the *Six Days of Creation*. The colors, lines of demarcation, and the space-age images alongside cave paintings encapsulate nearly all the issues involved with textual criticism, namely, the dating of sources and texts. In addition, the question of literary seams, i.e., the "cutting and pasting" of the ancient writer becomes much more understandable to the student. The two different visuals used for the two different creation accounts substantiate the thesis that there were two different authors. Even the omitted line corrected with an inserted verse in the margins helps to explain why some ancient manuscripts have one account of something and other manuscripts have another.

Archaeology

The Genesis page is self-explanatory on the importance of biblical archaeology and even paleontology. The depiction of the second creation story in Genesis 2 shows an African couple, Adam and Eve. This move reflects the current understanding that the evolutionary roots for all forms of human life stem from the African continent. In further lessons, when the discussion leads to the dating of Exodus, for instance, students will understand the importance of historical context in deciphering a biblical text.

The Hermeneutical Question

By using art to explain the text and to engage the discipline of scriptural study, the educational exercise employs analogy, and cultural historians are quick to note that analogy is a very Catholic way of perceiving reality, for it is the foundation of the sacramental system. So, by the means I employ at the very beginning, I am leading students to where I want them to go. That is, to see the sacredness of the text even in the limitations of its details. This exercise is also most conducive for underscoring those biblical accounts of particular importance to the Christian metanarrative. Combining text with image provides a dual approach to learning and comprehending the major stories and metaphors supporting the Christian faith. Other sections from the Bible for which I use this method include the *Ten Commandments, Isaiah's Temple Vision,* the *Suffering Servant,* the *Psalms,* the frontispieces for each of the four gospels, and select parables.

Students have been enthusiastic in their response to this instruction. For those who fear that the course will feature some kind of fundamentalist indoctrination, the use of images along with the variety of responses to them allays those fears. Likewise, those who are uncomfortable with biblical criticism are better able to understand the complexity of interpreting a biblical text. Images have a way of crossing over ideological divides and opening the imagination to new ways of thinking. But I also feel that there is something deeper at work, and I have to return to that experience in Italy.

Evangelization

Catholicism is nothing if it is not sacramental. Painting, sculpture, architecture, music, and dance and all the smells and bells that go with liturgy are part and parcel of faith. Just as the windows, carvings, and layout of medieval cathedrals taught people of that time everything about the Bible and salvation, good art today can do the same thing for students as well as the rest of the population. People are drawn to beauty, and beauty is a reflection of the glory of God. What better way to bring students to the Catholic tradition than by using the treasury of resources that the tradition has given birth to? If the duty of every Christian is to proclaim the Gospel, my experience with *The Saint John's Bible* has proven to me at least that drawing on the great patrimony of Christian art can connect us to the truths of the faith and give us a means to proclaim it to others in a manner that is respectful, challenging, and true, and there is no better place to start than in our own classrooms.[3]

---

[3] Readers can view *The Saint John's Bible* at http://www.saintjohnsbible.org/see /explore.htm.

Part 4

In Places of Struggle and Challenge

Catholic Social Teaching, Community-Based Learning, and the Sacramental Imagination

Susan Crawford Sullivan

I am deeply fortunate to teach at a Jesuit college, where I have had the opportunity to learn about the Ignatian notion of "finding God in all things." St. Ignatius of Loyola, founder of the Jesuit order, saw the divine in the ordinary workings of daily life, present in all of creation. Ignatian spirituality "invites a person to search for and find God in every circumstance of life, not just in explicitly religious situations or activities. . . . It implies that God is present everywhere and, though invisible, can be "found" in any and all of the creatures which God has made."[1] For a social scientist, this invites questions about what it means to see society and social structures through a sacramental imagination, as a "set of ordered relationships, governed by both justice and love, revealing, however imperfectly, the presence of God."[2] As such, the study of society and its interworking, the ways in which relationships and institutions shape our daily lives, can become an exercise in becoming a deeper beholder of grace.

---

[1] George W. Traub, SJ, "Do You Speak Ignatian? A Glossary of Terms Used in Ignatian and Jesuit Circles," in *An Ignatian Spirituality Reader: Contemporary Writings on St. Ignatius of Loyola, the Spiritual Exercises, Discernment, and More*, ed. George W. Traub, SJ (Chicago: Loyola Press, 2008), 253–54.

[2] Andrew M. Greeley, *The Catholic Myth: The Behavior and Beliefs of American Catholics* (New York: Macmillan Publishing Company, 1990), 45.

Sacraments, writes Michael Himes, are when omnipresent grace is made concrete. Beyond the formal established sacraments in Catholicism such as the Eucharist, "anything can be sacramental if one views it in its rootedness in the grace of God."[3] A sacramental worldview means that this grace can be found in the workings of the world, messy and imperfect though the world is. Himes also argues that education is at its core a spiritual act, as it can awaken and enliven the imagination and help students to deeply see and understand the world around them.[4] That said, as a sociologist teaching courses on poverty, religion, and civic engagement, I do not actively work to awaken a sacramental imagination in students as an aim of my classes. As a scholar, and aware that at a Catholic college, students come from a wide variety of backgrounds, I aim to teach sociology. However, as there are ways of looking at society that are consonant with a sacramental imagination, I provide students with tools that can further develop such an imagination. For students who are so inclined, these tools can act to deepen in them this way of looking at the world. Specifically, combining the introduction of Catholic social teaching with the pedagogy of community-based learning provides an excellent vehicle for helping students to more deeply see, understand, and experience the world around them. This does, I believe, end up deepening a sacramental imagination for some students.

Sociologist Andrew Greeley, who has written extensively about the sacramental imagination, states that the Catholic imagination basically sees the world as good place, where grace exists. Drawing from the theological concepts of David Tracy and putting them into a social science framework, Greeley argues that a Catholic imagination sees society as a sacrament of God, something that is good but flawed, and that the natural response to God's grace is social.[5] Greeley actually tests these theological concepts through large-scale rigorous national social science surveys, finding evidence indeed for a Catholic sacramental imagination

---

[3] Michael J. Himes, "Living Conversation: Higher Education in a Catholic Context," in *An Ignatian Spirituality Reader: Contemporary Writings on St. Ignatius of Loyola, the Spiritual Exercises, Discernment, and More*, ed. George W. Traub, SJ (Chicago: Loyola Press, 2008), 225.

[4] Michael J. Himes, "Finding God in All Things: A Sacramental Worldview and Its Effects," in *As Leaven in the World: Catholic Perspectives on Faith, Vocation, and the Intellectual Life*, ed. Thomas M. Landy (Franklin, WI: Sheed & Ward, 2001), 100.

[5] Greeley, *The Catholic Myth*, 45.

that "reflects an image of God that is present in creation" and subsequently emphasizes the importance of community.[6]

Sociology, as a study of social structure and the workings of society, thus can be intimately connected with the idea of the sacramental imagination. In the courses I teach on poverty, inequality, Catholic social teaching, social action, and similar topics, I see the notion of the sacramental imagination at play in three ways. First, through concepts appropriated from Catholic social teaching such as solidarity and the preferential option for the poor, students can come to view the poor in a different way and see grace amid difficult situations. Second, sociology asks us to think about how society can be better, structured more justly, and with more concern for those who are at the margins of society. A sacramental imagination can consider what needs to be done in order to bring our society more in line with a more loving, graced, and just vision of the world.

Finally, the idea of the sacramental imagination also ties to the concept of "everyday," or "lived" religion—that is, how faith is lived in daily life. Students, who are at a developmental stage of discerning their future vocations and the people they wish to become, can come to learn more about themselves and the role they want to play in the world. Sociologists of religion are paying increasing importance to the realm of everyday religion, moving beyond studying formal attendance, beliefs, practices, and rituals to studying how religion plays out in people's day-to-day lives. To study lived religion, states Robert Orsi, "entails a fundamental rethinking of what religion is and of what it means to be 'religious.' . . . Religion comes into being in an ongoing, dynamic relationship with the realities of daily life."[7] Students from a variety of backgrounds, some of whom may be disengaged from organized religion, appropriate concepts consonant with a sacramental imagination through their study of poverty through the lens of Catholic social teaching and direct work with the poor. Through this engagement, their "lived religion" may deepen in a sacramental way of viewing and interacting with the world, as they consider how they can help bring about a more just and graced social order.

---

[6] Ibid., 46.

[7] Robert Orsi, "Everyday Miracles: The Study of Lived Religion," in *Lived Religion in America: Toward a History of Practice*, ed. David D. Hall (Princeton, NJ: Princeton University Press, 1997), 7.

Pedagogy in Action:
Catholic Social Teaching and Community-Based Learning

As a principle undergirding the mission of many Catholic institutions of higher education, the Catholic social tradition asks students to confront issues of justice, responsibility, and the common good. Unfortunately, even in schools with explicit mission statements referencing social justice concepts, the majority of students at Catholic colleges and universities are unfamiliar with Catholic social teaching. However, Catholic social teaching provides an excellent framework whereby students can intellectually, emotionally, and spiritually grapple with troubling social problems. This is true whether students are Catholic, from a different religious background, or have no religion. Catholic social teaching can be a vehicle for students to more deeply analyze and understand the world, and for many, more deeply find grace in an imperfect world.

In my experience teaching sociology, Catholic social teaching's concern with the structures of society makes it an excellent complement to community-based learning in helping students to more fully behold their environment. Taken as a whole, several key themes emerge from Catholic social teaching as particularly pertinent. Catholic social teaching starts from the premise of the dignity of the human being, created in God's likeness and with a sacred worth. Societal problems that degrade human dignity, such as homelessness or exploitation, are thus in this framework spiritual problems as well. The theme of solidarity that undergirds Catholic social teaching emphasizes interdependence and common humanity as opposed to individualism. Solidarity means we are interdependent members of the same human family. Catholic social teaching emphasizes that as interdependent beings, we realize our full humanity only in interpersonal relations and community. Pope Benedict's 2009 encyclical letter *Caritas in Veritate* (Charity in Truth) indicates, "The more authentically he or she lives these relations, the more his or her own personal identity matures. It is not by isolation that man establishes his worth, but by placing himself in relation with others and with God. Hence these relationships are of fundamental importance."[8]

Another relevant Catholic social teaching principle is the preferential option for the poor, which charges members of society with special con-

---

[8] Pope Benedict XVI, *Caritas in Veritate* (2009), 53, accessed October 10, 2013, http://www.vatican.va/holy_father/benedict_xvi/encyclicals/documents/hf_ben-xvi_enc_20090629_caritas-in-veritate_en.html.

cern for vulnerable and poor people. In the 1986 pastoral letter "Economic Justice for All," the US Catholic Bishops reiterated that a society can be judged by how its most vulnerable members are treated. "Human life is life in community. . . . Catholic social teaching challenge[s] economic arrangements that leave large numbers of people impoverished. Further, it sees extreme inequality as a threat to the solidarity of the human community. . . . The obligation to provide justice for all means the poor have the single most urgent economic claim on the conscience of the nation. . . . The obligation to evaluate social and economic activity from the viewpoint of the poor and the powerless arises from the radical command to love one's neighbor as one's self."[9]

The notion of participation is one more theme in Catholic social teaching that is particularly relevant to the study of poverty and social action. Simply stated, all people are called to fully participate in society, a society which reflects God's goodness. People should not be excluded from full participation in society, whether it be in employment, in education, or in having their voice heard. Conditions which keep any members of society from full participation are conditions which need rectifying. William Bolan argues that Catholic social teaching can help students move beyond an attitude of altruism and charity toward a more profound vision of the common good. Through Catholic social teaching, students can evaluate the conditions they encounter in the communities in which they work in light of the Gospel.[10] In keeping with a sacramental worldview, Catholic social teaching articulates God's presence in an imperfect society, while calling for people to work toward societal arrangements that more fully reflect divine love and justice. Catholic social teaching emphasizes the notion of "subsidiarity" in addressing societal problems. Subsidiarity simply states that issues and problems should be handled at the lowest level possible, but that higher levels must be involved as necessary. Thus, for example, a problem could be handled within a family, a neighborhood, a local community, a local government, a state government, a national government, or through international involvement.

---

[9] US Conference of Catholic Bishops, "Economic Justice for All: Pastoral Letter of Catholic Social Teaching and the U.S. Economy" (1986), 63, 87, accessed October 10, 2013, http://www.usccb.org/upload/economic_justice_for_all.pdf.

[10] William P. Bolan, "Promoting Social Change: Theoretical and Empirical Arguments for Using Traditional Community-based Learning When Teaching Catholic Social Thought," in *New Wine, New Wineskins: A Next Generation Reflects on Key Issues in Catholic Moral Theology*, ed. William C. Mattison III (Lanham, MD: Rowman & Littlefield Publishers, 2005).

Problems which cannot be resolved at a lower level need to be addressed at a higher level.

Catholic social scientist Mary Jo Bane, of the Harvard Kennedy School, has written an excellent essay on what it means to study poverty and poverty policy through the lens of Catholic social teaching and a sacramental imagination. Bane describes how what she calls a "Catholic sensibility" can be brought to poverty policy analysis. This Catholic sensibility, or a Catholic sacramental imagination, sees the world as "created and redeemed by a God who takes a personal interest in the well-being of men and women, as a hopeful place that is basically good and in which redemption is always possible."[11] The formal sacrament of the Eucharist means that Catholicism is primarily a communal rather than an individualistic religion. Catholics are called to follow Jesus' model—as one who "loved, healed, and forgave indiscriminately."[12] To see the poor in light of Catholic social teaching and a Catholic sacramental imagination means that we must be attentive to the reality that some in our society lack the capacity to participate fully and to flourish—through lacking things such as education, income, shelter, or jobs. Bane states that a Catholic sacramental imagination toward the poor means an emphasis on God's love and empathy for all people—especially the poor—rooted in generosity, hopefulness, and a spirit of mutual responsibility for each other.[13]

The Role of Community-Based Learning

Community-based learning is an important teaching tool that, done properly, can develop in students a sense of solidarity with marginalized members of society. Pope John Paul II argued that solidarity is "not a feeling of vague compassion or shallow distress at the misfortunes of so many people, both near and far. On the contrary, it is a firm and persevering determination to commit oneself to the common good; that is to say to the good of all and of each individual, because we are all really

---

[11] Mary Jo Bane, "A Catholic Policy Analyst Looks at Poverty," in Mary Jo Bane and Lawrence M. Mead, *Lifting Up the Poor: A Dialogue on Poverty & Welfare Reform* (Washington, DC: Brookings Institution Press, 2003), 17.

[12] Ibid.

[13] Ibid., 49.

responsible for all."[14] Solidarity, he continues, thus calls us to see "the other" instead as "our neighbor . . . on a par with ourselves, in the banquet of life to which all are equally invited by God."[15] In community-based learning courses, students must consider issues of charity and justice. Often in doing community service, students are likely to see the people with whom they work as passive recipients of charitable good works. Catholic social teaching's emphasis on solidarity, interdependence, and a just social order calls students to rethink these assumptions—helping them to see community members as human beings of equal worth and dignity, people who best know the issues facing them and who are collaborators in providing solutions. This leads to questions of justice, beyond charitable provision of social services.[16] I have found combining these Catholic social teaching concepts with engaged learning courses often leads to students' more deeply seeing the grace, humanity, and compassion in the complex realities of the situations they encounter, leading to a fuller beholding of the world.

While Catholic social thought may be unfamiliar to many students, community-based learning has become increasingly common at colleges and universities. These types of courses engage students in experiential learning through work in the surrounding community in order to further the learning process. There has been considerable research that finds this type of engaged learning to be beneficial to students' intellectual and moral development.[17] Well-structured engaged learning courses that

[14] Pope John Paul II, *Sollicitudo Rei Socialis* (On Social Concern) (1987), 38, accessed October 10, 2013, http://www.vatican.va/holy_father/john_paul_ii/encyclicals/documents/hf_jp-ii_enc_30121987_sollicitudo-rei-socialis_en.html.

[15] Ibid., 39.

[16] Susan Crawford Sullivan and Margaret A. Post, "Combining Community-Based Learning and Catholic Social Teaching in Educating for Democratic Citizenship," *Journal of Catholic Higher Education* 30, no. 1 (September 2011): 113–31.

[17] For example, a longitudinal study of over 22,000 college undergraduates found that community-based learning courses positively affected students' academic performance, sense of self-efficacy, leadership activities and skills, self-rated leadership ability, interpersonal skills, choice of a career in service, and plans to continue participating in service after college. See Alexander Astin, et al., "How Service Learning Affects Students," *Higher Education Research Institute* (Los Angeles: University of California, 2000). Also, the Political Engagement Project of the Carnegie Foundation for the Advancement of Teaching, described in Anne Colby, et al., *Educating Citizens: Preparing America's Undergraduates for Lives of Moral and Civic Responsibility* (San Francisco: Jossey-Bass, 2003) counters a sometimes-heard critique that community-based learning courses are used to advance a liberal political ideology. This study finds that experiential education courses help develop students' citizenship skills but

clearly link academic theory with hands-on experiences can help students develop a deeper understanding of both the academic material of the course and relevant "real world" issues. Research indicates that instructors need to frequently connect the academic and experiential parts of such courses, through class discussion, analytical and reflective writing, and other means, for a strong learning experience.[18]

Putting Concepts into Practice

So how does this look translated practically into courses? Here are two examples of classes in which I have integrated Catholic social teaching and community-based learning in order to help students become better beholders of the world around them. One class is an advanced seminar on community organizing, leadership, and civic engagement entitled "Catholic Thought and Social Action." Taught in the sociology department, the interdisciplinary material draws on social psychology, social movement theories, the Catholic social tradition, case studies, and biography and autobiography. Students must spend approximately five hours per week as an "organizer," working with a leadership team in a campus-based or community-based organizing. They are tasked to achieve a measureable outcome by the semester's end.[19] Grading is based not on whether or not students achieve their outcome (learning by failure often proves very fruitful, in fact), but on their analytic writing and reflection connecting theory and practice.

Social science theories of social change and civic engagement are well-suited to pair with Catholic social teaching, given that Catholic social teaching deals with questions of justice in societal structures. In the seminar, students learn about the broad Catholic social tradition, encompassing official Catholic social teaching encyclicals, as well as action occurring through organizations such as Catholic Charities, Catholic

do not change their party affiliation or political ideology. See Sullivan and Post, "Combining Community-Based Learning and Catholic Social Teaching," 115–20, for further discussion.

[18] Lisa Boes, "Learning from Practice: A Constructive-Developmental Study of Undergraduate Service-learning Pedagogy" (PhD dissertation, Harvard Graduate School of Education, 2006). Also see Astin, et al., "How Service Learning Affects Students."

[19] See Sullivan and Post, "Combining Community-Based Learning and Catholic Social Teaching" for a fuller description of the course. The community organizing framework for the course comes from Marshall Ganz's work; see "Organizing," accessed October 10, 2013, http://isites.harvard.edu/icb/icb.do?keyword=k2139.

Relief Services, and Catholic hospitals, schools, and local parishes. Students read significant excerpts from a number of the key social encyclicals, from Pope Leo XIII's 1891 *Rerum Novarum* (On the Condition of Labor) to Pope Benedict XVI's 2009 *Caritas in Veritate* (Charity in Truth). The themes of these encyclicals, including justice for workers, war and peace, urbanization, poverty, inequality, and international development,[20] align well with the academic social science and historical literature in the course, and equally important, with the students' social justice interests and organizing projects. Letters from the US Conference of Catholic Bishops on issues such as economic justice and immigration help students understand how Catholic social thought plays out in an American setting.[21] Students also read from the Old Testament prophets on justice and read about lay Catholic leaders like Dorothy Day.[22]

Doing a community organizing project while reading Catholic thought on social justice brings up for most students the question of vocation. Students actively consider how civic, moral, and religious traditions (Catholic or other) may have shaped their motivation for doing this type of work and learn to articulate why they feel called to engage in social change leadership.[23] The notion of vocation is furthered by reading parts of biographies or autobiographies of people like Dorothy Day, Mother Teresa, Cesar Chavez, Martin Luther King, and Jane Addams—people who have lived out a vocation congruent with elements of Catholic social thought. I usually have students read selections focusing on the young adult lives of these people, seeing how these now-famous figures strove to determine their path and struggled to found movements of justice and charity.[24] The idea of vocation is furthered by guest speakers, such as local Catholic Worker members and others, who share their work and

[20] Thomas Massaro, SJ, *Living Justice: Catholic Social Teaching in Action* (Lanham, MD: Sheed & Ward/Rowman & Littlefield Publishers, 2000).

[21] Course readings from books such as Massaro's *Living Justice* and Kathleen Maas Weigert and Alexia Kelley's edited volume *Living the Catholic Social Tradition: Cases and Commentary* (Sheed & Ward, 2004) provide students with a good framing of the Catholic social tradition. Readings from Austen Ivereigh's *Faithful Citizens: A Practical Guide to Catholic Social Teaching and Community Organising* (Darton, Longman, & Todd, 2010) usefully link Catholic social teaching explicitly with community organizing.

[22] See Sullivan and Post, "Combining Community-Based Learning and Catholic Social Teaching" for an expanded discussion.

[23] Marshall Ganz, "What Is Public Narrative?" (unpublished paper, Harvard Kennedy School, 2007).

[24] See Sullivan and Post, "Combining Community-Based Learning and Catholic Social Teaching," 125–26.

their stories of how they came to live a life engaged with social justice ideals. These types of readings and speakers can also help deepen a sense of beholding. For example, the writings of Dorothy Day and Mother Teresa clearly reveal a sacramental imagination. Both of these women saw divine grace in the world around them and saw God in the poorest of the poor with whom they worked. Encountering these autobiographies, biographies, and role models of spiritually motivated social change, students may absorb their some of their sacramental view of the world. Students can also consider how they too might be instruments of grace in the world, in grappling with thinking through their own responsibilities to bring about greater love and social justice in their worlds.

Working with community organizations, students in the seminar have worked to mobilize support for legislative issues with regard to affordable housing, education, the environment, and school nutrition. Some students work to build campus-community partnerships and create new campus organizations, for example, on homelessness or youth mentoring. Mentored by experienced organizers, they have been involved in community efforts to help low-income youth get summer jobs and expand college access. Students have organized campus forums on issues ranging from genocide in Darfur to support for pregnant students on campus.[25] Working together with others toward a greater common good, learning to see poor and marginalized people with whom they may be working not as charity recipients but as brothers and sisters sharing a common dignity and humanity, people who are equals and partners in a struggle for a more just society—these actions often help students more deeply behold divine grace in the world around them.

It is likely that a considerable number of students at Catholic colleges would find more knowledge of the Catholic social tradition beneficial as they work in their communities and explore vocational options. Students find this seminar to be an intense, richly rewarding, experience. My favorite comment from the overwhelmingly highly positive student evaluations over the years simply states, "I have developed into a better person because of taking this course." To deepen a sacramental imagination by learning to see the poor as our brothers and sisters, to see grace in an imperfect world, and to learn skills to help bring about a more just society, is indeed to become a better person. What students are responding to here, I believe, is the sense of grace, hope, and possibility engen-

[25] Ibid., 126.

dered by concepts of Catholic social thought, on one hand—solidarity, interdependence, preferential option for the poor—and the skills needed for community-based collective action, on the other hand.

I find that whether or not students hold traditional religious beliefs or not, many feel a spiritual motivation to engage in this type of work.[26] Because many students find spirituality to be an important part of their motivation, readings from the Catholic social tradition on themes of hope, grace, solidarity, human dignity, and justice resonate strongly with them. Seeing their community-based learning project through the lens of Catholic social teaching leads students to see grace and dignity in the communities where they work. They feel a sense of solidarity with the people with whom they are working. Many connect the spiritual motivations for engaging in this type of work with a growing sense of responsibility, both as citizens and as people of faith, for helping their society to more deeply reflect divine love and justice. In all of these ways, their experiences in the course can deepen the sacramental imagination. It also becomes a way of "lived religion" in how their commitments and beliefs are lived in the world.

The course just described is an advanced seminar, typically attracting what I find to be unusually mature students interested in learning about Catholic social teaching and often arriving with long résumés of extensive campus and community-based volunteer experiences. However, the combination of Catholic social teaching and community-based learning also proves effective in helping a broader range of students to deepen their sacramental worldview. Another course in which I use this pedagogy is an intermediate-level course titled Women, Poverty, and Religion, which draws on my own research interests in the role of religion in the lives of mothers in poverty. Beginning with social science explanations of the causes and consequences of the "feminization of poverty" both in the United States and globally, this course considers the challenge of women's poverty to religion and the role that religion plays in the lives of poor women. The course addresses several key questions, such as how classical social science theorists have conceived of the relationship between religion and poverty, theological understandings of poverty and justice, how public policy and religious organizations address women's poverty, and the role of religion in the everyday lives of poor women.

[26] This was also true when I taught community-based learning courses on leadership and social change at a large secular research university.

These questions, of course, can be sociologically considered without involvement of either community-based learning or Catholic social teaching. The pure academic reading and writing demands of the course would make for a full load for students with no additional requirements for community engagement. However, it seems to me unfathomable to have students spending a semester reading sociological works about women in poverty without ever actually interacting with such women. So students must volunteer somewhere one or two hours a week where they will interact with low-income women or girls. For some students, this is new, as the background of students in this course varies widely with respect to volunteer background in the surrounding community. Some students have been previously involved, while others have not been involved at all. Students also have a range of motivation and desire to engage in community work, with some eager, some willing, and a small few resentful of this aspect of the class.

Catholic social teaching enters the class when we consider a variety of theological responses to the problems of poverty and deep inequality. In the course of presenting on a variety of religious traditions' teachings in this area, I note key themes of Catholic social teaching. The theme of solidarity, I believe, proves most important in this class in the development of a deeper sacramental imagination. While some students come from backgrounds of poverty, the majority of students at the college come from middle-class or privileged backgrounds and have had little interaction with the poor. Those who have experience, perhaps tutoring children or working in a soup kitchen, most often have seen themselves as providing charity to needy people who are "other." Many sociological studies, in studying and writing about the poor, have the unfortunate effect of intensifying this notion that the poor are indeed "other."

To underscore the importance of the notion of solidarity, the first class starts with a discussion of Julia Dinsmore's poem "My Name Is Not 'Those People,'" written out of her experiences as a mother in poverty. "My name is not 'Those People.' . . . My name is not 'Problem and Case to be Managed.' . . . My name is not 'Lazy, Dependent Welfare Mother.' . . . Before you give in to the urge to blame me, the blame that lets us go blind and unknowing into the isolation that disconnects your humanity from mine, take another look. Don't go away. For I am not the problem, but the solution. And my name is not 'Those People.'"[27] After

---

[27] Julia K. Dinsmore, *My Name Is Child of God . . . Not "Those People": A First-Person Look at Poverty* (Minneapolis: Augsburg Books, 2007), 20–21.

playing a short video clip showing Dinsmore reading the poem and talking a bit about her life and her struggles with poverty, we discuss the implications of the poem. The course soon turns to statistics, explanations of governmental policy toward poor women, and so on, but starting the class with a brief look at this woman in her humanity sets the tone for the whole semester. Although students may be learning statistical information and reading social science works about women in poverty, women in poverty are not "those people."

Students further encounter the humanity of those whom they are studying by encountering guest speakers who visit the class. One guest speaker is a former homeless mother and domestic violence survivor who now works at a homeless shelter and is involved in domestic violence prevention work. When she comes to class she shares not only her own story, but those of some of the women she encounters through her work. Another guest speaker is a dynamic Pentecostal pastor, local politician, and mother of six, whose work with at-risk youth in the city has earned her acclaim from many quarters. Her account of her faith motivation for the work which she does and her stories of the youth with whom she works often has a strong impact on the class members.

The community-based learning component further develops the theme of solidarity, along with the concept of preferential option for the poor. Students are engaged for the most part in ordinary volunteer activities, helping tutor disadvantaged teenagers or volunteering at the local homeless shelter. In keeping with Catholic social thought, it is emphasized that they are to "be with" and "do with" people; they should not see themselves as swooping down from the hills of our privileged campus to "rescue" "helpless and hopeless" people. One student, a middle-class sophomore with little prior community involvement, remarked in class how our academic sociology books, intentionally or not, seemed to write of poor girls and women in ways that divided people into "us and them." However, she continued, her community-based learning work (with low-income teenagers) more than anything made her feel like these were kids who at their core were no different than she—that in working with them, she found far more similarities than differences.

I believe that these types of community-based learning experiences, in connection with themes from Catholic social thought, can help some students deepen a sacramental imagination. In these encounters, students find that they share core humanity with people from very different backgrounds. They read in the Catholic social teaching documents that God loves all people deeply and equally, that all persons have dignity that demands protection, and that a measure of a just society is how it treats its poor and vulnerable. They read that grace is incarnate in the world and come to see divine grace at work in the homeless shelters and housing projects where they volunteer and in their hopes and actions for a better and more just world.

Catholic Social Teaching, Community-Based Learning, and the Sacramental Imagination

A sacramental imagination is cultivated in community. An incarnational, sacramental spirituality finds divine grace in the day-to-day encounters, relationships, and experiences of daily life. Fr. Peter-Hans Kolvenbach, former superior general of the Jesuit order, stated, "For the Society there is no such thing as an either-or approach to God and the world, however dangerous the latter may look. The encounter with God always takes place in the world."[28] The Ignatian vision sees the world as a gift that invokes gratefulness and wonder, seeking to find the divine in all cultures and communities.[29]

One way to become a beholder is to look fully and deeply at the world around you, aware of "finding God in all things." Community-based learning brings students outside of campus walls to interact with the broader world. Catholic social teaching helps them to see the world through a lens of grace and justice and a sense of solidarity. The combination of these pedagogies can lead students to embrace the world with "a fundamental trust, a wonder at the giftedness of life itself, a radical, universal and finally incomprehensible grace, a pervasive sense of a God of love who is never an 'inference' but an always-present reality to each and to all."[30] The world is imperfect, to be sure. Imperfect, however, does not mean forsaken. Teaching students to really look at their world, to fully experience relationships and situations they encounter in community-based work, and guiding students as some journey toward

---

[28] "The Jesuit University in Light of the Ignatian Charism," Address of Fr. Peter-Hans Kolvenbach, Superior General of the Society of Jesus, To the International Meeting of Jesuit Higher Education, Rome, May 27, 2001, accessed October 10, 2013, www.sjweb.info/documents/phk/university_en.doc.

[29] Traub, "Do You Speak Ignatian?," 395.

[30] David Tracy, *The Analogical Imagination: Christian Theology and the Culture of Pluralism* (New York: Crossroad, 1981), 311.

vocations as leaders of social change—all of these help develop a sense of truly beholding. Students can find grace in an imperfect world, see where the world needs to become better, and experience a "lived religion" which calls them to consider their own role in bringing about a more just society.

Solidarity through "Poverty and Politics"

William Purcell and Rev. William Lies, CSC

Throughout the last century the Catholic Church has articulated its mission in society through an ever more comprehensive social teaching. With encyclicals, statements, and pastoral letters, the pastoral leaders of the Catholic Church have continually advocated for those who are poor and have affirmed their confidence in social structures, networks, and organizations to assist in addressing the root causes of poverty and the deep need for solidarity among and for all. This is alluded to in a passage from Pope John Paul II's On Social Concern (*Sollicitudo Rei Socialis*):

> Solidarity is not a feeling of vague compassion or shallow distress at the misfortunes of so many people, both near and far. On the contrary, it is a firm and persevering determination to commit oneself to the common good; that is to say to the good of all and of each individual, because we are all really responsible for all. (SRS, 38)

In recent years, a growing political polarization, especially within the American political scene, has called many of these social structures of economics, education, and government into question and is among the reasons we have seen an erosion of the solidarity that the church is attempting to foster. Today's intensely divided political environment is the one in which present college students in the United States have come of age. Thus, a particular challenge for Catholic colleges and universities is to help students assess, especially in light of Catholic social teaching, the benefits and liabilities of these social structures that attempt to address the root causes of poverty. The Center for Social Concerns at the University of Notre Dame offers programs and facilitates courses throughout the curriculum that move students to awareness and action by deepening their understanding of the substance of Catholic social thought. This chapter's aim is to describe the efforts and outcomes of one such course, which focuses in a particular way on the principle of solidarity and demonstrates the tangible impact a greater understanding of the church's social mission can have on student attitudes, choices, and futures. In doing so, it will argue that our Catholic colleges and universities have an important opportunity, through their curricula, to foster values that will deepen students' sense of church as well as their sense of responsibility as citizens.

Introduction:
Catholic Social Teaching and Catholic Higher Education

The social justice teaching of the Catholic Church is rooted in Scripture, which calls the people of God to lives of justice and mercy, compassion and hope, solidarity and peace. The US Bishops have spoken articulately about this. In their report, *Sharing Catholic Social Teaching: Challenges and Directions*, the bishops state that two of the most vital gifts of our community of faith are (1) our remarkable commitment to Catholic education and catechesis in all its forms and (2) our rich tradition of Catholic social teaching.[1] They argue that there is an urgent need to bring these two gifts together.

Catholic social teaching is a distinct body of church doctrine with its own primary sources and literature. While its roots are in Scripture, its branches continue to grow today. Indeed, much of the tradition has been developed through the last century when the church has encountered new social situations, and as it has read anew the signs of the times in each new culture and age. This social justice tradition, say the bishops, is a central and essential element of our faith. It is built on a commitment to the poor and emerges from the truth of what God has revealed to us about himself. As the bishops clearly state,

---

[1] *Sharing Catholic Social Teaching: Challenges and Direction*, Reflections of the US Catholic Bishops, The Summary Report of the Task Force on Catholic Social Teaching and Catholic Education (1998), 1.

We believe in the triune God whose very nature is communal and social. God the Father sends his only Son Jesus Christ and shares the Holy Spirit as his gift of love. God reveals himself to us as one who is not alone, but rather as one who is relational, one who is Trinity. Therefore, we who are made in God's image share this communal, social nature. We are called to reach out and to build relationships of love and justice.[2]

Sharing Catholic Social Teaching was borne of a bishops' Task Force on Catholic Social Teaching and Catholic Education. The task force brought leaders of Catholic education and social ministry together to assess and strengthen current efforts and to develop new directions for the future.

In its overall assessment, the task force found much goodwill and many innovative efforts by Catholic educators to communicate the social doctrine of the church. At the same time, however, they were clear that in some educational programs Catholic social teaching is not really shared or is not sufficiently integral and explicit. As a result, they conclude that far too many Catholics are not familiar with the basic content of Catholic social teaching. More fundamentally, many Catholics do not adequately understand that the social teaching of the church is an essential part of Catholic faith. This poses a serious challenge for all Catholics, since it weakens our capacity to be both a church that is true to the demands of the Gospel as well as a sacramental sign to the world. They argue that we need to do more to share the social mission and message of our church.[3]

The report is explicit about some of the specific challenges in this regard, especially within Catholic higher education, where there is a perceived lack of emphasis on Catholic social tradition. Since the report's release in 1998, however, Catholic colleges and universities across the land have taken creative strides forward in their efforts to confront this challenge. These efforts include, among others, mission trips through campus ministry, community service, academic community-based learning, and courses and seminars across the curriculum, all built upon a Catholic social teaching framework. Based on almost thirty years of experience, the Center for Social Concerns possesses a track record of developing effective domestic and international community-based learn-

[2] Ibid., 1.
[3] Ibid., 3.

ing educational opportunities based in the Catholic social tradition. One such course is discussed here. Poverty and Politics is an interdisciplinary seminar for undergraduate sophomores with a community-based learning component. The course attempts to cultivate in its students a deeper sense of solidarity with others. We turn now to a consideration of the course, beginning with its prevailing ethos and pedagogy.

Confronting the Challenge through Innovative Pedagogy

"Poverty and Politics" is a college seminar course in the College of Arts and Letters at the University of Notre Dame. The college seminar, designed for all sophomores in Arts and Letters, is defined by the college handbook as "a unique one-semester interdisciplinary course in which students and faculty explore a significant question on such topics as faith, reason, and identity, while developing students' speaking skills." The central focus in this particular college seminar, which is team taught by the authors of this chapter, is United States domestic poverty and the politics around it. It essentially asks the question, "Why are people poor and why should we care?" This question is considered then through various disciplinary lenses, including the humanities, the social sciences, and the arts. Sixty-five percent of the student's grade is based on oral communication and presentation. The goal for the student is to research, write, and present on a creative solution to poverty in a particular area: education, immigration, children in poverty, health care, etc. But even more fundamentally, the goal is to expose students to the realities of their world through a lens of Catholic social teaching, inculcating in them a deep sense of solidarity.

Throughout the semester, as they examine how poverty can be addressed systematically, they are challenged to address what has come to be known as social sin. Sin is the opposite of grace and justice. It cannot be understood without the acknowledgement that at its heart lies the accumulation of individual sin, yet social sin itself is a crucial concept. John Paul II speaks of it in *Reconciliatio et Paenitentia* (Reconciliation and Penance).[4] "To speak of social sin," John Paul says, "means in the first

---

[4] *Reconciliatio et Paenitentia* (On Reconciliation and Penance), Apostolic Exhortation, December 2, 1984, accessed October 10, 2013, http://www.vatican.va/holy_father /john_paul_ii/apost_exhortations/documents/hf_jp-ii_exh_02121984_reconciliatio -et-paenitentia_en.html.

place to recognize that, by virtue of human solidarity which is as mysterious and intangible as it is real and concrete, each individual's sin in some way affects others." He goes on:

> In other words, there is no sin, not even the most intimate and secret one, the most strictly individual one, that exclusively concerns the person committing it. With greater or lesser violence, with greater or lesser harm, every sin has repercussions on the entire ecclesial body and the whole human family. According to this first meaning of the term, every sin can undoubtedly be considered as social sin. (*Reconciliatio et Paenitentia*, #16)

This form of sin exists within any structure in society that oppresses human beings, violates human dignity, restricts freedom and increases inequity. Social sin affects the community so as to penetrate its laws, customs and policies. Unfortunately, change becomes extremely difficult in overcoming its presence. Catholic social thought encourages the development of solidarity in addressing and responding to social sin. The responsibility lies in the relationship of individuals and groups to one another, through family, through church, through society and its structures, and through the human family as a whole. Poverty and Politics focuses on the principle of solidarity, in particular, in addressing social sin and in the healing of relationship. Solidarity is the goal.

The beauty of the principle of solidarity is that it helps sum up all the elements of Catholic social teaching. Solidarity is an expression of how God's love gets carried out in caring for poor and vulnerable people. "Solidarity is a Christian virtue. It seeks to go beyond itself to total gratuity, forgiveness, and reconciliation. It leads to a new vision of unity of humankind, a reflection of God's triune intimate life" (*Sollicitudo Rei Socialis*, #40). Ultimately, the students come to be transformed from their head to their heart through the realization that, all together, we make up the Body of Christ. Human dignity is recognized because of this interrelationship. There exists one human family. Solidarity calls the students to work toward the elimination of poverty, to speak against injustices, and to shape a more just and peaceful world. "There can be no progress towards the complete development of the human person without the simultaneous development of all humanity in the spirit of solidarity" (*Populorum Progessio*, #17).

Faith-Based Community-Based Learning

As a Catholic university, a primary goal is to inspire students to live moral lives based in Christ Jesus, and to strive to build a more just and humane world. The work of the Center for Social Concerns at Notre Dame enacts this through a pedagogy of community-based learning and community-based research so that the students are transformed enough that they live their particular vocation in faith. Jesus provides the best model of solidarity. Christ entered into ultimate solidarity by becoming human and sacrificing himself for our salvation. He used everyday experiences with people to teach about living in relationship with God, other people, and all of God's creation. Stories and symbols become the archetypes to explain and understand how people are called to relate to one another, and students are often surprised by the grace that is borne of understanding and, ultimately, of solidarity.

The Poverty and Politics seminar employs a community-based learning approach that relies on experience as a key learning tool. As a pedagogy, community-based learning attempts to develop students' understanding of their academic disciplines and commitment to civic responsibility, even as it enhances colleges' and universities' engagement with their local communities. Throughout higher education, community-based learning takes various forms, including one-week immersion seminars, long-term summer placements, and semester-long courses. For Catholic colleges and universities, community-based learning also has the potential to teach values congruent with Catholic mission and identity, and specifically to demonstrate the relevance of Catholic social teaching to contemporary social issues.[5]

Faculty, in partnership with representatives of community organizations, design service-learning projects based on two main objectives: advancing the students' understanding of specific course content and related civic learning objectives, and responding to community-identified needs and assets.[6] Strong reflective and analytical components are built

[5] See Mary Beckman and Angela Miller McGraw, "Understanding Catholic Social Teaching through Community-Based Learning: Perspectives from Notre Dame," *Catholic Education: A Journal of Inquiry and Practice* (forthcoming), for a more comprehensive treatment of this issue.

[6] Several comprehensive guides to service-learning have already been published, and "how-to" information with sample syllabi from various disciplines is readily available via websites. See Janet Eyler, Dwight E. Giles Jr., and Angela Schmiede, *A Practitioner's Guide to Reflection in Service Learning: Student Voices and Reflections* (Nashville: Vanderbilt University, 1996). *See also* National Service Learning Clearinghouse's

into the course to help students analyze relationships among their service, the course's curriculum, and its impact on their values, vocations, and professional goals.[7]

Community-based learning also includes social analysis and the practical applications of social justice. Social justice seeks long-term solutions. Those doing justice develop relationships among stakeholder groups, including those "in need of service." Doing justice entails a learning environment that continually uncovers structural or root causes of inequities or injustices. For example, those engaged in doing justice ask why people are hungry now and then seek to change the social and institutional structures that contribute to hunger, through advocacy regarding public policies, community organizing, and other forms of civic engagement.[8]

In this Poverty and Politics course, students engage weekly with people in poverty at a local nonprofit in the South Bend community to put a face on the issues they are examining. Journal writing assists students' reflection on this local site interaction. Case studies connected to community organizing are also presented in order to build awareness of community in action. The design of the course is based on the pastoral circle of immersion, social analysis, theological reflection and a plan of action, something about which the students only become aware through the course of the semester. As Catholics we ask the question, "Why should we care?" from a rich faith tradition which demands that we see God in all things. Catholic social tradition is the intellectual, moral, spiritual, and pastoral framework which addresses the social structures and individual behaviors that contribute to poverty. Students' prejudices and assumptions are challenged through concrete experiences with impoverished and marginalized communities.

---

website at http://www.servicelearning.org/; Campus Compact's website, accessed October 10, 2013, http://www.compact.org/; and Community Campus Partnerships for Health's website at http://depts.washington.edu/ccph/. Research on community-based learning over the last three decades has revealed that it facilitates the development of leadership skills, self-esteem, teamwork, communication skills, and acceptance of cultural diversity (Brandell & Hinck, 1997; Shumer & Belbas, 1996; Wade, 1997). See Beckman and Miller McGraw for more.

[7] This definition is slightly modified from the definition offered by the Midwest Consortium for Service Learning in Higher Education. See http://www.midwest consortium.org/mission.html, accessed July 9, 2011.

[8] Jennifer Reed-Bouley, "Service and Justice: Understanding the Relationship through Community Service-Learning," *Listening: Journal of Religion and Culture; Teaching and Doing Justice in Higher Education* 37, no. 1 (Winter 2002): 53–63.

The Structure of the Course

Teaching social analysis to students begins broadly and then narrows through the semester in this seminar on poverty and politics. The first time the class meets, the students are asked to write a brief essay on the definition of poverty. During the second class, students are given a general quiz on basic poverty statistics for the United States, which often reveals some of the common misconceptions people have about domestic poverty. By this second class, the students are also assigned to one of four local South Bend community agency sites where they will volunteer two hours a week throughout the semester. Experiences at these sites, students attest, help them to put a face and a name to poverty, as well as to make connections between what is happening in our classroom with real-world issues in our local community and beyond. Students keep a journal entry on their local service work experience. The guideline for the journal asks them to identify an event each week, analyze the incident, and then provide an insight on poverty they may have acquired. These journals become an excellent means of incarnating a preferential option for the poor as they document and reflect upon the experiences of individuals who struggle for human dignity.

Early in the semester, students study the history of institutions which deal with poverty in the United States from the colonial period to the present age. This context allows students to examine trends in Americans' sympathies in dealing with poverty. They come to understand England's role of church and government translated over to the colonies and influenced its development. The *Statute of Charitable Uses* by Elizabeth I allowed bishops to enforce civil law and to hold charities accountable to the public.[9] Leaders like Benjamin Franklin formed voluntary associations in early America to take care of the needy and community needs. Around the same time, James Madison argued for a strong, more centralized federal government to help foster a common understanding of the needs of the whole community and to manage the factions in the diversity of the nation. The social movements of antebellum reform, the progressive period, the New Deal reform, and the Great Society reveal how structures can play a key role in addressing the needs of poor and oppressed people. The devolution of government assistance with the Reagan Revolution and Clinton's Bridge to the New Millennium with

---

[9] *Statute of Charitable Uses*, accessed October 10, 2013, http://www.hks.harvard.edu/fs/phall/01.%20Charitable%20uses.pdf.

welfare reform are also discussed. Providing YouTube links to different presidential speeches addressing poverty has proven a compelling way of providing a historical context to this digital generation.

Throughout the semester, classes generally consist of two parts. The first part focuses on a particular aspect of poverty and the second on discussion of that focus and the related assigned readings. Based on these readings, students prepare a one-page reflection or analysis with questions and observations that have emerged from the readings. These one-page assignments, required for every class, assist the students in engaging the relevant topic and greatly enhance the depth of class discussion. Classic literary works are assigned to draw students into the nuanced realities of poverty, even as they help students develop a foundational framework for understanding poverty and solidarity. *The Jungle*, by Upton Sinclair, has provoked strong responses from students since the novel is so descriptive and useful in developing empathy, especially for its main character, Jurgis Rudkus.[10] There are many works, however, that can offer similar perspectives, both among classic and contemporary fiction. Steinbeck's *The Grapes of Wrath* offers a fruitful example of such a classic; and, if one were to look at poverty outside the US context, *Great Expectations*, by Charles Dickens, or the more contemporary *City of Joy*, by Dominique Lapierre, would also serve well.[11] Throughout the course and its readings, students are prompted to make connections to poverty today. One activity that students have found compelling is the simple exercise of figuring out one's monthly budget in an urban area.[12]

Reading the signs of the times, students frame the problem of poverty in the United States in the contemporary context. With US Census information on poverty, students begin to understand the vastness and complexity of the issue. In order to provide balance, on the website for the class there exist resources with differing ideological analyses of social problems ranging from the Heritage Foundation to the Brookings Institute. An important overview on the welfare reform of the 1990s helps students to see a paradigm shift in government's approach to poverty.

---

[10] Upton Sinclair, *The Jungle* (New York: Doubleday, Page and Company, 1906).

[11] John Steinbeck, *The Grapes of Wrath* (New York: Penguin Books, 1992); Charles Dickens, *Great Expectations* (London: Macmillan and Company, Limited, 1904); Dominique Lapierre, *City of Joy* (New York: Grand Central Publishing, 1988).

[12] Depending on the socioeconomic status of the students, this could be more or less effective. This exercise and other useful pedagogical resources can be found in *Just Neighbors*, accessed October 10, 2013, http://www.justneighbors.net/.

Social sciences are incorporated in the course to allow critical evaluation of poverty in urban and rural settings, as well as in race and gender areas. An economist speaks to the class on deindustrialization, while readings in sociology are used to deal with poverty and race. Using an ethnographic study like William Julius Wilson's *There Goes the Neighborhood* allows the students to see a contemporary comparison of poverty in the same neighborhoods in Chicago where the events of *The Jungle* took place.[13] Often the students speak of their surprise at the blatant racism that still exists in some sectors. They are also asked to examine contrasting secular political philosophies through works such as *Why Social Justice Matters*, by Brian Barry, and *Ill Fares the Land*, by Tony Judt.[14]

The role of faith in poverty and politics is initiated through the incorporation of Catholic social tradition documents. Over the five years this course has been offered, we have focused on encyclicals like *Sollicitudo Rei Socialis* (On Social Concern) by John Paul II or *Caritas in Veritate* (Charity in Truth) by Benedict XVI, since they are social doctrine which specifically address the role of government in addressing economic justice.[15] Each year we have also had the students present aloud, "This Land Is Home to Me," the rich, poetic pastoral letter of the Appalachian bishops.[16] The letter addresses rural poverty issues, especially exploitation, and continues to hold strong relevance for our time.

The fine arts are a focus of several classes as the course presses beyond the intellectual content to the emotional and deeply human understanding of solidarity. For instance, in one class students select and share a piece of music that expresses for them an understanding of poverty. In doing so, they must articulate their rationale for the piece as well as their experience of it. In another, students visit the university art museum for a photography exhibit on scenes of poverty from throughout the

[13] William Julius Wilson and Richard Taub, *There Goes the Neighborhood: Racial, Ethnic and Class Tensions in Four Chicago Neighborhoods and Their Meaning for America* (New York: Vintage Books, 2006).

[14] Brian Barry, *Why Social Justice Matters* (Malden, MA: Polity Press, 2005); Tony Judt, *Ill Fares the Land* (New York: Penguin Press, 2010).

[15] John Paul II, *Sollicitudo Rei Socialis* (On Social Concerns) December 30, 1987, accessed October 10, 2013, http://www.vatican.va/holy_father/john_paul_ii /encyclicals/documents/hf_jp-ii_enc_30121987_sollicitudo-rei-socialis_en.html. Benedict XVI, *Caritas in Veritate* (Charity in Truth), Encyclical, June 29, 2009, accessed October 10, 2013, http://www.vatican.va/holy_father/benedict_xvi/encyclicals /documents/hf_ben-xvi enc_20090629_caritas-in-veritate_en.html.

[16] "This Land Is Home to Me," Bishops of Appalachia, 1975; see www.ccappal.org /CCAbook040307.pdf. Accessed October 10, 2013.

twentieth century in the United States. These compelling photos hearken back to previous topics and readings of the course—Chicago newsboys from the same time period as *The Jungle* or suffering families in the Appalachian region. Students also take advantage of several campus films that have poverty themes. Some of those viewed in the past have included, *God Grew Tired of Us*, about refugees coming from Sudan; *Trouble the Water*, following the life of a family during and after Hurricane Katrina in New Orleans; and the classic, *A Raisin in the Sun*.[17]

The final portion of the course attempts to move students from under-standing the complexities of poverty to envisioning solutions. The frame-work for action that is provided is borne of the Catholic Church's social tradition. Students analyze case studies of social projects rooted in Catholic social tradition and present on the process through which these community organizing groups throughout the nation have overcome poverty.[18] After a long semester of sobering literature and readings, along with the intense experience of difficult realities, this turn toward practical action comes as an important moment of hope and transformation. As a final project, then, students complete a research project that focuses on a particular area of poverty. They are encouraged to consider solutions for their area of focus and then present their study as a final presentation to the class. The areas of poverty from which they choose include: chil-dren in poverty, race, worker issues, immigration, women in poverty, the government's role, and energy and the environment. This presenta-tion requires students to do thorough research, provide thoughtful analy-sis, integrate Catholic social tradition into their work, sharpen their oral skills, and use their creativity in an area they have become passionate about over the semester. Most students integrate their local community-based learning experience into their presentation as well. On the final day of class, the first-class-day essays on the definition of poverty are returned to the students and discussed. The insight and depth of that conversation is remarkable as students grapple with their earlier, often naïve understandings of poverty and now wrestle with the beginnings

---

[17] *God Grew Tired of Us*, written and directed by Christopher Dillon Quinn, codi-rected by Tom Walker (Newmarket Films, 2006); *Trouble the Water*, produced and directed by Tia Lessin and Carl Deal (Zeitgeist Films, 2008); *A Raisin in the Sun*, a play by Lorraine Hansberry, 1959. For the 1961 film, see *A Raisin in the Sun*, directed by Daniel Petrie (Colombia Pictures, 1961); for the 2008 television film, see *A Raisin in the Sun*, directed by Kenny Leon (Sony Pictures Entertainment, 2008).

[18] *Living the Catholic Social Tradition: Cases and Commentary*, ed. Alexia Kelly and Kathleen Maas Weigert (Lanham, MD: Rowman and Littlefield, 2005).

of comprehension of the enormously complex issue and their responsibility before it.

Student Reactions

The major fruit of this course for students has been the obvious expansion of their knowledge of the politics of poverty and its complexity, and
the increased capacity to discuss and think critically about poverty and
its solutions. The more important outcome, however, may be the deepened sense of solidarity it engenders among and within its students as
they come to see their place within these complex issues.

Seeking a student perspective on the outcomes of the course, we asked
two students—Jim Ogorzalek and Beth Simpson—to reflect on the course
and its impact.[19] As their reflections have no need of commentary, they
follow here in succession.

> What continues to strike me as the most significant knowledge I
> gained from "Poverty and Politics" is a recognition of the interrelated
> nature of distinct aspects of poverty. In other words, the subtle move-
> ment between seemingly unrelated topics through case studies,
> volunteer work, and social science analysis led me to finally recog-
> nize a web of interconnectedness that permeates throughout all
> aspects of life in poverty in the United States.
>
> My volunteer experience at a free health clinic in downtown
> South Bend brought me into contact with the community of South
> Bend more fully than almost any of my peers who did not experi-
> ence "Poverty in Politics." My experience, therefore, remains a vital
> piece of my intellectual and emotional growth while at Notre Dame.
> Its significance lies in the simple fact that working with those in
> poverty—serving them and learning their stories—took the emphasis
> off of me. Certainly, I reflected upon these experiences as they related
> to me, but the main character in my journal entries was seldom
> myself. Perhaps it was in working in a field in which I had no previous
> knowledge that I was able to (ironically) most fully immerse myself
> in this experiment with social justice. Being unaccustomed to the

[19] These two students were not chosen randomly. They were chosen because of
how articulate they have been about the impact of the course. That said, they do
represent students of different political perspectives, and their reflections (if perhaps
more articulate) are somewhat typical of most of the students who have experienced
the course.

work of the clinic and the life of the patients encouraged me to make a full effort to speak with employees and patients alike to learn as much as possible about the plight of those in poverty and the abysmal access to quality healthcare tolerated by so many in this nation.

Further, this course insists upon a recognition that the work cannot be completed during the course—the work of social justice for me began with this course that served as a gateway to a way of life. Of course, I return to the texts we used in this course from time to time when debating issues with friends. But the most lasting impact of "Poverty and Politics" is this very insistence that it is not "completed" in one semester. Most likely, I will never physically return to that free health clinic in downtown South Bend. But I return to it often in my daily reflections on what I want to accomplish with my life. While working with the poor and with those serving them, I became conscious of my role in that interrelated web. In my eyes, that is solidarity. Because of "Poverty and Politics," I have personal experience of the plight of the poor and a general fluency in the policy issues that allow systemic poverty to occur. In this way, I have become part of the story—the ongoing struggle—of poverty. The burden of those in poverty became mine. The burden of those working to eradicate poverty became mine. Transformed in this way, I carry this burden with all of my peers who have met poverty, studied it, and have been charged to work to end it.

—Jim Ogorzalek (Notre Dame, Class of 2011)

By becoming attentive to the harrowing reality of social sin, I learned to distinguish and articulate the structures in our society and political system that perpetuate sin. My own responsibilities as a Catholic and Christian became ever more clear, as did the importance of effective and just policy. "Poverty and Politics" was integral to my discernment of vocation. I think that a clear understanding of the political, social reality and a foundation of Catholic values are inherent to discerning one's vocation. While opening my eyes to the reality of poverty in the United States, the seminar helped me to identify also effective models and policies of change. With great concern for the persistent poverty in this county, I root my hope in Christ. As such, I have discerned more clearly my vocation and responsibility to work actively to reform policies that perpetuate poverty and inequality.

Having grown up in a political family, political talk was as common fare at the dinner table as my grandmother's steamed broccoli, which is to say that it graced every family gathering. My grandfather served as United States Senator for Wyoming for eighteen years and as the Republican Whip for ten years, following his father who served as US Senator and Wyoming State Governor. With a hereditary affinity for political life and deep admiration for my family's public service, I contemplated whether I too might enter public service. Upon entering college, however, I recognized my longing to explore more deeply and grow in faith. I struggled to discern how politics might coalesce with my deepening life of prayer. During sophomore year, through the Center for Social Concerns Poverty and Politics College Seminar taught by Fr. Bill Lies and Professor Bill Purcell, I was exposed for the first time to a fruitful integration of faith and politics alongside a critical examination of poverty in the United States. I recognized the imperative for living the Christian faith within the political sphere. Whereas, I had previously considered faith and politics as two disparate qualities, I now experienced these passions converge—and I discerned a fundamental theme of Catholic social teaching, being rights and responsibilities.

It is the responsibility of the Catholic university to put intellectual learning at service to the human community. Through "Poverty and Politics" we learned not only how we might serve with our hearts by living in solidarity with the poor, but we also learned how to serve with our minds. We discerned how we might engage intellectually and spiritually with issues of poverty and inequality. As such we challenged persisting structures of political and social inequality and distinguished new models of change. If liturgy is the sharing of God's work on Earth, the classroom served as the thinking place where we conceived of how to integrate our minds and hearts in the service of God in the human community. While as Catholics we should identify how we are transformed by living in Christ through the sacraments, "Poverty and Politics" revealed to us our imperative to share this transformation with the human community. By direct political and social action in service to justice and the dignity of the human person, we share in the liturgy. As it integrated faith, reason, and service, "Poverty and Politics" helped us to realize the Christian life and sacramentality.

—Beth Simpson (Notre Dame, Class of 2011)

Conclusion: Solidarity

A more comprehensive understanding of justice and solidarity comes through the course of the semester as students engage ever more deeply the complexities of economic poverty and as they enter relationships with people oppressed by it. All of the world's religions call people of faith to work for justice. The holy writings of the major faiths call each person to serve poor people: feed the hungry, clothe the naked, shelter the homeless, and free the oppressed. Many New Testament verses about the poor build upon the Old Testament tradition of caring for the widow, orphan, alien, and stranger. The students are enticed to reflect upon who are the widows, orphans, aliens, and strangers in our midst today.

The development of courses like Poverty and Politics is vital to living out the mission of Catholic education. According to the 1971 World Synod of Bishops statement, *Justicia in Mundo* (Justice in the World), education needs to be seen as a liberating force.[20] "Education demands a renewal of heart, a renewal based on the recognition of sin in its individual and social manifestations. It will also inculcate a true and human way of life in justice, love and simplicity" (*Justice in the World*, #51). The University of Notre Dame, too, acknowledges this role for education when, in its mission statement, it affirms:

> The University seeks to cultivate in its students not only an appreciation for the great achievements of human beings but also a disciplined sensibility to the poverty, injustice, and oppression that burden the lives of so many. The aim is to create a sense of human solidarity and concern for the common good that will bear fruit as learning becomes service to justice.[21]

By affording our students the opportunity to be witnesses to the suffering and joys of the local community, even as we attune them to the cry of the poor through the arts and literature and the social sciences, the aim is that they will apply these new insights to their academic and research interests and, ultimately, to their vocational and professional pursuits. By the time students walk out of the Poverty and Politics course, the practical ways of living a just life have become more apparent to them. Many students have acknowledged that their trajectory of studies has been impacted by this deeper understanding of solidarity. Through the awareness of Catholic social tradition and justice education, these

---

[20] *Justicia in Mundo* (Justice in the World), Synod of Bishops, 1971; for an outline summary see: http://www.educationforjustice.org/system/files/justiciainmundo.pdf.

[21] *Mission Statement of the University of Notre Dame*, see http://nd.edu/aboutnd/mission-statement/.

students not only understand how to work for others through direct service and advocacy but also through empowerment and solidarity.

Ultimately, Christian solidarity deepens our belief in Christ Jesus, motivates us to share his Good News, and makes us responsible to transform the world. Christian solidarity, therefore, is possible only inasmuch as it cultivates communities who are willing to be both contemplative and action oriented. Over the course of a semester, students' definition of solidarity and of justice changed precisely because together they engaged in interdisciplinary learning, prayerfully integrated the wisdom of Catholic social teaching, and built authentic relationships with their classmates and community. They became faithful to one another and to their brothers and sisters in Christ, growing as prophetic witnesses and agents of solidarity.

Exorcizing Taboos:
Teaching End-of-Life Communication

Michael P. Pagano

"Death has always been a subject that I avoid talking about because the thought alone scares me."

(Kelly, 2010, Self-reflection paper 1)[1]

With an organizational mission of educating the whole person—mind, body, and spirit—I struggle to help my students recognize the importance of end-of-life communication for their intellectual, physical, and spiritual well-being. Classroom discussions about death and dying clearly made the overwhelming majority of my students uncomfortable and inevitably eroded to silence, or to frequent comments that reaffirmed their communication fears. "As I am sure it is for a majority of people, death is a terrifying fact of life and it is natural to try and avoid thinking about it at all costs" (Christopher, 2010, Self-reflection paper 1). As their teacher, I have my own discomfort when it comes to applying a religious lens to a critical analysis of end-of-life communication. While I grew up in a Catholic family, I am not a religious person. However, I believe it is imperative to recognize the spirituality (religious and humanistic) that frequently accompanies end-of-life conversations. Therefore, students are encouraged to discuss their views, observations, and analyses from either a religious or humanist perspective in our analyses of death and dying communication.

Teaching a variety of communication courses at a Jesuit university has afforded me an opportunity to help develop men and women for others. Throughout this exploratory journey, I have used a variety of teaching

[1] All students' names are fictional.

methods including: service-learning, interdisciplinary offerings, as well as applied approaches. However, with the topic of dying these methods consistently proved less than successful. Students constantly resisted any efforts at self-reflection or analysis regarding end-of-life communication behaviors.

After much consternation and contemplation, I decided to try a multi-method approach to overcoming students' reticence and fears (as well as my own views on religion's role) and provide them with an opportunity to apply the communication theories they were studying to an interdisciplinary, service-learning experience with dying patients and their families. This essay will detail the course that was developed, the students' and my own responses to it, and what we all learned through the experience.

After more than two decades of teaching health communication courses to undergraduate and graduate students, I decided to create a course called End-of-Life Communication that was cross-listed for undergraduate and graduate students in the spring of 2010. I didn't want this, however, to be just another lecture, or even seminar course, where students passively learn and/or discuss theories about death and dying topics. I wanted the young adult and older students to spend some time around people who were dying—to talk with them, but most importantly, to listen to them. Having worked as a health-care provider for over three decades, I knew these folks had many life lessons to share with the students—if I could only help my class overcome their fears of the unknown (finite and infinite). The overwhelming majority of students in my classes had experience with wakes or funerals, but not communicating with dying people or their loved ones. One student, Jenna (2010), stated in her first self-reflection paper, "when I was younger, I was fortunate that I never had anyone close to me die, and never knew many people that died. Of course people died, but it was not until I was in middle school that my parents thought I was ready to go to my first wake." Almost all of my students identified some experience of parental protection against death and dying. Therefore, in order to accomplish the experiential learning intended for this course I needed to find a place for students to meet dying people in a context that would be supportive, safe, and life affirming. Conversely, I was concerned that having students go to a hospital to interact with individuals who were dying would eliminate too many of the potential psychosocial aspects of the interaction and make it more about the biological or life-extending perspectives of modern health care.

Transformative Experiential Learning

Helping students grow and evolve is one of the real joys of higher education. However, only infrequently in my twenty-plus years of teaching undergraduates and graduate students at colleges, universities, and professional schools have I seen students transformed by their newfound knowledge and abilities to apply their learnings to everyday life. In this course, even the most skeptical students found the experience "life changing" and used those terms to describe it. As Marie (2011) wrote in her third and final self-report paper, "now that I have experienced ten hours at the Connecticut Hospice, I can say that my outlook on life and death is completely different. I can truly say that I have a greater appreciation for every day of my life." A contrarian might question if twenty-year-olds who make such emotional statements are being introspective. However, the breadth and depth of all the class members' responses leads me to conclude that these feelings were not conjured up for a paper or a grade (they knew their responses were not being graded, just their abilities to communicate them), but the fact that these students reaffirmed their statements in multiple class discussions, papers, and in their final anonymous class evaluations makes it much more likely that they are reporting what they feel.

Matt (2010) documented his feelings about the course and its impact on his future when he wrote in his final self-reflection paper,

> This past Saturday (May 1, 2010), I was in Westbrook, Connecticut for my dad's wedding. I was the best man. Of course, whenever you are my age and attend an event where you are surrounded by family and friends you have to be ready to answer an onslaught of questions. This particular night the question du jour was, "so Matt, do you know what you are going to do after you graduate?" Many people were in shock when I told them I was seriously considering a path in palliative care, particularly a career working in pediatric palliative care. The responses varied, but many people assured me how "noble" the work I would be doing was. I had to explain to them what it was really like, and that in fact it is not noble because as I have all semester, I always walk out of the hospice doors feeling like I have taken a lot away from my experience. How could a situation where I feel like I am gaining so much value also be considered a "noble" thing to do?

As I begin preparations for my fourth year of teaching this course I am aware of the enormous satisfaction I receive from the students' responses in class, in their papers, and in their course evaluations. But perhaps even more rewarding are the comments I get from the staff at the hospice who see the students evolve, become more independent, and interact with dying strangers in ways that help both the students and the patients grow and benefit from the experience. The students describe, both from a religious and a humanist perspective, their observations of interpersonal family-patient, friend-patient, staff-patient, and volunteer-patient perspectives. The students relate in their narratives how the patients share stories about their families, loves, and life experiences. However, what begins for most of the students as a detached participant-observer experience nearly always evolves into an interpersonal relationship between the student volunteer and a particular patient or family member. And most importantly, from my perspective, is that they use this relationship with someone who is dying to embrace a new understanding of the life cycle and their place in it. They more closely examine what the future offers for them and their loved ones. Many of them describe those feelings as a little less scary. One of the students, Lynn (2010), in her final self-reflection paper noted,

> Volunteering at the hospice has reminded me that it's the little things in life that count. Simply sending a smile or engaging in a small conversation can light up someone's day. It may sound like a bit of an oxymoron, but the more time I spend at the hospice, I realize that death does not encompass its rooms, but rather all the life from the patients and the overwhelming amount of love that comes with them. Photographs, drawings, books, blankets, and other mementos surrounding the patients' beds serve as a reminder that these people are loved and have lived long lives. Yesterday I sat and spoke with a man for about forty-five minutes about his life and family. While he was trying to remember the name of a town, he said to me "don't grow old kid, you start forgetting things." I smiled and said to him, "one day I hope to be as lucky as you, with so many memories and a big family to love and remember me." He smiled and told me that I had a point there. I used to be afraid of growing old, but I'm gradually letting that go.

This quote illustrates the humanist aspect of experiential learning in this course. However, before the students could grasp the realities of death and dying as a natural component of the life cycle, they needed to understand how traditional health-care providers typically view patients with an illness, injury, or terminal condition.

Biomedical Versus Bio-Psychosocial Models

To help students understand the role of hospice in patients' end-of-life experiences and communication, it is critical to be sure they recognize the distinction in modern health care between the biomedical and the bio-psychosocial approaches to patient care. Medical practitioners have traditionally focused on identifying the biological and medical causes for patients' health problems, and then prescribing the appropriate treatments. This approach views patients as biological entities with illnesses or injuries that can be cured or fixed. Clearly if a patient has pain in the right upper quadrant of the abdomen, the biomedical model allows a health-care provider to determine the cause of the pain and what the most appropriate treatment option is. For a patient with such pain, removing the gallbladder if it is inflamed will likely solve the biological cause. However, not all health-care problems are related to biological etiologies. Therefore a narrow, objective, scientific approach to wellness and illness leaves little room for an appreciation of the spiritual, psychological, or sociological aspects of human health.

One of the first lessons students must learn is the distinction between curing a health problem and patients' quality of life. In some cases, as in the example above, if a problem/illness/injury can be identified and treated successfully—removing a diseased gall bladder—then curing and quality of life may be synonymous. However, when a person has a terminal illness, there is no cure. Health-care providers working from a biomedical model have nothing to offer these patients. In such circumstances, providers generally do one of two things: they either continue to treat the patient even though treatment cannot cure the condition, or they tell the patient that there is nothing else to be done and stop seeing him or her. Obviously, for a patient with a terminal illness, being treated unnecessarily may decrease his or her quality of life. But being dismissed as "hopeless" can be equally painful. Students need to recognize that the spiritual aspects of being human have little impact on providers who practice health care from a biomedical model. This dichotomy between cure and quality of life from a health-care provider's perspective is eye-opening to students who have frequently never considered the role quality of life can play in dying patients' lives. Luckily, most hospice providers, as well as others, utilize a bio-psychosocial approach to health care and seek to address a patient's spiritual, mental, and relational health issues as well as his or her biological ones.

As students begin to explore the differences between the biomedical and bio-psychosocial approaches to health-care delivery, they quickly recognize the dialectical tensions between the two as they apply to terminally ill individuals. Classroom discussions explore how patients, and especially family members, often seek to stay alive "at all costs," instead of enjoying what time a person has left to live. With today's technology, pharmaceuticals, and medical services, dying patients can be treated up until they die. Sometimes these treatments can prolong life, but at great costs in terms of hospitalization, loss of autonomy, pain, emotional suffering, and loss of financial resources. However, all too often health-care providers either do not inform patients and their families that these treatments are only prolonging the inevitable, not preventing it, or they justify continued therapy with the hope of a "miracle cure." Students can then examine what quality of life means to them, and what it might mean to a dying person. They can begin to analyze their own perceptions of the spiritual, psychological, and sociological aspects of life that might be more important than medical treatments with little or no chance of extending their lives and the great likelihood that they would make life more difficult, painful, or uncomfortable. Not surprisingly, students generally communicate their desires to stay alive at all costs. At that point in their self-reflections and analysis they are asked to do a textual analysis of the film version of the play *Wit* (2001).

Wit is a fictional, first-person account of a middle-aged, female professor's interactions with health-care providers as they do everything possible to treat her terminal illness but fail to address her quality of life. The complete disregard of the physicians and other providers for the patient's feelings, concerns, and spiritual needs are clearly portrayed. The recognition, even though it is a fictional representation, of the possible realities of the biomedical approach is not lost on the students. While they are never forced to discuss their own deaths, the class is generally much more vocal as the course progresses about their views on the dialectical tensions between treatment at all costs and quality of life. This discussion provides the ideal opportunity to explore how patients respond from a psychological and sociological perspective to a terminal prognosis.

Accepting Death

To help students understand the psychological aspects of a terminal diagnosis, this course used Kübler-Ross's *On Death and Dying* (1969). This text served as a vehicle for discussions about how patients and their families go through a variety of stages in their acceptance of their condition and how those stages may impact their communication behaviors, treatment decisions, and/or quality of life. These theories proved extremely thought provoking for young adults who generally saw life as eternal. The discussions about people having a terminal illness suggested that students only perceived this as a problem for their grandparents or other older adults. In order to help them recognize the random nature of the life cycle and end-of-life realities, the students viewed Dr. Randy Pausch's (2007) "Last Lecture" at Carnegie Mellon University.

The juxtaposition of the Kübler-Ross (1969) text and the Pausch lecture allowed the students to see how a forty-year-old theory could be illustrated in a contemporary context. But even more importantly than the realization that Dr. Kübler-Ross's theories could be applied to "everyman" was the students' awareness that a healthy appearing forty-year-old person not only accepted his own death but was able to communicate about it and about the value of using the time he had left to continue doing the things he wanted to do, including educating others about dying. In addition, Dr. Pausch specifically mentions that he is not in denial and explains that he and his wife have used end-of-life communication to make plans for the family's life after his death (moving closer to family in a different state, etc.). This lecture and the Kübler-Ross book were stimuli for students' discussions of end-of-life decisions and communication—not just for some hypothetical grandparent or elderly individual, but for their parents or even their friends. The students were fascinated with Dr. Pausch's humanist approach to sharing his dying experiences, anecdotes, and perceptions in the same way that he teaches his courses. Once the students could internalize the realities of death and dying, they could then reflect on how people who were dying might want to communicate with family and others during their remaining days, weeks, etc., and might want to spend more time reflecting on their lives, their relationship with their God, and being with their loved ones. This realization led to the class's introduction to hospice care in America.

Hospice and Health Care

As the students' realizations and understanding of death and dying in the life cycle evolve, the earlier discussions of biomedical versus biopsychosocial approaches help them recognize the importance of a more humanistic, compassionate, patient-centric alternative to medicine's traditional "fix it" mentality. At this point in the course they do research into alternatives to hospitals, long-term care facilities, and efforts to cure every illness.

This exploration helps students discover the distinct differences in hospice versus nonhospice health-care delivery. Discussions about their research help the class examine the mission and goals of the diverse health-care organizations. Students are then better able to easily recognize the spiritual and psychosocial distinctions between being treated as an entity with a disease versus being helped to have the best quality of life possible. The students are able to recognize the unique role of hospice in serving the patient's wishes and needs, as compared to the patient being controlled and following "orders" from health-care providers. These realities lead to further discussions of who can utilize hospice services and when.

The students' research promotes further understanding of the financial and legal issues related to hospice utilization. They begin to understand that health-care services are not, as most of them have enjoyed, available for everyone at any time. The students quickly realize that not just anyone can utilize hospice services. For some students, the reality that health care is rationed based on age, income, and/or disease state creates interesting conversations about the moral and ethical issues surrounding the care of others in our society. These conversations provide an opportunity to further discuss their responsibilities as men and women for others in a variety of social and health-care-related contexts. The potential value of a humanistic and/or religious approach for patients who are dying and should not have to be concerned with mounting bills, Medicare approvals, and quality of life issues is clearly verbalized by the students.

The question of treatment versus hospice care creates another powerful teaching opportunity with students. I ask them what they would recommend for their parents or grandparents if they knew they had six months to live. This question, which for many of them is the first time they have really considered their parents' finiteness, leads to much self-reflection and to discussions of dialectical theory and the tensions between wanting loved ones to live at any cost versus wanting the best quality of life for them in their remaining time. The potential benefits of knowing that a person is dying are discussed from both a patient and family perspective. For most of the students in this course, the notion that a person can be relatively certain she or he is going to die in a specific time frame, both philosophically and medically, is a completely new reality. While the class can refer back to Dr. Pausch's (2007) lecture as an example, the context of his talk—a lecture hall, his physical appearance—healthy and energetic, and his upbeat tone all seemed surreal and in some ways similar to the "virtual" worlds they are familiar with. The realization, however, that Dr. Pausch is moving his family closer to relatives to aid in his care at the end of his life (in a few months) and for support after his death, forces students to accept the reality of his situation.

Just prior to the midterm in the course, the students are introduced to a new text, Mitch Albom's (1997) *Tuesdays with Morrie: An Old Man, a Young Man, and Life's Greatest Lesson*. A critical reading of this book is intended to prepare the students for their upcoming orientation and volunteer efforts at the hospice. Using this text in the course continues to build on our exploration of death and dying communication. The Albom book plunges students into an interpersonal relationship that began years earlier as professor and student and reemerges as a friendship. This text provides an opportunity for the students to apply the social science theories they are learning to an analysis of Albom's narrative of Morrie's decisions and discussions about dying at home with family and friends. Morrie uses his professorial role to help Mitch understand that death and dying are the final stage in the life cycle and therefore something to be shared with family and friends, not hidden away or avoided at all costs (medical, emotional, and spiritual). Students respond to the weekly discussions of the text by verbalizing their own anticipation for the next Tuesday with Morrie.

As Morrie's health visibly fails, the students are eager to see if Mitch will learn what his former professor is trying to teach him. The students clearly see Morrie trying to help Mitch become more self-reflective, to verbalize and acknowledge his fears and feelings and to ultimately accept Morrie's death as the professor has. This acceptance of death is important to the students because Kübler-Ross (1969) postulates that until a person accepts his/her own death, s/he cannot truly relate to someone who is dying. At this point the class starts to recognize that the interactions between Mitch and Morrie are really mutually beneficial. The students discuss how Morrie gets to spend his final months, weeks, and days, sharing himself with others. His friends and family get to spend more time with him in an environment that is conducive to communication— as compared to a hospital or nursing home. Therefore, the issue of the context for dying takes on more relevance in their appreciation for the psychological and sociological possibilities for dying individuals and their loved ones.

Hospice Orientation

It is at this point in the course, just before spring break, that we travel together to an hour-long orientation at the hospice. I believe it is important that we do this together, both the commuting and the orientation, because the students have some time to talk about their anxieties and learn that everyone has anxieties about the new experience. Once we arrive at the hospice, they are very vocal about their evolving perceptions of the facility. It is a modern-looking, four-story structure with a glass wall on one side that provides unobstructed views of Long Island Sound from every patient's room.

The director of the hospice and the director of volunteers from the Music and Arts Department spend an hour or more explaining the history of the institution—the first in the United States. They involve the students in discussions about why the building was designed the way it was, the use of volunteers, and the goal of making patients' quality of life the organization's primary mission and goal.

The students ask questions about availability of doctors, pain medication, and if the patients can leave and go back to a hospital if they wish. The staff assures them that the patients are in complete control of their tenure. They have physicians and nurses caring for the residents, and patients are encouraged to request pain medication whenever they need it. However, the students are frequently reminded that the hospice is there to serve the patient, so if a patient wants to go home, or to a hospital for traditional medical care, she or he is always free to do so.

On the trip back from the orientation students are very open about their prior concerns and how seeing the facility and learning more about it have helped them feel better about their upcoming twenty hours of volunteer work. This new realization, however, is frequently accompanied by a statement of concern about what it would be like to be around dying people. In her second self-reflection paper, Gina (2010) described the dialectical tension she felt post-orientation and prior to her first volunteer experience.

> I was a bit nervous because the first time we visited as a whole class we never actually saw any patients or had any interaction with them. I pictured in my head that every patient would be in the same condition as my grandmother: immobile, not entirely coherent, and hooked up to various machines. Thankfully at this hospice there were maybe one or two patients that I saw in that condition while the other forty were mobile, talkative, and very "with-it."

This reality, that in spite of the discussions of theories, hospice myths and realities, of Morrie and Randy, etc., is the entire reason why this course needs to include a service-learning experience. While students can assimilate the various texts' explanations of death and dying, end-of-life communication, and hospice care, for most students it was still extremely abstract and illusive until they started to meet and interact with dying patients and their families. In her second self-reflection paper, Madison (2010) wrote,

> Everyone at the hospice works as a complex team. The building is constantly humming with a positive energy as nurses complete their rotations, social workers help bridge the communication gap between admitted patients and their families, families spend time with their loved ones, and the volunteers interact with the patients who are alone for the day. As I learned my way around, I was constantly greeted with smiles. I felt as if my presence was truly appreciated, something that I haven't felt in a long time. Volunteering at the Hospice has reminded me that it's the little things in life that count. Simply sending a smile or engaging in a small conversation can light up someone's day.

This sense of both giving and receiving something uplifting was reiterated time and again in the students' discussions, self-reflection papers, and final research projects. The interaction with dying patients, their families, and the hospice staff helped the class recognize the realities, medically and spiritually (from a humanist or religious perspective), of life and death in a hospice facility, as compared to reading about it in a book.

Volunteering/Participant Observation

In the final weeks of the course, students were expected to volunteer in randomly assigned groups of two for three- to four-hour shifts at the hospice. It was my feeling that working as a team would be less stressful on the students than going to the facility and volunteering individually. The hospice required that the students work with a staff member for their first four hours at the facility to assure they understood the policies, logistics, documentation requirements, etc. Students were required to enter into the patient's medical record their visits, observations, etc.

These cooperative visits helped ease the students into their roles at the hospice but also assisted them in seeing the value of using the arts to enhance dying patients' lives.

One student, Julie (2010), described her initial positive experiences with a member of the arts staff in her second self-reflection paper.

> There was one specific experience that was memorable on the first day. The [staff member], my classmates, and I went into the room of Catherine, who was ninety-nine years old. She has nine children, four of whom were present in addition to grandchildren and other relatives. They agreed to have the [staff person] sing a song with her guitar. [We] sang songs like "Danny Boy" and "We've Got the Whole Word in Our Hands " Catherine opened her eyes and smiled numerous times. The family was thrilled that Catherine was enjoying the music, so they all participated and even waved colorful scarves around. This intervention made me realize how significant the arts could be in end of life and why hospices offer them. This experience was not only touching for Catherine and the family, but for us as volunteers as well. After leaving that hospice visit, I felt a warm and rewarding bubble of happiness inside of me. Knowing that I brightened someone's day and contributed to the positive energy in the room made me feel important. Witnessing this touching moment at hospice between the patient and family put me in a mood of high spirits, as ironic as that sounds. I noticed that Catherine had rosary beads tied to the side of her bed. I interpreted the presence of these as her sign of hope. It was evident that her family members also had hope as they sang along and did everything they could to make her happy and comfortable.

This student's discussion touches on the humanistic roles they observed and participated in with the patient and her family. This opportunity, to see how staff and volunteers can help change a dying person's experience to something that is rewarding, not just for the patient and family but also for everyone involved, is one of the amazing benefits of this course for students. At the same time, the students' contributions provide benefits for the patients, family members, and staff. Beyond the student's recognition of how this experience can help a dying person and his/her family cope with the situation, however, is the student's appreciation of the value of helping others. Julie's reflection and ability to verbalize her own feelings about such an interpersonal experience are quite unique in my experiences in undergraduate education. Her statement "I felt a warm and rewarding bubble of happiness inside of me. Knowing that I brightened someone's day and contributed to the positive energy in the room made me feel important" elevates this class beyond theory and assimilation of information to the experience of being men and women for others. Faculty and administrators can theorize about, and encourage, our students to be more caring and more giving of themselves, but until students actually participate and witness the benefits of their behaviors, the personal rewards are likely to be under-valued or unimagined.

Finally, the student's quote above provides an interesting glimpse into her own thinking. She discusses her role in communicating with a dying ninety-nine-year-old woman and her family, and in spite of the student's clear awareness of the woman's impending death, she is no longer afraid to be in the room or unsure about how to behave in such a context. In fact, the student is communicating as she might in a variety of contexts, sharing herself, her talents, and her humanism with others. Clearly a transformation from the person who ten weeks earlier did not know how to think about communicating around a dying person. And instead of the student's denial of death and fears of it, she writes "I noticed that Catherine had rosary beads tied to the side of her bed. I interpreted the presence of these as her sign of hope. It was evident that her family members also had hope as they sang along and did everything they could to make her happy and comfortable." This is a student who now verbalizes the benefits for the patient and the family of the interpersonal communication and of their religion, and how both provide everyone involved a sense of hope and community.

We can all question whether a dying woman who only opens her eyes to communicate made the decision to put a rosary on her bed. But the student clearly perceives this sign of hope as emanating from the patient, and we can also see how the student's sense of religion and humanism lead to her own sense of hope. Whether that hope is for a longer life, or for life after death, or for a good life for the patient's family—is unclear. What is clear however, is that the student uses her volunteer experience to analyze a communication setting and recognize the role end-of-life communication plays in not only the patient's life but also in the family's, hospice staff's, and volunteers' lives. This realization of the importance of end-of-life communication not just for the dying but for family, friends, and others was a true discovery for every member of the class and re-peated again and again in countless student discussions, self-reflection papers, and final research projects.

Other Implications

It should be noted that this course is very different from almost any other communication course in our curriculum. In fact, I've been told that no other communication department has a course totally devoted to end-of-life communication. I think the reason why this course is both different and difficult for other programs to offer is that the topic is truly taboo in our culture. While we've managed to overcome other taboos in our course offerings, however, this particular topic requires the professor and the students to accept the finite nature of each other's existence. Students enroll with little or no experience talking about dying and then spend four months sharing their fears, thoughts, observations, and personal experiences with death and dying issues. This approach is vastly different from most other communication courses.

One of the interesting theories emerging from teaching this course is that the benefits of this type of experiential learning might be applicable to other settings (as well as other disciplines). As we strive to teach our students to be men and women for others, I wonder if a psychology, sociology, communication, or nursing service-learning course that included volunteering at homeless or domestic abuse shelters would not provide a similar opportunity for students to apply their classroom theories to social injustices. Caitlin (2010) in her first paper summed up the possibilities for similar types of service-learning courses, "I think that this course, by offering the experience of firsthand interactions with people who are dying, will have an even bigger impact on me because I will not only be observing but also actively participating and immersing myself completely in the volunteering." Based on this course and my students' responses, my goal is to find more ways to immerse my students in learning, and in doing so help them share themselves with their communities so they can truly be totally educated—mind, body, spirit, and practice—being men and women for others.

Bibliography

Albom, Mitch. *Tuesdays with Morrie: An Old Man, a Young Man, and Life's Greatest Lesson*. New York: Doubleday, 1997.

Kübler-Ross, Elizabeth. *On Death and Dying*. New York: Scribner, 1969.

Nichols, Mike. *Wit*. HBO Films, 2001.

Ragan, Sandra, Elaine Wittenberg-Lyles, Joy Goldsmith, and Sandra Sanchez-Reilly. *Communication as Comfort: Multiple Voices in Palliative Care*. New York: Routledge, 2008.

Randy Pausch Last Lecture: Achieving Your Childhood Dreams. http://www.youtube.com/watch?v=ji5_MqicxSo, 2007.

Who Decides?
Encountering Karma and
Catastrophe in the Catholic Liberal Arts[1]

Michael Bathgate

"Who decides?" Although neither I nor my students realized it at the time, the first real question of my teaching career was also arguably the best. I had been hired out of graduate school to teach a semester-long survey of the Buddhist tradition at a Catholic university. My students' first reading assignment was to be a passage describing the Buddhist worldview, the unending cycle of rebirth and suffering in which Buddhism holds us all to be bound, and from which the Buddha offered us escape. In strikingly specific terms, the text described the consequences of our actions in this life for the next, including:

> By passionate attachment to sensual pleasures, people are reborn as geese, pigeons, donkeys, and other passionate animals; those who have erred through stupidity are reborn as worms.
> Anger and malice cause rebirth as snakes; the prideful become lions; haughtiness causes rebirth as an ass or a dog.

---

[1] I would like to thank my fellow participants in Collegium 2009, who did not shy away from discussing the problem of evil raised by the sacramental imagination, as well as my colleague Jason Aleksander, whose repeated invitations to visit his class on *The Divine Comedy* not only reflects the best tradition of interdisciplinary teaching but also provides a welcome forum for discussing the kind of comparative theodicy elaborated here. Most importantly, these reflections would not have been possible without the questions and insights of my students.

People who are hostile and selfish become, after death, tigers, cats, jackals, bears, vultures, wolves, or other meat eaters.

People who steal others' property and give out nothing whatsoever will never themselves become wealthy, strive as they may.

One who, in this world, makes donations of alms food will be reborn ever-happy: endowed with long life, good complexion, strength, good fortune, and good health.

By virtue of a gift of a lamp, a person will come to have good eyes; by the gift of a musical instrument, a good voice; by the gift of beds and seats, ease and comfort.

All karmic rewards resemble the acts of which they are the natural outcome: suffering from sin, happiness from good deeds, and a mixture of the two from a mixed deed.[2]

I assumed that virtually all of my students were already familiar with the notion of karma, and was expecting to use the text as a point of departure, to confirm some of what they already knew, and to explore the implications of this doctrine for the teachings of and about the Buddha. But my student's deceptively simple question asked for something (indeed, perhaps a number of things) quite different from what I had planned. At issue was not only how this tradition envisions the world but also how that knowledge might inform our own view of the world.

"Who decides?" On one level, the question could be taken to address the *agent* of karmic justice. That is, where is the judge who decides the individual cases? Contrary to Christian or Islamic images of the Day of Judgment, karmic justice—at least as it is presented in this account—is essentially mechanistic: you can no more appeal to karma about extenuating circumstances than you can beg gravity for forgiveness when you are falling down the stairs. At the same time, however, Buddhist texts routinely supplement the mechanistic imagery of karma with a more judicial imagination, where the dead are brought on trial before the King of the Underworld, and where character witnesses—and, in some accounts, even bribes—are admissible. Exploring the tensions between these two visions raise some interesting questions about the way the Buddhist tradition imagines the unstable boundaries between justice and goodness. The moral physics of karma, after all, presents an image of the world as perfectly just, in which every action produces an equal and opposite reaction, but it is a justice without appeals, and ultimately one without mercy.

[2] John S. Strong, *The Experience of Buddhism: Sources and Interpretations* (Belmont, CA: Wadsworth, 1995), 29–31.

"Who decides?" On another level, the question touches on the nature of religious knowledge, and the authority on which it is grounded. Like the *contrapasso* suffered by the damned in Dante's *Inferno*, the imagery of karma depends upon a kind of retaliatory fitness between cause and effect. Yet who decided that a particular consequence "resembles" a specific action, rather than some other? Some of the post-mortem fates described in Buddhist sources seem perfectly consistent with my students' intuitive grasp of poetic justice, while others seem out of place, even bizarre. Ignorant worms and prideful lions usually pass without comment, but what about passionate geese or haughty dogs? Investigating these incongruities not only illuminates some of the historical and cultural assumptions behind these accounts but also brings to light the fundamental tensions between the (presumably universal) nature of cosmic justice and the (culture-bound) efforts of human beings to understand it.

"Who decides?" I would like to report that—having only just passed my qualifying exams—I recognized all of the complex ramifications of my student's question in a sudden flash of insight, and deftly rethought my approach, not only to the class, but to the course as a whole. To be honest, however, I can barely recall what I said before returning to my all-too-carefully prepared class notes, except that it was both superficial and utterly unsatisfactory. In retrospect, I am disappointed by my response, less because I failed to exhaust all the implications of my student's question (the class, after all, was only fifteen weeks) than because I allowed the most crucial element of the question to pass unexamined: not who decides the unfolding of karma in the world of the text or the world of its authors. Rather, who decides right here, in the college classroom? Who decides what aspects of that vision are questionable in the first place?

"Who decides?" To some extent, of course, my task as an instructor is to point out questions that my students hadn't thought to ask: this, more than the answers to those questions, is what it means to introduce students to an academic discipline. Nevertheless, if those new questions are to represent anything more to my students than the quaint customs of yet another academic tribe in their whistle-stop tour of the disciplines, they must be grounded in students' own experience, or, perhaps better yet, in the troubling contradictions between their experience and the materials at hand. It is, after all, precisely where readings like these *fail* to meet our (often unexamined) preconceptions—that justice, for example, requires the presence of a judge—that we are most likely to take note. Indeed, whether we are considering the attitudes and practices of our religious ancestors or the worldviews and values of our neighbors, it is often through the juxtaposition of differences that we are best able to perceive what we so often take for granted about our own commitments. I have come to think that it is this exploration of our own religious orientations, often more deeply held and unexamined than the doctrines to which we publicly assent, that provides the central role for the academic study of religion (especially religions other than students' own) within the Catholic tradition of the liberal arts.

"Who decides?" Given my failure to take advantage of this moment the first time it arose, I count myself fortunate that, over the course of fifteen years teaching at the same Catholic institution that first saw fit to hire me, my students have never once failed to ask this question. In that time, I have gradually modified both my readings and my assignments in order to tease out some of the implications of this question, to better explore, not simply the foundations of the Buddhist tradition, but my students' own fundamental orientations to the nature of justice, the goodness (or perhaps even the existence) of God and his creation, and the problem of evil that it necessarily begs when we struggle to reconcile those orientations with our experience.

Comparative Theodicy in the College Classroom

This is, of course, hardly uncharted territory. Since at least 1922, karma theory has been understood as one of many responses to what Max Weber described as "the problem of theodicy."[3] Coined by Leibniz in 1710, the term theodicy (literally, "divine justice") initially referred to a form of apologetic theology, concerned with defending God's omniscience, omnipotence, and omni-benevolence in the face of our day-to-day experience of injustice, suffering, and waste. The question, as David Hume posed it, represents a fundamental challenge to commonplace images of the divine: "Is he willing to prevent evil, but not able? Then he is impotent. Is he able, but not willing? Then he is malevolent. Is he both able and willing? Whence then is evil?"[4]

For Weber, this tradition of theological argument (and that of its cultured despisers, from Voltaire to Christopher Hitchens) is best understood as part of a more general category of religious expression, the effort

---

[3] Max Weber, *The Sociology of Religion* (Boston: Beacon Press, 1963), 139.
[4] David Hume, *Dialogues Concerning Natural Religion* (New York: Penguin Books, 1990), 108–9.

to reconcile an image of a perfect God (or a perfectly functioning cosmos) with "the imperfection of the world."[5] That effort will necessarily differ from one tradition to another: the Christian question of whether or why a good God permits the suffering of innocents, for example, would seem to have little in common with the Zande notion that misfortune is inevitably the result of witchcraft, or the idea, found among adherents of Sūkyō Mahikari, that illness may be the result of one's failure to perform devotional rituals correctly.[6] Yet they may be productively compared, as efforts to preserve what Peter Berger has described as the "plausibility structure" of a tradition.[7] At stake is nothing more or less than our ability to continue living in our worldview as we go about living in our world.

Placing the history of Buddhist reflections on karma into this comparative perspective permits my students and me to view it as bound up not only with the fundamental principles of Buddhist ethics and soteriology but also with the equally fundamental problem of human meaning in a world were suffering appears inescapable. This sense of theodicy as a common problem expressed and resolved in manifold ways—not only between traditions but within them—represents an invitation to explore the problem of evil, less as a question with a definite answer (whatever the vocabulary, whether in the jargon of systematic theology or the pat slogans of popular dogma), than as a perennial dilemma, a struggle at the intersection of expectation and experience. In this regard, my comparative interest in the Buddhist theodicean imagination is driven less by a sense of its logical consistency, moral utility, or emotional appeal than by its heuristic value: precisely because karma represents an approach to the problem of evil that is different from theistic formulations so much so that it strains the etymological limits of the term "theodicy" itself it serves to draw our attention to what we so often fail to examine in our own traditions.[8]

The profundity of the problem and the fragility of the answers make the differences between the Buddhist tradition and my students' own

---

[5] Weber, *The Sociology of Religion*, 139.

[6] E. E. Evans-Pritchard, *Witchcraft, Oracles, and Magic among the Azande* (Oxford, UK: Clarendon Press, 1976); Winston Davis, *Dojo: Magic and Exorcism in Modern Japan* (Stanford, CA: Stanford University Press, 1980), 227.

[7] Peter L. Berger, *The Sacred Canopy: Elements of a Sociological Theory of Religion* (New York: Doubleday, 1967), 58.

[8] In this, my approach is quite different from that of scholars like Whitley R. P. Kaufman ("Karma, Rebirth, and the Problem of Evil," *Philosophy East and West* 55, no. 1 [January 2005]: 15–32), yet in the course of my discussions with students, we arrive at many of the points he raises.

worldviews pedagogically useful in another respect, as well: it provides a degree of analytical distance, in which they can begin to consider these fraught questions vicariously, through the lens of a tradition very different from their own. Indeed, many of my students admit to having enrolled in my classes precisely because the religious traditions that I teach represent something new, even exotic, a departure from the worldviews, values, and practices with which they are familiar (and, not infrequently, bored). While I am happy to benefit from this perspective, I take it to be one of my central tasks to illustrate to them the ways in which the exploration of these new religious territories ultimately require them to reevaluate the very religious landscapes they are often so eager to ignore. In the time I have served at my institution, the student body has become considerably more diverse (and has come to include a sizeable minority of Muslims along with virtually every Christian denomination). Nevertheless, the Buddhist tradition has thus far remained firmly in the realm of the religious Other.

The most basic venue for this encounter between the Buddhist theodicean imagination and students' own presuppositions is assigned readings from a variety of primary sources. Those readings are always accompanied by a brief writing assignment—usually on the order of once a week—where they respond to a few specific, but typically open-ended questions (asking them, for example, to identify what they take to be the most and least fitting examples of karmic cause and effect), as well as asking them to identify what they find to be particularly confusing or troubling. The point of this exercise is not simply to direct their attention to what I expect will be the most productive areas for later discussion in class, but to require them to begin practicing what is in fact some fairly challenging hermeneutics: to bring the text—with all its internal tensions—into conversation with their own points of view without allowing the one to eclipse the other. It is a task that most of my students find difficult to understand at first, let alone to perform. In the first weeks of each semester, one of the more assiduous (or simply grade-conscious) students will inevitably suggest that I might have the timing of the assignment confused: if they were asked to write their reflections *after* we discussed the texts in class rather than beforehand, they would be more likely to "get it right." They often find my response that the point of this exercise isn't so much to demonstrate their understanding as to explore their confusions less than satisfactory. Indeed, many students will struggle with this notion in virtually every assignment of the semester. I tell them that they may well receive a poor grade if they tell me that they "don't get" a reading assignment, but only if they stop there. Often, some of the best responses begin with that complaint but then go on to explain in detail what they "don't get" and why. Is it because the text seems to contradict some idea that we've discussed earlier in the term? Or is it because it seems to contradict some element of what the student takes to be common sense? Identifying and exploring those contradictions, I suggest, are precisely where understanding begins. These assignments often provide the raw material for me to reformulate both my questions and the readings I assign, less to eliminate student confusion than to focus it and make it a suitable topic for class discussion.[9]

The Story of the Monk and the Crow

One of the recurring questions related to the problem of who decides has to do with the matter of intent: my students have frequently asserted that an act isn't bad karma if it isn't intentional. We can, and do, discuss the traditional division of karmic "seeds" (i.e., the deeds that give rise to karmic consequences, or "fruits") into actions of body, speech, and mind in Buddhist doctrine, but the implications of this doctrinal distinction are perhaps most strikingly illustrated in narrative. A story from one ninth-century Japanese text, for example, describes a monk who unknowingly kills a crow when he idly throws a rock into the bushes where the bird is hiding. This crow, we are told, is later reborn as a wild boar, who in turn dislodges some rocks while rooting for food on the mountainside, creating an avalanche that—just as unintentionally—crushes the monk.[10] Most of my students are quick to object to such an account, often couching their challenge in the best tradition of vernacular ethics, as "unfair." It usually requires a bit of careful analysis on all of our parts to unpack what makes it so unsatisfactory.

To begin with, this account appears to emphatically reject what for many of my students appears to be a basic—if unquestioned—element

---

[9] For obvious reasons, I am not inclined to grade these assignments for their polish but for the degree of interpretive effort they evidence. A perfectly formatted (and accurate) synopsis is ultimately less useful to my purposes than a more inchoate collection of questions, especially if they provide the underlying reasons for those questions.

[10] *Miraculous Stories from the Japanese Buddhist Tradition: The* Nihon ryōiki *of the Monk Kyōkai,* trans. Kyoko Motomochi Nakamura (Surrey: Curzon Press, 1997), 222.

of their moral sense: that unintended consequences are not properly within the domain of ethics. In the end, however, most are willing to withdraw this knee-jerk reaction, if only grudgingly. Our own justice system, after all, distinguishes between involuntary and premeditated homicide, and we can easily imagine that, had the monk carefully and maliciously planned to stone the crow, he would have been guilty, not only of a bad bodily action but of a negative mental action, as well, an additional karmic seed that would have given rise to further unpleasant fruit. Taking up the judicial metaphor, some of my students have also suggested that, precisely because the monk didn't take appropriate precautions when he threw the stone, he could be found guilty of a kind of depraved indifference. Sometimes, the very fact that a consequence is unintended may suggest a prior moral failure on our part, a reckless— and even willful—ignorance of the larger world in which we act.

As our discussion progresses, however, we also begin to see that this account begs a number of still larger and more troubling questions. Insofar as the crow's death at the hands of the monk caused the monk's death at the snout of the boar, for example, what caused the monk to kill the crow in the first place? That is, if the boar was acting as a kind of agent of karmic justice, bringing retaliation for the monk's act of involuntary avicide, what sins had the crow committed to put him in the path of the monk's stone? And should we expect the boar, in turn, to be killed again by the monk, now reborn in some new form (say, as an intestinal parasite)? If, as this story suggests, even accidents are bound up in the cycle of karmic cause and effect, to what extent can we really speak of moral guilt or innocence? And where, in this apparently closed moral ecology, is there room for free will? For some of my students, the questions raised by this account quickly pile up, outstripping the ability of the story itself to support any answers.

Yet this line of inquiry provides an invaluable insight into why the Buddha taught not simply the importance of scrupulous moral behavior for ensuring a good rebirth but also the need to escape from the cycle of rebirth altogether. Like many systematic accounts of karma and rebirth, the text with which I began these reflections describes karmic cause and effect as a series of one-to-one correspondences, between a specific seed and the fruit to which it gives rise. The hostile and selfish, we are told, become carnivorous animals, but what then becomes of those carnivores? Surely a tiger or jackal (or intestinal parasite) has few opportunities for the kinds of moral actions that might lead to a better rebirth in future. We can, in other words, begin to see where the utter justice of karmic cause and effect may be just as utterly unsatisfactory for the Buddhist tradition as it is for us.

The image of the monk and the crow—locked in an eternal cycle of murderous retaliation, ignorant of the karmic drama that frames their actions—also puts into perspective the urgency of Buddhist admonitions for us to realize the rarity of life as a human being, and to turn that life over to the search for salvation. The cycle of rebirth may well offer us a virtually limitless opportunity to "play the game" of life over again and make our choices differently, but the law of karma suggests that those choices necessarily—even brutally—curtail the kinds of choices we will be able to make in future.

The Story of the God and the Rabbit

If tales like this encourage us to consider the long-term implications of our choices, they also prompt us to think about the ways in which those choices are bound up with the moral lives of others. It is a notion that arises in interesting (and often surprising) places as the course unfolds. One of my favorite Buddhist stories, for example, tells of one of the Buddha's own past lives. According to the tale, the god Śakra felt his heavenly throne grow warm, a sign that somewhere on earth a being was performing the kind of religious practices that would one day cause him to surpass the gods themselves. Going in search of this being, Śakra discovered not a man but a humble rabbit, performing austerities. Taking on the form of a beggar, he approached the rabbit to ask for alms. Other animals happily provided the beggar with what he needed—the jackal brought him food taken from a farmer's hut and the otter brought him fish taken from a fisherman's lines—but the rabbit had nothing the beggar could eat except his own flesh. He asked the beggar to build a roaring fire, and just as he was about to leap into the flames, the beggar caught him, and revealed his true identity. In honor of the rabbit's supreme act of compassionate generosity, the god reached up into the heavens and painted his portrait on the surface of the moon, an image it still bears today.[11]

More than a fable or a just-so story, the tale of Śakra and the rabbit represents an early form of Buddhist hagiography, in which the character

---

[11] *Original Buddhist Sources: A Reader*, ed. Carl Olson (New Brunswick: Rutgers University Press, 2005), 23–25.

of the Buddha is elaborated by describing the karmic seeds that made him what he was in his final rebirth. Like many of these accounts, the central theme is, curiously, not the Buddha's wisdom or insight, but rather his compassion and generosity. As some of my students have pointed out, however, the tale also has some intriguing things to say about the nature of generosity itself. Whatever this tale may have to say—or not say—about the religious life of rabbits, or why a god would find it necessary to intervene (was Śakra testing the rabbit or tempting him?), it is at heart a story about a moral dilemma: How can the protagonist accomplish his religious duty to offer alms when he has nothing that the beggar needs? Or, to put it another way, is generosity a virtue restricted to the rich? To what extent does wealth (itself the fruit of past karmic seeds) expand our power to do good? Does poverty (the consequence of past negative deeds) limit our moral opportunities?

My students seldom fail to note that while it may be impractical to offer our bodies as meat for the hungry (most panhandlers, after all, are not cannibals, although the Buddhist tradition is replete with tales of holy men who offer themselves to hungry tigers or other predators), we might still be able to offer ourselves—our time or our effort—even when we can't offer goods or money. As one of my more astute students has noted, however, the tale may imply that an offering of ourselves may be the *only* morally unambiguous choice. The other characters in the story—the jackal and the otter—may have been able to offer the beggar suitable alms, but their wealth was in fact grounded in theft. That is not to say that all riches must be inevitably ill-gotten, but it does force us to consider the extent to which the disparity of wealth that makes charity necessary in the first place may be grounded in a history of less-than-virtuous action.

Telling Our Own Stories: Of Road Rage and Disaster

These conversations about morality, justice, and suffering in the Buddhist tradition set the stage for later assignments, when I ask students to apply these ideas (and, more importantly, the questions that they raise) to their own experience. In the course of our discussion of the Buddhist Path, for example, I ask them to engage in a fairly rudimentary exercise in the practice of meditation. Right Effort—one of the elements of the Noble Eightfold Path toward enlightenment—is the foundation of Buddhist meditation, a commitment to do no more or less than take responsibility for one's own physical and mental activity. And in order to do that, one must first pay attention.

Their assignment is to keep track of their karmic activity over the course of forty-eight hours. I don't ask them for a detailed log (my class, I remind them, is neither reality TV nor the confessional), but rather a general summary and analysis. How many of their actions (of body, speech, or mind) were directed to the benefits of others, and how many to their detriment? And to what extent did their positive actions outweigh their negative actions? In the class discussion that follows this assignment, the daily commute to class or work is commonly noted as an arena of moral conflict: a few students are willing to allow other motorists to merge ahead of them (especially those who remember that they are recording their karmic account books for that day), but many admit to closing the gap between cars when they see a turn signal. And most acknowledge that rush hour is a dangerously fertile ground for bad karma of both speech and mind.

This exercise offers its fair share of opportunities for laughter, but the overarching point is really rather grim: most students admit that their lives are characterized by a host of little injustices and hurtful remarks, a tide of petty evils that is seldom matched by the good they do. Given what they've learned of the immutable law of karma, many share a sense that—in the perfectly just world envisioned in these texts—their next rebirth would be unlikely to be as good as the one they now enjoy. More than an opportunity to demonstrate their growing familiarity with the Buddhist worldview, this exercise also provides many of my students with a vantage from which to appreciate the daunting character of any call to moral purity—whether it is couched in the Buddha's own admonition "to avoid all evil, to cultivate good, and to cleanse one's mind" or Jesus' command to "be perfect, therefore, as your heavenly Father is perfect"—when that call is grounded in an affirmation of absolute justice.[12] At the same time, it provides an insight into the welcome gratuitousness of mercy or forgiveness on the part of savior figures in either tradition. If theodicy asks us to affirm the justice of the cosmos, it may well be the possibility of compassion that makes that vision tolerable.

Perhaps the most illuminating—and for my students, the most troubling—of these exercises is when I invite them to consider the implications of these ideas, not only for the daily struggles of individuals, but

[12] Dhammapada 14:183; Matthew 5:48.

for the catastrophes that affect hundreds, even thousands. And these have never been in short supply: it seems that each semester brings some fresh and awful tragedy for our consideration, from terrorist attacks and wars to industrial disasters and killer storms. Yet I am hesitant to join those who would describe our students today as "the disaster generation." Whatever role modern media may play in bringing them to our attention, it seems that every generation is marked by disasters of one kind or another and must struggle with the effort to derive meaning from (or despite) them. Indeed, it is precisely when calamity strikes whole communities—without regard to age, reputation, or wealth—that the more common and comfortable affirmations of theodicy begin to seem labored, even shrill. In many respects, the earthquake and tsunami that devastated northeastern Japan and sent shockwaves through the world economy in 2011 has as its spiritual antecedent the earthquake and tsunami that ravaged Lisbon in 1755, prompting Voltaire to pen *Candide*, his mocking dismissal of Leibniz's confident assertion that, our suffering notwithstanding, we live in "the best of all possible worlds."

By the end of these conversations, we often conclude that the meaning of such overwhelming human suffering may be found less in the way it reveals the just or benign unfolding of the cosmos than in the opportunity that it offers for us to experience compassion and to practice acts of mercy. This conclusion strikes me as especially apt, if only because, insofar as it dodges the question of theodicy altogether, it reflects my students' overwhelming resistance to this particular subject. Given the profound challenges (both intellectual and emotional) implicit in this line of inquiry, it would not be surprising for students to be uneasy in pursuing it. More than an expression of discomfort, however, I have found that my students frequently object to the discussion *in principle*, arguing that this topic is essentially out of the proper bounds of academic investigation.

For some students, the straightforward discussion of justice (let alone goodness, mercy, or compassion) in the face of such appalling ruin brought to mind the hateful smugness of certain contemporary religious leaders, the pious *schadenfreude* of those keen to use disasters as a means of blaming those with the temerity to disagree with them. Others objected on the grounds that theodicy was, in their experience, an academic exercise in the meanest sense of the term: a discussion of the complexities of karmic cause and effect (or the goodness of a God who presides over human suffering) may be intellectually engaging, but it is at best a diversion. Bringing that merely theoretical discussion into the realm of real human suffering is a fundamental act of disrespect, a trivialization of victims' pain. Still others found themselves in agreement with one student-athlete, who put the matter concisely: you can give credit to God for a game-winning performance, but you should never blame God when you lose. It is, in other words, in poor taste at best (and is at worst impious) to pursue the question of the justice, goodness, or simple intelligibility of the cosmos in the face of adversity. For these students, thanksgiving, not the defiant protests of Job, is the only proper register for theological expression. Insofar as truly mass suffering makes thanksgiving untenable, it is better to avoid the question altogether, or to declare it meaningless, the work not of a good God but of bad luck.

I have found it revealing to explore some of the preconceptions that inform each of these objections in class. On further reflection, however, I am inclined to think of them as variations on a single theme, a common sense of the limits of religious inquiry grounded in an essentially secularist worldview. Rather than atheist or irreligious (although there are always at least a few students who would claim those labels), this is a vision that acknowledges—perhaps even celebrates—the importance of religious community and conviction but limits their scope to the private sphere. I take my students' struggles with the religious meaning of catastrophe to be less a product of secularism as a coherent system of political thought (e.g., the Jeffersonian "wall of separation between church and state," on which the continued flourishing of a religiously diverse society may well depend) than the unintended consequences of a more popular form of politesse: the maxim never to discuss religion or politics at a party. From this perspective, public discussion should be reserved for subjects that—either because they are trivial or because the venue is comprised entirely of the like-minded—are expected to be uncontroversial, or to provoke an argument for which the stakes are comfortably low. In such a climate, religious language seldom has the opportunity to address concerns beyond the narrowest confines of private life, a sphere that seems to grow narrower with the transformations of our technological environment. As a result, religious inquiry—theodicean or otherwise—is easily reduced to platitudes, with little capacity to address the richness or profundity of our experience. However comfortable these platitudes may be, they are unlikely to be particularly comforting in the face of genuine suffering. Challenging these commonplaces (and the preconceptions about public and private that permits them to go unexamined) may be unwelcome at a cocktail party, but they are, I think, essential in the classroom.

Discernment and the Catholic Liberal Arts

In my experience, discussions like these can provide valuable insights, but they seldom provide the sort of answers that at least some of my students (and, over the years, a few of my colleagues) seem to expect. The comparative enterprise, not unlike the problem of theodicy itself, is ultimately driven more by the encounter with unexpected contradictions than by neat solutions. Essential truths or ironclad schemata seldom survive either endeavor unscathed.

If this represents a problem for the specifically Catholic character of the Catholic liberal arts, I would argue that it is one at the heart of the tradition. Rather than the common parlance of catechesis (concerned more with religious instruction than with religious studies) or the contemporary language of marketing (concerned with affirming a "niche identity" as the foundation for a university's "brand"), I would suggest that these academic endeavors be understood as part of a process of discernment, an exploration of and engagement with the troubling (even tragic) complexities of experience, in order to appreciate the resources available to us as members of a particular tradition. In so doing, students may come to consider the goodness of creation less as a doctrine to be accepted (or rejected) as a solution to an intellectual puzzle than as a question that drives their lives.

Beholding the Eschaton: Transforming Self and World through the Study of World History

Eric Cunningham

Introduction

First, let me apologize for the boring title. I would have preferred to call this essay "Beholding the Eschaton: An Apocalyptic, Psychedelic, Postmodern Guide to Transcending the Historical World, Including Some Practical Exercises on How to Avoid Becoming a Zombie at the End of History." I figured my chances of getting any such title accepted in the early stages of editorial screening would have been difficult to say the least, so I toned it down a bit. I only mention it now to give some indication of the tantalizing complexity of the topic at hand.

For nearly ten years now, I have started every semester by telling my History 112 (World Civilizations since 1500) students two important things about the course. The first thing I tell them is that the study of history is holy, hermetic work, and I warn them that if they are not willing to experience a significant personal transformation during my class they should drop immediately and enroll in another, less existentially demanding section. It is a suitably dramatic way to begin the course, and it invariably grabs their attention. I have not collected any statistics or devised any instruments that would tell me the degree to which my students are actually transformed (an admission that could probably land me in hot water with our local outcomes and assessments trackers), but I receive a respectable number of evaluations each year in which students convey their appreciation and surprise that my course was not "boring like most history classes." I take such remarks as great victories, considering that most of my students take world history as part of their university core, which is to say, under compulsion, and not out of any particular love for the subject.

It is very difficult, to paraphrase C. S. Lewis, to irrigate the mental deserts of our results-oriented, outcomes-driven college students.[1] But with each passing year, I find myself struggling with an irresistible urge to bypass Bloom's tedious taxonomy and dedicate myself to recapturing the spirit of the early teachers of the Society of Jesus. There exists, even for a layman like myself, no greater "objective" in Catholic pedagogy than to draw as closely as possible to the traditional, God-centered ends of the Jesuit educational mission. As the *Ratio Studiorum* of 1599 states, it is "one of the leading ministries" of the Society of Jesus to teach its students "all the disciplines . . . in such a way that they are aroused to a knowledge and love of our Maker and Redeemer."[2] As Catholic scholars, it is our privilege as well as our duty to lead our students to "become beholders" of the God who not only created our world but remains always present, always active, and always loving within it. If we are not actively looking to find and reveal God in all of our disciplines, then we are doing great injury to the Catholic intellectual tradition we have been privileged to inherit, and missing a golden opportunity to plant new seeds for world-transformation. If our teaching mission is to become nothing more than the presentation of content and teaching our own tests, a state university is just as effective, and a good deal more affordable.

The second thing I tell them is that the modern historical world is coming to an end and that the most important part of the holy work of studying history is to figure out a way to bring the modern world to a satisfactory conclusion. We can only do this, I tell them, if we are willing to figure out what the process of history means, where modernity fits into that process, and what its conclusion should actually entail. Unfortunately, the best textbooks on the market today provide little insight as to how one might do this. Despite their beautiful graphics, their politi-

---

[1] C. S. Lewis, *The Abolition of Man* (New York: MacMillan, 1947; reprint, 1978), 24.
[2] *The Ratio Studiorum: The Official Plan for Jesuit Education*, trans. Claude Pavur, SJ (St. Louis: Institute of Jesuit Sources, 2005), 7.

cally correct treatment of all vital world regions, and their ecumenical inclusion of all current subfields, world history books come up short when it comes to explaining what the purpose of history may be.

Modern historians tend to treat history as an essentially aimless process of political, economic, ecological, social, and cultural change, all of which takes place against an apparently static background of time and space. The process is filled with all kinds of interesting things, to be sure, but it has no knowable origin, no knowable end, and no particular purpose. For what it's worth, I strenuously disagree with this common opinion, but the "official" ambiguity of the historical process leaves plenty of space for my students to come up with their own theories, which I encourage wholeheartedly. I am always hopeful that by the end of the term, they will consider the possibility that the meaning of history is intimately enfolded into the End of history, and that the End of history is intimately enfolded into the various ends of their own lives.

To avoid the linear predictability that results from starting with the Renaissance, the Reformation, or any other such well-acknowledged "dawn" of the modern era, we commence our fifteen-week journey with the headlines of the daily news, which give the best indication of the moment upon us and then circle back upon the past to see how we got here. At this late stage in history, I tell them, it makes no sense to rehash the common narrative line—we already know where it leads, and it does not leave us with much to crow about. The primary task of the historian and the history student today is not to reaffirm the interpretations of past events according to conventional narrative models, but to craft a more satisfying narrative that allows us to prepare ourselves and the world we inhabit for the smoothest end-of-story possible. Then and only then can we truly behold the Logos behind History, and use this vision to inspire the creation of a new world.

As you can imagine, such an introduction to an entry level core history course invites no small amount of confusion and rebuttal. Students will invariably ask "haven't there *always* been people predicting the end of the world? What's the big deal?" To this question, I invariably answer that there really have not *always* been people predicting the end of the world—just occasionally, and during those times that people have said the world was ending, they were usually right. The world ended for the Romans; it ended for the Azetcs, it ended for the Ming dynasty, it ended for Tokugawa Japan—there are numerous cases in world history in which entire empires disappeared in the space of a few years, and in each case there was a loud eschatological buzz in the popular culture preceding the fall. So maybe what's actually happening is not that the *world* is about to disappear, but that some major change—on the order of the Aztec conquest, for example—is on the horizon. The question we face (as we listen to our own resounding eschatological buzz) is this: how do we prepare for the end of a world? My answer (and challenge) to my students is this: Go out and meet it—prepare for the end, and start now to rebuild what comes afterward.

Eschatology, or the study of the end times, is not a topic that most modern people are all that comfortable discussing. Young people in particular, I have learned, find the whole notion of "world-ending" to be highly disturbing, and given the generally pleasant circumstances of their lives as undergraduates on a student-friendly campus, they are loathe to contemplate the possibility that "all of this" could disappear before they get a chance to optimize their enjoyment of it. Like most moderns, young people seem to be hardwired with what is commonly called today a "normalcy bias." This refers to the tendency of people, when confronted with the possibility of any crisis, no matter how severe—from the collapse of the economy to the threat of world annihilation—to assume that all will turn out for the best and that any upsetting conditions will return to normal in due course.[3] For better or worse, I have never been prone to any such bias, and would work strenuously to overcome it if I did!

My own preference has always been to search out the uncanny, the bizarre, and the outré, not only because "weirdness" is more interesting than normalcy, but also because I believe that the unexpected episodes we encounter in life have much more to tell us about the nature of reality than any of our earnest modern attempts to create a secure, predictable world. That having been said, I need to make it clear that the reason I stress the eschatological modalities of history in my classroom is not because I want to project my own dark apocalyptic fantasies on otherwise well-adjusted young people, but because after fifteen years of focused research into this topic, I am convinced that the Eschaton *is* the meaning of our historical process. If we can learn to embrace it creatively, we will find the keys both to world redemption and personal salvation.

---

[3] Use of the term "normalcy bias" has become common in news journals, blogs, and internet sites in describing peoples' responses to recent natural disasters. For an academic treatment of the phenomenon, see Katsuya Yamori, "Revisiting the Concept of Normalcy Bias," *Japanese Journal of Experimental Social Psychology* 48, no. 2 (2009): 137–49.

I recognize that these are bold claims for any kind of professor, let alone for a history professor, whose "proper" function is to interpret the past and leave grandiose predictions about the future of the world to more qualified commentators—stockbrokers or candidates running for political office, I suppose. Nevertheless, a careful consideration of eschatology will show that this peripheral yet universal domain of knowledge is of special importance to the historian. To make it work, though, the historian has to sidestep the strict confines of modern materialist linearity and integrate into his or her thinking the possibilities presented by what Daniel Andreev refers to as "metahistory." Andreev, a Russian mystic who spent ten years in a Soviet prison camp, defined metahistory as "the sum of processes . . . as yet outside the field of vision, interest and methodology of science . . . that take place on planes of being existing in other time streams and other dimensions and are sometimes discernible through the process we perceive as history."[4]

Among the processes we might include under the umbrella of metahistory are the study of dreams, spiritual visions, film, psychedelic hallucinations, insanity, schizophrenia, apparitions, psychic intuitions, and artistic imaginaries, all things which are palpably real to their observers, yet difficult to categorize qualitatively according to the protocols of objective science. For the remainder of this essay, I will focus on three specific "metahistorical" arguments that justify the adoption of an eschatological approach as a best means of beholding the God of History.

1) The contemporary world is inundated with aesthetic, spiritual, and psychic evidence that "the world as we know it" is coming to an end.

2) All historical narratives are *inherently* eschatological.

3) Eschatology provides the most effective means of explaining the acute and general crises of modernity and helps make the concept of postmodernism more intelligible.

In addition to clarifying each of these points, I will also provide some practical journal and discussion exercises I have used with great profit in my own history courses.

---

[4] Daniel Andreev, *Rose of the World* (Great Barrington, MA: Lindisfarne Books, 1997), 73.

The contemporary world is inundated with aesthetic, spiritual, and psychic evidence that "the world as we know it" is coming to an end.

When I began doing serious research into eschatology in 1996, the current hype and anxiety over the "2012 phenomenon" was barely a blip on the psychic radars of most Americans. Apart from the "crazies" who belonged to apocalyptic cults such as "Heaven's Gate," and the insomniacs who faithfully listened to Art Bell's *Coast to Coast AM* every night on the radio, there were few people who gave much thought to the apocalyptic streams that run so deeply yet so close to the surface of our collective consciousness. There were, of course, growing concerns about the Y2K computer bug, and speculations on how it might bring the cyberworld to a halt, but that particular dud of an apocalypse did more to diminish than enhance the legitimacy of millennial prognosticators. The proximity of a new millennium, however, managed to evoke a number of dormant apocalyptic concerns in the collective consciousness of modern Westerners. It seemed clear that after two thousand years of Christianity and five hundred years of modernity, both of which have been considered the psychic property of the West, we had far more things to lament than celebrate. Even if the world was not ending, there was little evidence that it was heading anywhere good. The World Trade Center attacks in 2001, followed immediately by an open-ended war on terrorism, were hardly an auspicious opening for the new Christian millennium.

As if to compound the effects of the millennial turn, we now find ourselves on the far side of 2012, a year which became the convergence point for a multitude of popular eschatological impulses. Even the most cursory web search still yields *hundreds of millions* of links to websites dealing with the 2012 phenomenon. Most of these sites dutifully describe the ancient Mayan belief that on the winter solstice of 2012, when the sun ostensibly rose at the intersection of the ecliptic and the Milky Way galaxy, a new era of peace and harmony would begin. Many 2012 sites offer less verifiable evidence to predict the onset of other transformational events as well. These range from the second coming of Christ to the Advent of the transhuman singularity[5]—with every conceivable type

---

[5] Transhumanism, an emerging field embracing science, philosophy, and technology, has been enjoying a boom in print and internet publishing in the last five years. For a readable theoretical background to transhumanism, see Ray Kurzweil, *The*

of war, natural disaster, celestial disturbance, and economic catastrophe in between. So whether or not people know or care anything about the Mayan Calendar and its long prophesied fulfillment on December 21, 2012, the year has come to serve as a cipher for some great shift in human consciousness. Whether or not this is good news would seem to depend on how deeply one is invested in the prospects of modern civilization.

The modern rationalist, acting in accordance with "good common sense" (read "normalcy bias") may treat all of this "2012 stuff" as either a pure delusion or a clever commercial scheme, but nobody can argue that something *strange* is going on out there in our nice, predictable, Newtonian world. When we survey the number of books, magazines, TV shows, and movies that have been bombarding us with images of world destruction and dystopia, it is clear that pop eschatology has crept in to take over the human imagination. Moreover, the external world is clearly rushing to cooperate with the collective unconscious of our popular culture, bringing into reality a series of events that make the news of the world look like something out of a third-rate science fiction screenplay. We have catastrophic oil spills, "Arab springs," mad industrialists creating the scourge of global warming, mad scientists fudging their data about the cause of global warming, revolutionaries who want to destroy the constitution, revolutionaries who want to restore the constitution, despotic leaders who make Hitler and Stalin seem like rational men, earthquakes, tsunamis, nuclear meltdowns, flash mobs, political corruption, financial collapse, and war breaking out in every sector of the globe. These bizarre and frightening phenomena, which have become downright commonplace, force us to ask the question: which came first, the apocalyptic screenplay or the CNN headline?

I like to make time in class to discuss the recent history of apocalyptic cinema, not only because of my interest in these films, and because students can relate so directly to them, but because they provide the most compelling and instructive metahistorical evidence of the coming Eschaton. If we look at the evolution of the apocalyptic film, a genre which gained recognition during the Cold War,[6] we can locate number

---

Singularity Is Near: When Humans Transcend Biology (New York: Penguin, 2006). For a comprehensive guide to the "canonical" writings on this topic, consult http://neo humanism.org/t/tr/transhumanism.html. Accessed October 10, 2013.

[6] See Charles P. Mitchell, *A Guide to Apocalyptic Cinema* (Westport, CT: Greenwood Press, 2001) for a comprehensive guide to the millennial genre of film.

of distinct and significant turns that reveal the degree to which our imagination brokers have lost the ability to envision any satisfactory future.

At the cusp of the millennium, films like *Independence Day* (1996), *Deep
Impact* (1998), and *Armageddon* (1998) portrayed the Earth as the victim
of either an alien invasion or an asteroid collision. The response to the
unwelcome appearance of the Alien Other in these movies was essentially the same: the nations of the world rallied to the United States, and
under the inspired leadership of its wise and dynamic president, they
dealt with the threat by obliterating it with nuclear weapons. While it
was undoubtedly a sad commentary on modern civilization that the
apparent Ultimate Solution to Big Problems was the creative use of
nukes, at least there was a sense, way back in those carefree, sunny, pre-
Y2K days that Big Problems *could* be fixed. This would not be the case
for long.

The next wave of apocalyptic cinema, which began around 2005,
brought the release of several films that implied that earthlings were no
longer the innocent victims of a hostile cosmos, but rather the creators
of their own doom. *Serenity* (2005), *V for Vendetta* (2005), *I am Legend*
(2007), and *Doomsday* (2008) to name only a few, all showed the end of
civilization as the result of some botched government-sponsored medical
experiment, followed by the callous extermination of masses of people
for the sake of preserving political stability. The message of these films
seemed to be that modern civilization itself was the Alien Other and that
the crowning achievements of modernity—rational civil government
and medical science—were just as likely to serve as agents of enslave-
ment and annihilation. More disturbing, perhaps, than the notion that
we had created the mechanisms of our own destruction was the fact that
none of these films showed us any way out of the dystopia to come.
While there were hints that the surviving protagonists made it to places
of sanctuary, no portrayal of what happened in the post-apocalyptic
world was ever given—the reason for this, I submit, is that *we simply do
not know* what a postmodern, post-historical world is supposed to look
like. We intuit that modern civilization is ending, but we do not know
what comes next, and we cannot envision it. This is the historical trap
that we have set for ourselves by buying into the false notion that material progress is a never-ending enterprise. Because we are no longer
beholders of the transcendent transhistorical, we are stuck with dystopic
visions of world disaster and diminished human prospects.

Perhaps the most alarming cinematic turn has been the emergence of
the "Zombie apocalypse," a new take on the genre of zombie films that

began with George Romero's *Night of the Living Dead* (1968) and have lurked on the periphery of the apocalyptic genre for decades. In recent years, the Zombie apocalypse has come into its own as an indicator of what may await post-historical humanity if some recapturing of spiritual value does not take place soon. Films such as *The Zombie Diaries* (2006), *Planet Terror* (2007), and *Zombieland* (2009) take one of the persistent themes from the second phase of apocalypse films, i.e., the violent and deranged subhuman byproduct of the medical mishap, and carry it to a frightful conclusion—that modern civilization possesses the capacity to create a new subhuman species. The Reavers of *Serenity*, the Dark-seekers of *I Am Legend*, and the cannibal marauders of *Doomsday* show us what may lay in store for our species should hope and humanity go extinct. While I would be reluctant to define the exact set of conditions that would constitute a real fall from the human status, the very existence of the concept of transhumanism would suggest that the human-being-created-by-God is neither a fixed nor permanent category of the species *Homo sapiens*. I would also argue that the thoroughly bored—yet somehow also thoroughly enraged—packs of young people sparking riots and flash mobs throughout the modern world differ more in degree than in kind from the brain-dead zombies of film who roam the city streets and shopping malls of the postmodern world with no apparent aim other than to gain immediate satisfaction by feeding on the flesh of the living.

What does it mean then, to live in an era that seems to have become preoccupied with the destruction of the world and the degradation of the human species? While there undoubtedly exist any number of psychological, anthropological, economic, political, or sociological explanations, the historical answer, as best as I can tell, is that our modern civilization is out of ideas. Modern consciousness is done, but we have not figured out what comes next, because modern civilization makes no provision for any valid subsequent reality beyond itself.

One may argue that it is irrational to make such bold conclusions on the basis of Hollywood's vision of the world because these are, after all, only movies. What contends with this normalcy reflex is the argument that movies may actually represent the shadows of future consciousness being reflected into the present day, giving us a vivid, if symbolic portrayal of the post-historical human condition.[7] If it is possible that we

[7] Terence McKenna, "New Maps of Hyperspace," in *The Archaic Revival* (San Francisco: Harper, 1991), 96.

bring the future into being through the products of our visual imagination, then the world really is coming to an end. The great tragedy here is not that we lack the technology or talent to avoid self-destruction—it's that we lack the *imagination*. Modernity, the historical narrative that defines our reality, is simply inadequate to deliver us beyond its own aesthetic constraints. All the strife and anxiety we now see in the world is taking place because the modern world is seeking its end, but we who inhabit this world have no real concept of how to bring the end about. Nevertheless, history, like all good stories, must end—but it may be up to us to write our own ending.

Mental Exercise Number One

Imagine that you are a surviving character who has found safe haven at the end of one of the following movies: *I Am Legend*, *War of the Worlds*, *The Road*, *Doomsday*, *Children of Men*, *Deep Impact*—or any other apocalyptic film of your choosing.

What happens tomorrow? How is your new community organized? What are its values, its goals, its aspirations?

History Is Inherently Eschatological

In purely functional terms, all histories serve as a means of organizing and interpreting human experience as it changes according to the temporal modalities of past, present, and future. If we had no experience of past, present, and future, we would have no history. This statement, while obvious enough, invites us to consider what the organization and interpretation of human experience would look like if the awareness of the passage of time did not exist; if, for example, we happened to be gods, angels, ghosts—or even prehistorical human beings. Stuck as we are inside our modern three-dimensional historical consciousness, it is difficult for us to form any idea of what human experience was like before history, but since the vast majority of human experience was actually spent in a prehistorical mode, we know that "prehistorical consciousness" is a real thing—so what is it?

As I encourage my students to reflect upon this question, I introduce them to the ideas of two particularly thought-provoking modern thinkers, the Austrian seer Rudolf Steiner and the American ethnobotanist Terence McKenna. These men, by means of native clairvoyance and psychedelic vision, respectively, obtained insights into the nonmaterial world that enabled them to articulate theories of prehistorical consciousness, as well as explain humanity's "descent" into history.

According to Steiner, our ancestors lived for untold millennia as semi-spirit beings in a condition of consciousness similar to what we know as the dream state. In order to fulfill the evolutionary purpose of acquiring more enhanced ego-understanding, human beings descended from the spiritual world into a physical, time-and-space-bound world. To return, after many more eons, from this state to the spiritual world (having learned what ego can teach us) constitutes, in a broad sense, the meaning of history. McKenna, for his part, on the basis of psychedelic visions (and over thirty years of nonpsychedelic empirical research in pharmacology, mathematics, and history), maintained that our ancestors lived in an almost perpetual state of hallucination, owing to the likelihood that they consumed the psilocybin mushrooms that grew from the dung of their cattle herds as part of their regular diet. Over time, McKenna believed, as the African veld dried up and mushrooms became increasingly scarce, people slowly withdrew from the psychedelic consciousness and began to adapt to the three-dimensional environment that we now define as reality. Sensing that they were losing contact with the spirit world, they began to conserve their mushrooms, and saved them for periodic forays into the imaginary domains. In these psychedelic rituals, which researcher Gordon Wasson believed were first human religious ceremonies,[8] anointed members of the community known as shamans would eat the "sacramental" mushroom, behold the indwelling god, and bring back sustaining wisdom from the realms of image and spirit.

While the scope of my course (and this essay) does not allow anything but a cursory treatment of these idiosyncratic theories, it has been my experience that students find these ideas, as well as their obvious resonances with the biblical story of creation and the Fall, the Mass, and the Eucharist, quite compelling. Discussing these seemingly far-fetched theories also gives me a chance to remind the students that many of our civilization's greatest discoveries began as little more than dreams, visions, or wild imaginations. Of course, I remind my students that for those researchers who lack clairvoyant vision and wisely choose to avoid

---

[8] See R. Gordon Wasson, *Mushrooms, Russia, and History* (New York: Pantheon Books, 1957), for Wasson's theories on the role psychedelic mushrooms may have played in the history of religion.

psychedelic gnosis, the best way to gain an understanding of prehistoric consciousness is to look at whatever texts and practices remain from prehistoric times.

Modern anthropology confirms that in the shamanic tradition, priests, wise women, and medicine men conveyed spirit lore to their communities in the form of stories; whatever we know today of these ancient stories has come down to us in the mythology that ultimately passed from the oral tradition into writing during the Bronze Age (c. 3000–600 BC). If this interpretation holds true, then myth would appear to be the *narrative expression* of the activity of the spiritual world. What exactly does myth tell us about this activity? To answer this question would require us to layer speculation upon speculation, except that we do possess, straight from the world of hard science, a working model for spiritual activity, or, as physicist Thomas Campbell calls it, "the Fundamental Process of Consciousness."[9]

According to Campbell, Consciousness *is* the ground of all reality, and it is purely spiritual in substance. Its fundamental evolutionary process can be described as a three-part sequence of changes that begins with consciousness existing in some original state, then moving out from itself through a change or distortion of that original state, and then returning to the original state, substantially transformed as a result of the change. As a description of process, Campbell's three-stage consciousness movement resembles the familiar Hegelian dialectical scheme in which a preexisting reality (thesis) encounters a contradiction (antithesis), resulting in a new reality (synthesis), thus it "works" well for history students. In Campbell's theory, spiritual evolution is an iterative multiplication of such changes in which consciousness continually seeks optimal profitability through its creative experience. It only goes to reason (if we want to think of the entire universe as a fractal piece of this primordial consciousness) that this movement "out and back" from self is replicated in the shaman's journey. It follows too that the myth narrative itself would also adhere to the "out and back" pattern, which may explain why so many myths take the form of the "hero's journey."[10] In this mythic archetype, the hero responds to a call to adventure and embarks upon a quest, encountering hardship and trials along the way. Upon successful

[9] See Thomas Campbell, *My Big TOE: Awakening, Discovery, Inner Workings* (Lightning Strike Books, 2010).

[10] See Joseph Campbell, *The Hero with a Thousand Faces* (Princeton, NJ: Princeton University Press, 1968).

completion of his ordeals, he returns to his place of origin, glorified, transformed, and blessed.[11] As mythologist Joseph Campbell (no relation to Thomas Campbell) explains:

> A hero ventures forth from the world of common day into a region of supernatural wonder: fabulous forces are there encountered and a decisive victory is won: the hero comes back from this mysterious adventure with the power to bestow boons on his fellow man.[12]

If we permit ourselves to think of human consciousness as the hero of its own world process, it is not difficult to see the entire mythic experience as a narrative expression of that process—an epic complete with "separation," "initiation," "return," and all the subsidiary steps that lead the hero out on his quest, returning to him or her "home" in a new and transfigured state.

What distinguishes the mythical consciousness from the historical consciousness is the fact that while myths are always "finished," human history is still open-ended, at least according to our perceptions from within it. It is clear that a certain point in the development of our consciousness—perhaps this was indeed "the Fall"—we moved out of what Mircea Eliade calls the "sacred time" of myth into the profane time of history, and we have been stuck there ever since.[13] Yet history, like myth, demands closure, because if myth is the narrative expression of spiritual activity, history is the space-time expression of myth. History *must* return to myth and *must* recapture the capacity to end in order to fulfill the evolutionary imperatives of spirit. Unfortunately, since the historical process has become overdetermined by modern thinking, even imagining the end has become an uphill battle.

[11] Ibid. The steps/phases of the Hero's Journey described in this book are: (1) The Call to Adventure, (2) Refusal of the Call, (3) Supernatural Aid, (4) Crossing the First Threshold, (5) The Belly of the Whale, (6) The Road of Trials, (7) The Meeting with the Goddess, (8) Woman as the Temptress, (9) Atonement with the Father, (10) Apotheosis, (11) The Ultimate Boon, (12) Refusal of the Return, (13) The Magic Flight, (14) Rescue from Without, (15) Crossing of the Return Threshold, (16) Master of the Two Worlds, (17) Freedom to Live.

[12] Ibid., 30.

[13] Mircea Eliade, *Myths, Dreams, and Mysteries: The Encounter between Contemporary Faiths and Archaic Realities*, trans. Philip Mairet (New York: Harper and Brothers, 1960), 31.

Mental Exercise Number Two

Imagine you are a mythic hero approaching the end of your life. Map out the story of your life as myth, including the nature of your fundamental quest, your primary challenges, and some idea of what a successful journey entails. You have obviously not lived most of this journey yet, so try to be creative. How can you bring your own myth into reality in the time-and-space-bound historical world?

Eschatology Provides the Most Effective Means of Explaining the Acute Crises of Modernity

In his 1949 classic *Meaning in History*, a book I routinely assign in this course, the German philosopher Karl Löwith traces the steps of a major transition in Western historical consciousness from the late Roman Empire up to the modern era.[14] Examining the writings of historical philosophers from St. Augustine through Jacob Burckhardt, Löwith shows how the Western philosophy of history began in an eschatological conception of time rooted in faith in the action of divine providence and gradually shifted toward its current status as an exclusively secular worldview based on modern "faith" in endless material progress. This transition was slow and subtle in the centuries prior to the Reformation but became much more pronounced in the seventeenth and eighteenth centuries when Enlightenment thinkers such as Voltaire and his philosophical descendants redefined world history without any reference to God, providence, or specific purpose. In the modern world, history has, in a real sense, become meaning*less*.

Löwith, a Christian thinker, was clearly concerned by the modern crisis of history, but he had no concrete solutions to propose. At the time *Meaning in History* was published, the world had only just emerged from nearly twenty years of global crisis in which totalitarian regimes in Germany, Italy, and Japan had actively sought to overthrow the modern liberal West.[15] In a world recovering from the brutal excesses perpetrated by these fascist states, there seemed little possibility that a healthy critique of modernization could ever take place. Who, after the Second World War, would ever question the idea that the modern liberal society

---

[14] See Karl Löwith, *Meaning in History* (Chicago: University of Chicago Press, 1949).

[15] Eric Cunningham, *Hallucinating the End of History: Nishida, Zen, and the Psychedelic Eschaton* (Palo Alto, CA: Academica Press, 2007), 298.

was the greatest guarantor of peace, prosperity, and happiness in the history of human experience?

As it turned out, peace and prosperity in the West were exactly what *did* inspire new inquiries into the validity of the modern narrative. The staid homogeneity of postwar bourgeois life, the tensions of the Cold War nuclear standoff between America and the Soviet Union, and the growing awareness of social injustice at home and around the newly polarized world, led to nagging doubts about the ability of modern materialist progress to provide a universally satisfactory future for humanity. Throughout the postwar era, a new generation of intellectuals, artists, and clerics raised provocative questions about the prospects of modernity, and began to ponder the possibility of a "postmodern world."

One of these intellectuals, Jean Francois Lyotard, published an important summary of modern and postmodern epistemology called *The Postmodern Condition: An Inquiry into Knowledge* in 1979. Lyotard characterized the postmodern condition as an "incredulity toward metanarratives," [16] in particular the "grand narrative" of Enlightenment progress, the same narrative of expanding secular freedom and scientific rationalism that Löwith had earlier identified as having had replaced the narrative of divine providence. What Lyotard's work implied—something that Löwith himself had intuited thirty years prior, was that the dominant narrative of progress was itself as vulnerable to replacement as the earlier providential model had been. The historiographical problem with this, which Löwith also foresaw, was that without some informing narrative, providential or progressive, the historical process had nowhere to "go." Unfortunately, this is precisely where the postmodern turn has left us—in the middle of a progressive, never-ending narrative that is no longer even progressing. When we stop to consider the range of problems plaguing our modern (or is it now officially postmodern?) society, we find there are almost too many things to list: a lingering threat of nuclear annihilation, warfare, poverty, religious conflict, environmental degradation, moral decline, energy depletion, global terrorism, political despotism, financial collapse—the list is essentially never-ending. What was once the most forward-looking and optimistic civilization in human experience has become a global cult of doubt and despair.

To the normalcy-biased modernist, all of these problems are caused by bad politics, bad social programs, bad economic policies, and misplaced

---

[16] Jean-François Lyotard, *The Postmodern Condition: An Inquiry into Knowledge* (Minneapolis: University of Minnesota Press, 1984), xxiv.

priorities in education—and they will be fixed as soon as their party (whichever one it is) takes control of the Congress, the White House, the courts, etc. To the creative eschatological historian, these problems are the result of flawed aesthetics and neglected religion and will never be fixed until the narrative itself is replaced and God is once again beheld in the historical process. We are trapped in the wrong story and we need to rewrite it. The various meltdowns of modernity are simply what we get when we individually and collectively buy into the false myth of historical materialism and attempt to live in the counterfeit culture that this worldview inevitably engenders. Once again, we must embrace the Eschaton, behold the transcendent, and work to bring the modern world to a creative and holy end.

Mental Exercise Number Three

You are a historian living in the age that immediately follows the modern age. The end of the modern world was so decisive and complete that we don't even use the word "postmodern" anymore. What does the age call itself? You are writing a book about how the modern historical world came to an end. What were the underlying and immediate causes of the end? Since the end of modernity, is the world a worse or a better place? Explain.

Conclusion:
Embracing the Eschaton; Practical Considerations

I realize that this essay is somewhat long on theory and short on specific recommendations, but I have found it true in my life and my teaching career that a good theoretical seed, properly planted, can often yield more fruit than a hundred scattered "helpful practical hints." The exercises I have included in this essay have proven helpful in encouraging students to place themselves outside the predictable patterns of their modern life and to bring before their consciousness the idea that they are the authors not only of their personal biographies but of the historical world-narrative they inhabit. In addition to these mental exercises, I also encourage them, on their own time and in their own ways, to acquire or improve upon a number of personal supporting habits that I can guarantee, from experience, are effective in bringing one closer to a sustained state of beholding.

1) Prayer, to open themselves to the eternal God beyond time and space.

2) Meditation, to experience what it is like to exist beyond time and space.

3) The pursuit of some artistic or aesthetic hobby to take part in, rather than merely consume, the creative process.

4) The keeping of personal journals to record changes in their own thoughts and dispositions over time.

These practices, while simple, allow us to reduce the ambient noise in our lives and focus our attention on a few core principles. As a Catholic by birth and calling, and a history professor by trade, the core principle I try to live by, and hope to instill in my students, is, again, the idea that history is a story looking for fulfillment and that it demands our heroic and engaged participation in order to bring it to that ending of bliss and beatitude that already exists in God's design and in humanity's purest aspirations. To embrace the Eschaton is to live in the full and vivid awareness of our life with the Almighty, and to behold those realms of divine splendor of which the historical world, with all its complexity, is only a pale replica.

Part 5

Appreciating Where We Stand and What Others See

Shiver of Wonder:
A Dialogue about Chemistry with
Sr. Angela Hoffman, OSB

Karen E. Eifler

From time to time, faculty members in the sciences note their perception that embracing and articulating a sacramental worldview is more natural for their colleagues in the humanities than for themselves. Such an argument might hold that it makes sense to posit God's presence in great works of art and literature, perhaps even acknowledge God as the source of inspiration for such things but that what scientists work with are objective facts and laws about how the physical world functions. They hold up the vast repositories of chemical formulas, bones' names, and engineering principles they must help their students master on their way to medical school, construction firms, and research laboratories. Even if it is conceivable to articulate the presence of God in the connective tissues of living organisms, the sheer volume of knowledge and skills to be transmitted, some might say, precludes the luxury of bringing the Divine into a science classroom or lab. Sr. Angela Hoffman, a world-class biochemist who also happens to be a Benedictine sister, rejects that argument. This gentle, dreamy-eyed master teacher with the tart wit and total command of her demanding field, with its life-changing discoveries occurring every day, wants to make it clear to nascent scientists and especially to their professors, that honing people's abilities to see and honor the graced nature of chemical elements is not only possible, but unavoidable when one takes the time truly to behold what is right there under the microscope. She opened her office, mind, and heart to one of her colleagues to talk about how it is only natural to see an omnipresent God at work in the stuff this earth is made of.

KAREN: This conversation is about teaching top-notch chemistry in a Catholic university, so I want to confirm that you, Sister Angela Hoffman, are in fact a top-notch chemist. You hold four patents for your work on recovering paclitaxel from soils and plants to use in cancer-fighting drugs such as Taxol, and this year you were named a Fellow in the American Chemical Society. Those are stellar credentials for anyone, let alone someone who, like you, teaches as many as four courses and labs per semester at the University of Portland, a smallish comprehensive school that focuses most of its energy and resources on undergraduate education in the liberal arts tradition. You are also a member of the Order of St. Benedict.

SR. ANGELA: Yep, that's me.

KAREN: My first question is whether being a Benedictine sister makes a difference in how you teach chemistry. Are you conscious of that ancient spirituality having an impact on your teaching or work with students in the lab?

SR. ANGELA: Well, there has never been a time in my life when I *didn't* think that everything is a sign of the presence of God, which is of course a big part of Benedictine spirituality. But I didn't just start thinking like that when I became a sister; it was always part of my life. Everything has a chance to reveal something about God, and if that's not happening, you need to do something about it! That awareness is definitely something I want to pass onto my students, but I think it just comes out in the way I interact, and the subjects we study, not from my consciously saying, "Okay class, today we are examining the fact that electrons don't repel each other when they're paired up; what do you think God is trying to say to us here?" I'm more inclined to ask them to think through why it might be a bad thing for electric signals within a cell to be in conflict with the other two hundred or so other things that are going on there. I think the sense of mystery can't be missed when we simply start trying to explain what it is we are seeing. The sense of mystery comes from seeking physical answers, not spiritual ones. Because what we are trying to do in most of my chemistry classes is understand the way life is put together. That's pretty momentous.

KAREN: You just used the word "mystery," which sometimes pops up in the same conversations as "grace" and "sacrament." Do you mean it to?

SR. ANGELA: I'm a biochemist, and I'm not sure that words like "grace," which is paired with "redemption" in my mind, is a good fit for what we do in biochemistry. Of course I'm not antigrace, but I just think that it makes more sense to talk about "wonder" and "mystery" when what we are doing is trying to explain why things work so well. There's a reason things are put together in our bodies, in animal and plants' bodies, the way they are. If you want to say that this is a sign of God's care, that is perfect, because what the physical evidence demonstrates over and over is that things work. Everything is connected to everything else in some way, and our job as biochemists is to figure out those relationships. We approach these mysteries by asking questions, lots and lots of questions. Because that's what science does. It doesn't provide answers, it asks questions. Things work, and when they don't work correctly, biochemists ask if we can do something about it, by working with things the way they are meant to work.

I tell my students that we come at this work from a point of wonder, not a point of mechanism. For example, we investigate atoms and at first it's like a black box and we want to see what God put into it before hitting the "On" button. So we make a model to see if that explains what we are seeing, and when it doesn't work, that means our model doesn't match what's there. We need a different model to help us understand how things are working, and we make bigger and more interesting mistakes as we are figuring these things out. And I love that, because those bigger mistakes are bigger opportunities for wonder. Because when we *do* make a model that actually seems to explain what is going on inside that atom and then we step back to see what we now think we know . . . well, we have just spent all that time to figure out this tiny little corner of creation and there are now lots more questions and new models to build to see if those match what is going on. This is something I have to communicate to my students who think they are going to get all the answers out of their textbooks: science is about the unknown, whereas textbooks are about the known. A chemist's entire life's quest might end up being two sentences in a textbook, because real chemistry is not about books. It's about the next set of questions and students have to learn that.

KAREN: Sounds like patience is a skill or a disposition that you are teaching along with the facts and the questions.

SR. ANGELA: It sure is, and that is one way to bring sacramentality or wonder into a chemistry classroom. It's a way of seeing, taking the long view. It takes confidence to fail big and it takes faith to keep trying. But teaching students how to fail well is an important aspect of my teaching. They make a lot of mistakes. Their experiments and models don't explain how life works the way they planned them to. I am always telling them that failing is the surest chance of learning, and not to waste a chance to learn by failing to learn from your mistakes.

Let's take something basic, like the transport of information through cell membranes. This happens through receptors made out of molecules I can't even pronounce, by several things happening at once. To explain a mystery like this takes a lot of different perspectives. Many points of view are necessary. So we do a lot of investigations in teams, where students have to start with what they see and explain it in terms that make sense to them and that are defensible to others beholding the same phenomenon. I tell them that a good memory for facts is okay, but arranging those facts into a defensible explanation is infinitely better. We write a lot in my chemistry classes and I try to ask questions that, for the most part, can't be answered by parroting the textbook. I want to stress that it is in no way creative writing; it has to be defensible based on what we can see, not by what we wish we were seeing.

A lot of my students come in with the hope that they can cure cancer. That's a wonderful hope, to save lives. I don't want to stifle that hope, but as a biochemist, I want them to flesh out that hope by being excellent at working with what *is*, right this moment. The first words in the Rule of St. Benedict are to "listen with the ears of your heart," which is fine. But someone told me once that a goal of a university education is to learn to "listen with the ears of your ears and see with the eyes of your eyes," by which he meant that students are in our classes to hone their eyes and ears to notice and comprehend what they are seeing and hearing to the fullest extent possible. In the kinds of problems we explore in chemistry, it takes everybody using their senses and instruments well to be correct, and by correct, I mean defensible, consistent with the data.

KAREN: Describe a specific example of a classroom practice that helps you teach those skills to your students, and how you are able to foster the kind of patience and resilience you are describing. Please.

SR. ANGELA: Before I give one example, I'll say that a common thread in all my assignments and lab activities is insisting that students make their thought processes visible. Remember: our job as chemists is to figure out what is happening and to report that accurately. So let's say we are poking around the world of potassium-sodium ion channels. That is not a static thing. It is an elaborate set of interacting processes. I assign them the task of drawing a model of what they think that situation looks like. They then have to explain why their model makes sense, given all the facts we have acquired from lectures and lab and reading. And they have to link that model and their own argument to another chemical reality. Again, what they are doing is making their thoughts and reasoning very visible. They have to defend those to others who did the same task.

Students are always saying that this makes them think of stuff they never dreamt of on their own, and it almost always leads them to ask more questions and see more possibilities of "correct" answers in the most unexpected places or in the places right in front of their noses: literally, like the student who found herself wondering, after one of our model-building/describing sequences, how many moles of air there are in a typical human breath. Someone else was reading a 1994 Saturn Owner's Manual and got to wondering how much sodium azide it would take to fill up the car's 4-liter airbag. It's those kinds of questions that make me know I am teaching real scientists, not parrots.

KAREN: Do your students get to see your own thinking made visible?

SR. ANGELA: Sure. I show them that all the time. Take my paclitaxel research—which my upper division students are involved with, by the way. I'm up front in my conviction that God puts things together for a reason. I was looking at this one compound in yew trees and wondering why it might be that a plant would produce something—paclitaxel—that could possibly cure human cancers. Could that same chemical be in the plant as a kind of self-protection? What does a plant need to protect itself from? Something in the environment? If this model of explanation works, can we use it or adapt it to a human environment? These questions all have long, intertwined answers that can all be traced back to the premise that God puts things together for a good reason, and those knots can be loosened if we do our biochemistry really well. I'm not afraid to use that language, and my sense has been that students who enroll at a place like ours are not only receptive to that spiritual dimension, they come in expecting it . . . but they also want to learn excellent biochemistry that prepares them for graduate research and medical school. I never apologize for the wonder in my voice when I am explaining something like potassium-sodium ion channels; I really hope that shiver of wonder comes through. I've never had a student complain about it. I have had atheist students say that they sense something different—"something special from the inside out" was the way one person put it—in my courses and labs. It's impossible for me to separate good teaching from spirituality.

KAREN: You've made it clear that a sense of wonder and a willingness to fail often and to fail big are the foundations of anything we want to call a sacramental approach to biochemistry in your classroom and lab. One last question: how do you teach students the resilience necessary to keep moving beyond those failures and keep seeing failures as opportunities to learn?

SR. ANGELA: Look at the set-up immediately to your left hand on my desk there, Karen. There's a big box of Kleenex and a box of cookies. That cookie box opens up in your direction, not mine. You're sitting exactly where students sit when they come in disappointed by a lab result or from bombing an exam. The first reaction has to be one of hospitality, and tending to their immediate need for human comfort.

KAREN: I can feel St. Benedict grinning down at you.

SR. ANGELA: Oh, he's not the only one. You'll notice that right past the Kleenex and cookies is an icon of Hildegard of Bingen. St. Scholastica is here too. Benedictine hospitality is my first rule of interacting with students, especially when they are falling apart. Building human relationships with students is number one, and every failure they experience in my class is an opportunity to build a stronger relationship. Moving beyond that initial disappointment is next. Often, my supersmart students are receiving the first "Cs" of their lives and they have no coping mechanism for dealing with that. But I don't want to show them how to change the "C" into an "A." I want them to wonder about the concept and figure it out, so that they understand, not so they get a better grade. Insisting they show me their thinking means I can help them figure out where their solution went off the rails, where their model breaks down. Those are little cracks where I can squeeze in some new teaching and help them comprehend more deeply. If everyone blows a problem, they'll get another chance to use the same concept on another test. Not the same problem, because that would just reward memorizing, but working through the same concept. When I offer extra credit, I offer it to everybody, and it is immensely challenging work, because everyone deserves a chance to try and solve big, interesting problems. This is all more cyclic than mere repetition, because as their understandings change, they are in different places than they were with their earlier mistakes. I'm in a different place by then, too. Remember: in my discipline our business is to figure out how life is put together. Mistakes are part of our life, so my job is to help students figure out how those fit into some bigger picture, being absolutely convinced that they do. I'll let someone else have the last word on why I go at biochemistry this way, focusing on cultivating wonder and human relationships. It's as simple as this: "that in all things, God may be glorified."

"Finding the Unfamiliar in Familiar Places":[1] The Regis Community-Based Spanish/English Exchange Project; Journeys in Place

Obdulia Castro and Elizabeth Grassi

"Finding the unfamiliar in familiar places" is what students who participate in the Regis Community-Based Spanish/English Exchange Program (CB-SEEP) are asked to do every semester. This program, initially modeled after the Community-Based Spanish Program developed by Dr. Ethel Jorge at Pitzer College,[2] was implemented at our institution with the cooperation of the Regis College Center for Service Learning and two faculty members in two different departments: Modern and Classical Languages, and Education.[3] It was implemented to connect the

[1] Diego Baena, personal communication, 2011. We thank Diego Baena, a self-described wanderer in the spirit of Antonio Machado, for giving us permission to use his words in quotes in this title.

[2] We thank Professor Ethel Jorge and her colleagues at Pitzer College. Pitzer's original idea of having college students visit the home of Hispanic families continues to be at the center of our project, but our implementation and curricular design include important differences, some of which will be addressed in this chapter whenever appropriate.

[3] At Regis, we thank Melissa Nix for believing in this program and offering steady support. We owe great debt to Paul and Rosa Burson for their invaluable contributions to this project and the students and families who participate in the CB-SEEP program. We also extend our appreciation to Tom Reynolds, Patricia Ladewig, and Paul Ewald for their continued support of the CB-SEEP program. Our sincere thanks also go to Gabriela DeRobles for her careful reading of this manuscript. This project was initially funded by two consecutive Regis Sponsored Projects Academic Research Council (SPARC) grants.

assets and knowledge of two different cultural and socioeconomic communities—Regis College students and Latino immigrant families in the Regis community. Through this program, Regis students visit the homes of Hispanic families in the Denver area. The participating families are selected through contacts with local schools that enroll Hispanic children from the university neighborhood. Students are grouped in threes and visit the homes of Hispanic families once a week for two hours. During this time, students participate in the family's daily activities, explore the character of the Regis neighborhood, and discuss issues of importance to immigrant families living in the United States. The first hour of the visit is conducted in Spanish only. The second hour can be conducted in English or Spanish as our students become homework and/or language tutors for the family.

The combination of being exposed to the unfamiliar within apparently familiar surroundings immerses our students in a path of learning and self-discovery that will hopefully prepare them "for living what, following Socrates, we may call 'the examined life.' "[4] In this chapter, we follow our students' paths in an attempt to show the unique road they followed to incorporate transformative experiences. We do this by using direct quotes from journals, reflective essays, interviews, and evaluations done by our students at different stages of the program.[5] It is our hope that, paraphrasing Stephen Crites,[6] the narrative quality of their experiences will add to the larger narrative imagination.[7]

[4] Martha Nussbaum, "The Old Education and the Think Academy," in *Cultivating Humanity: A Classical Defense of Reform in Liberal Education* (Cambridge, MA: Harvard University Press, 1997), 9.

[5] This project was approved by the Institutional Review Board (IRB) of Regis University regarding appropriate use of human subjects, review number: 257-10 (C#039-036). All participants in this project signed consent forms agreeing to have their comments quoted in presentations and publications, provided their anonymity was guaranteed. All students completed anonymous evaluations of the program, and some students agreed to participate in a promotional video and also agreed to be interviewed about their experiences in the program.

[6] Stephen Crites, "The Narrative Quality of Experience," *Journal of the American Academy of Religion* 39 (1971): 291–311.

[7] For more information on "narrative imagination," see Martha Nussbaum, "The Old Education and the Think Academy"; "Democratic Citizenship and the Narrative Imagination," *Yearbook of the National Society for the Study of Education* 107, no. 2 (2008): 143–57; *Not for Profit: Why Democracy Needs the Humanities* (Princeton, NJ: Princeton University Press, 2010); Moira von Wright, "Narrative Imagination and Taking the Perspective of Others," *Studies in Philosophy and Education* 21, nos. 4–5 (July 2002–September 2002): 407–16.

In colleges across the country, the goal of immersing students in diversity, whether it be cultural, social, economic, or linguistic, has usually been attempted through three main different avenues: classroom teaching, study abroad programs, and/or service and community-based learning experiences. The project described here immerses students in "difference" by combining all three of these avenues: the safety of the classroom, the openness of a study abroad program, and a richer and more nuanced view of "service."

Although some parts of this program do take place only within the walls of the classroom, and some take place within a foreignlike setting, they all happen within the assumed and perceived level of safety of the city where our students live. At our institution, we are firm believers in the importance of international experiences and, therefore, strongly encourage our students to participate in study abroad. Nevertheless, some students either cannot afford to do it or choose not to participate. One of the founding goals of the program described here is to give students who are unsure and/or anxious about studying abroad the opportunity to try a somewhat similar experience in a space closer to home. At the same time, this program serves as a reentry point for students who are coming back from international experiences. More often than not, upon returning to their home country, these students experience a sense of not belonging (a kind of reverse culture shock) and struggle to find their bearings. Students coming back from Spanish-speaking countries in particular have a hard time identifying with Hispanic immigrants in the United States while trying to reconnect with American culture.

When students participate in traditional study abroad programs, it is expected that they will experience some sort of culture shock.[8] After all, they are in foreign and, therefore, unfamiliar territory. For CB-SEEP participants' "culture shock" happens in their own backyard, making them feel like foreigners in what is supposed to be familiar territory.

The world of higher education, as most everything else in our so-called postmodern world, deals with contradiction on a daily basis. On the one hand, the walls of academia strive to provide a safe environment where learners can dedicate themselves to the pursuit of pure inquiry without having to be concerned about mundane problems. University campuses,

---

[8] Colleen Ward, "Psychological Theories of Culture Contact and Their Implications for Intercultural Training and Interventions," in *Handbook of Intercultural Training*, 3rd ed., ed. Dan Landis, Janet M. Bennett, and Milton J. Bennett (Thousand Oaks, CA: Sage, 2003), 185–216.

especially in the United States, aspire to offer a monastic-like refuge from daily worries in order to provide the appropriate medium for immersion in the pursuit of knowledge. On the other hand, pressing issues related to the use and abuse of privilege in the world today make it imperative that learners be exposed to this reality before they join the "real world." At Regis University, in an attempt to provide students with the opportunity to be citizens of a larger and more inclusive community,[9] we developed the Regis CB-SEEP. We implemented this program at our campus to provide students with opportunities to leave their comfortable and/or familiar surroundings and experience "otherness."[10]

Participation in this program has allowed our students to venture outside of the classroom walls and establish unique relationships with neighbors they would not have met were it not for this project. At the same time, students are able to come back to the safety of their regular classrooms to compare experiences with their classmates and professors.

Program Methodology and Ignatian Pedagogy

Based initially in the life and teachings of Ignatius of Loyola, expressed in his *Spiritual Exercises*,[11] the 1599 *Ratio Studiorum*[12] developed a pedagogical vision revisited by The International Commission on the Apostolate of Jesuit Education (ICAJE) in 1993.[13] The methodology used in

---

[9] Nussbaum, "The Old Education and the Think Academy"; "Democratic Citizenship and the Narrative Imagination"; *Not for Profit*.

[10] Fean-François Staszak, "Other/Otherness," *International Encyclopedia of Human Geography* (Amsterdam, Netherlands: Elsevier, 2008).

[11] Ignatius of Loyola, *The Spiritual Exercises*, trans. Elder Mullan (New York: P. J. Kenedy & Sons, Printers to the Holy Apostolic See, 1914). Published as PDF-document by ixtmedia.com, the Digital Catholic Bookstore: http://www.jesuit.org/jesuits/wp-content/uploads/The-Spiritual-Exercises-.pdf.

[12] *Ratio Studiorum: The Official Plan for Jesuit Education* (*Ratio atque Institutio Studiorum Societatis Iesu*), trans. Claude Pavur (Saint Louis, MO: Institute of Jesuit Resources, 2005). *Ratio atque Institutio Studiorum Societatis Iesu*, vol. 5, *Monumenta Paedagogica Societatis Iesu*, ed. Ladislaus Lukàcs. Vol. 129 of the series *Monumenta Historica Societatis Iesu*, 357–54 (Rome: Institutum Historicum Societatis Iesu, 1986).

[13] International Commission on the Apostolate of Jesuit Education (ICAJE), *Ignatian Pedagogy: A Practical Approach* (World Union of Jesuit Alumni, 1993).

the implementation of the CB-SEEP incorporates the three main elements in Ignatian Pedagogy: experience, reflection, and action.[14]

Experience, the first element of Ignatian Pedagogy, can be vicarious or direct. In most classrooms, we expose our students to vicarious experiences by getting them to interact with texts, ideas, facts, and/or imaginations. It is assumed that by vicariously reading about the experiences of others, they can begin to understand different perspectives, therefore, developing their narrative imagination.[15] We can also offer students access to direct experiences by using hands-on activities, service and/or community-based learning, and immersion opportunities such as study abroad.[16]

The second element in Ignatian Pedagogy, reflection, gives students the opportunity to create meaning and show knowledge acquisition and personal growth. It is only after careful reflection that students can really understand what was learned and integrate it into their lives. We hope that after reflection, students will be moved into action, the third element in Ignatian Pedagogy, with the intent on making choices and acting on them for the greater good.

Prior to the three previous elements, at the beginning of the learning process, the Ignatian Pedagogy Paradigm also asks instructors to pay careful attention to the learning context to make sure that experience, reflection, and action can take place. When looking at the learning context, we need to pay attention to the student's previous knowledge and life experience. We also need to look at the learning situation: the environment where learning is supposed to take place together with the social, political, historical, and/or educational realities surrounding the student and the learning environment.

Within Ignatian Pedagogy there is also one more aspect that needs to be included: evaluation, an objective way to assess if learning has taken place and, if so, what was learned. As we were putting together the design elements of the project described here, we decided to be very

[14] These elements also resonate in Paulo Freire's "Pedagogy of the Oppressed." See Paulo Freire, *Education as the Practice of Freedom* in *Education for Critical Consciousness* (New York: Continuum, 1973); and *Pedagogy of the Oppressed* (Harmondsworth: Penguin, 1972).

[15] See Nussbaum, "The Old Education and the Think Academy"; "Democratic Citizenship and the Narrative Imagination"; *Not for Profit*; and von Wright, "Narrative Imagination and Taking the Perspective of Others."

[16] George D. Kuh, Jillian Kinzie, John H. Schuh, and Elizabeth J. Whitt, *Student Success in College: Creating Conditions That Matter* (San Francisco: Jossey-Bass, 2005).

intentional about our program's goals. Therefore, from the beginning, we established a research and assessment program to have a clear idea of what this program was doing for our students and our community as we followed them in their journey through this experience. As recommended in Pascarella and Terenzini[17] and Pascarella[18] we wanted to assess how and why exposure to diversity would affect our students' learning while collecting both quantitative and qualitative data to compare results.[19]

Program Implementation

Students in the Education Department of Regis College participate in this program as a requirement for one of their classes, whereas participation is voluntary for students enrolled in Spanish classes at all levels. Those students who choose to participate have to follow specific guidelines determined by course and level. All Education and Spanish students participating in the program are required to write a weekly journal, or reflective essay entries describing and reflecting on their experiences with the families. Spanish students share their experiences in Spanish with their classmates either in class and/or on an online discussion board, conduct formal oral presentations, and write a formal final paper reflecting on their experiences in the program. They are expected to write their journal entries and/or reflections in Spanish. Education students reflect weekly in class discussions in English where they connect their experiences with the families to educational theory and future classroom teaching of immigrant students. In their journals, all students are asked to describe their experience, discuss any new learning, and note any feelings/challenges they experienced.

[17] Ernest T. Pascarella and Patrick T. Terenzini, *How College Affects Students: A Third Decade of Research* (San Francisco, CA: Jossey-Bass, 2005).

[18] Ernest T. Pascarella, "How College Affects Students: Ten Directions for Future Research," *Journal of College Student Development* (2006): 508–20.

[19] See Elizabeth Grassi and Obdulia Castro, "Learning from Our Neighbors: Teachers Studying 'Abroad' with Local Immigrant Families," *AccELLerate! Quarterly Review of the National Clearinghouse for English Language Acquisition* 4, no. 1 (2011): 10–12, for more specific details and results of this research project.

Program Beginnings: Two Worlds Apart

Regis College is located on a beautiful and serene small campus. It can be described as an island in the middle of urban sprawl: a fitting space for a Jesuit university. But students here only ventured to the "other side" of the street to catch the bus. They never went inside the ever-present Hispanic restaurants or clearly Hispanic-owned businesses in the area. The campus is a well-protected bubble that keeps the students separate and safe from the world around them. Students were afraid to venture into the neighborhood, terrified to cross Federal Boulevard: "Federal Boulevard is Mexico" a friend from the Canary Islands said when being shown around Denver. For most of our students, Federal Blvd. is indeed a different country. It is next door, they see it from campus, and they travel through it to get to and from school, yet it is far and foreign. When we told our students how excited we were about all the restaurants and businesses around campus and asked them for references to good places to eat or shop, they told us they never visited any of these places. It was then that we realized how far apart these two worlds were. We needed to find a way to allow these two parallel words to intersect and, if possible, come together.

Finding the Unfamiliar in Familiar Places: Initial Program Design

After attending a workshop at the 2005 American Association of Teachers of Spanish and Portuguese (AATSP) National Conference in New York and having been offered the opportunity to visit, observe, and learn from the community-based program designed and organized by Dr. Ethel Jorge at Pitzer College, the idea of organizing something similar at Regis started to take shape. Dr. Jorge's invitation to visit and observe her program at Pitzer coupled with the opportunity to participate in Collegium at St. John's University during the summer of 2006 offered the luxury and privilege of having the time to put together the final touches of our vision. By the fall of 2006, we piloted the first offering of what was then called the Regis Community-Based Culture and Language Acquisition Project (CB-CLA).[20]

---

[20] Obdulia Castro and Elizabeth Grassi, "The Community-Based Cultural and Linguistic Acquisition Project," *The Voice of Hispanic Higher Education* 15, no. 3 (2006): 4–5.

We were fortunate to have two faculty members in two different departments, Spanish and Education, who were interested in implementing this program as an intrinsic part of their classes as well as the support of the Center for Service Learning at our institution willing to put together the necessary resources to coordinate the program. With this infrastructure in place, we proceeded to design and research what is presently known as the Community-Based Spanish English Exchange Program (CB-SEEP);[21] a program that has been integral to both the Spanish and Education departments for the last seven years.

Why This Program? Why Now? Rationale for Implementation

Due to rapidly changing demographics in the foreign language student population, Spanish departments in the United States are faced with new challenges.[22] The ever-increasing numbers of native Spanish speakers within the US territory have created a community of speakers who are a valuable resource to the study of Spanish as a second language, but at the same time are in great need of maintaining and/or developing literacy in both their native and second languages. This project, by putting together Hispanic families with college students, has sparked interest in language study and higher education for children in these families.

The 'teaching and learning' literature emphasizes the need for experiences beyond the classroom and the need for a diverse community.[23] By being exposed to the realities faced by Hispanic communities in the United States, our students have a unique insight into a different component of the wider and complex set of Spanish/Hispanic cultures. This immersion experience allows students to establish connections and make comparisons within a multicultural environment in their own backyard.[24]

---

[21] Elizabeth Grassi and Obdulia Castro, "Learning from Our Neighbors," 10–12.

[22] Kim Potowski,"Experiences of Spanish Heritage Speakers in University Foreign Language Courses and Implications for Teacher Training," *Association of Departments of Foreign Languages Bulletin*, 2002. http://www.adfl.org/bulletin/V33N3/333035 .htm.

[23] Kuh, et al., *Student Success in College*, 308.

[24] The American Council of Teachers of Foreign Languages (ACTFL) has identified five standards for foreign language teaching known as the five Cs: Communication, Cultures, Connections, Comparisons, and Communities (ACTFL 1996, 1998, 2006). http://www.actfl.org/publications/all/national-standards-foreign-language -education.

Demographic shifts of teachers and students in this country require teachers in our public schools not only to value cultures and languages other than their own but to actively collaborate with culturally and linguistically diverse students, their families, and their communities. By placing our preservice teachers in this program, we have found that our teachers learn manners of communicating with the "other" and actively work to bridge the gap between teachers, students, and communities in our local public schools.

This local immersion program has also provided a bridge between language studies in the United States and abroad. It has provided baseline orientation for students going to study abroad in Spanish-speaking countries as well as a reinsertion opportunity for students coming back from study abroad.

This project has taken our classrooms into the neighborhood and the neighborhood into our classrooms. We have found that, through participation in this project, our students go through all the stages of a deep process of transformation.

Pathways to Transformation: Reflections on Student Journal Entries, Interviews, and Evaluations

Facing the Unfamiliar: Anxiety and Disorientation

> I painted my nails so I would look nice when I met my family. When I was sitting talking with J., I started picking my nail polish off because I was so nervous. I am not one to pick at my nails, especially right after I have painted them—but I was so nervous I developed a new habit.
>
> —Student participant, first reflective essay[25]

This quote indicates that this student is experiencing something very powerful, but she does not have an appropriate way to react to it. She does not know why she is feeling this way. She can only attest to her feelings. We find a sense of what she is experiencing in the words of another student who had already participated in not one, but two study abroad programs before participating in the CB-SEEP:

[25] Only quotes from students who gave informed consent allowing the researchers to use their written materials have been included in this paper. Any names used in student quotes are pseudonyms.

It's been profound. Before I left the country I had the idea of foreign
as something different, something you had to take a plane or a pretty
long bus ride to get there, but now you realize they live down the
street from your university.

—Student participant interview

"Foreign" is expected to be "different" and we are supposed to experience "difference" in foreign places, but we do not expect that to
happen in our own backyard. That "plane trip" or "long bus ride" provides a needed point of transition from the familiar to the unfamiliar.
Whether long or short, that transition provides a resettling of the senses
and a self-awareness that we are moving from the "same" to the "other."
This "time in between" allows us to explain away any uncomfortable
feeling of not belonging and gives us reasonable excuses for not behav-
ing properly. Also, when we prepare for a trip abroad, we go through
what sometimes looks like an infinite number of required rituals: visa,
vaccinations, passport, prescriptions, packing, etc. In order to be ready
for that "long ride" we make sure we are ready to leave the familiar for
a specific amount of time and prepare accordingly.

The students who participate in our program are not given an opportunity of a period of transition. They go from their natural surroundings to a foreign environment without the time and space in between
provided by a plane trip or a long bus ride. We provide an orientation
to give participants a sense of what to expect, but they go from this
orientation in a familiar room within the college to (for some of them)
across the street to an unfamiliar situation. Without transition, they find
themselves lost and disoriented in a new environment. Their language
is taken away from them. They do not know how to behave or how to
react. If the students have taken a language class, they may be familiar
with some of these feelings. However, when they are in class, they know
it is a class, they know they are in a safe and choreographed environment
where making mistakes is encouraged. In the house of our participating
families, students are far from anything perceived as "previously choreographed." This newfound environment is real, and they are expected
to respond and perform in real time.

When students study abroad, culture shock often happens after a short
period of time, days or weeks. However, for the CB-SEEP students culture shock happens immediately, within the first five minutes. For our
students, life cannot possibly be that different across the street. This
difference is not expected, and our students are thrown into culture shock
the moment they enter the families' houses.

The surprise of encountering the unfamiliar in familiar spaces is what our students share in their diaries and reflective essays at the beginning of the experience.

> I literally left the house with a headache and feeling sick to my stomach. I believe I felt this way because I was out of my comfort zone. I didn't know what to say (because I don't know Spanish that well) I didn't know how to act (because I don't know their customs) and all I wanted to do was cry because I was so frustrated.[26]
>
> —Student participant, first reflective essay

Study-abroad students have attested to this level of discomfort, especially students who have not taken language classes before. The feeling of not having the ability to use words to make oneself understood is clearly overwhelming. Nevertheless, there is something else underneath all of this. In the first language-learning process, we are capable of developing the ability to communicate in a natural and safe place. As first language learners, we have the support of our culture as we go through the process. Indeed, the language we learn first is filled with all the nuances of that culture. The sense of powerlessness students experience when they cannot communicate using their native language is compounded and related to the fact that they also lack the knowledge of how to behave in a different culture. When this happens to students in a foreign country, it is, somehow, easier to understand. After all, they are in a "foreign country" where situations are expected to be different and strange. But when it happens in one's own backyard, our students confront something not only unexpected but unexplainable.

As humans, we tend to develop a sense of security about the world around us and the things we are capable of doing. Finding out that all of that can be taken away in a moment, makes us feel uncomfortable and insecure. Coming to terms with our frailty is disconcerting and sends us in a downward spiral. However, this disorienting sensation is a necessary and integral pathway to transformation. Indeed, it reflects a notion of "sacramentality" as presented in Himes,[27] where the visible reality serves as a launching point to unveil a deeper reality that would remain

---

[26] As cited in Grassi and Castro, "Learning from Our Neighbors," 10; and Joan Armon and Elizabeth Grassi, "Developing Justice-Oriented Teachers," *Jesuit Higher Education* 1, no. 2 (2012): 73.

[27] Michael Himes, "Finding God in All Things: A Sacramental Worldview and Its Effects," *As Leaven in the World*, ed. Thomas Landy (Franklin, WI: Sheed & Ward, 2001).

unknown if we were not confronted with diverse human experiences. We need to get out of our comfort zone to get to know others while learning about our own culture and ourselves.

Changing Places

> In the first hour of our visit we are only allowed to speak Spanish, and while I know a little I felt very out of place. It was very apparent that in that situation I was the one that needed to be taught and had a very difficult time learning.
>
> —Student participant, first reflective essay

In most service learning situations, students go in with the sense that they are in power and they are there to provide a service to someone in need or to teach something to someone who needs help learning.[28] When meeting the families and being asked to speak only Spanish for the first hour, our students quickly realize that it is the families who will teach them and that what they need to learn is not going to be as easy as they thought. In the process, both groups become subjects in the learning context.[29] This sense of surprise about who does the teaching and who does the learning works both ways. The following comment from a young boy, member of one of the participating families, is eye opening:

> Era interesante estar con personas más grandes que estaban interesados en aprender algo que tú ya sabes. (It was interesting to be with older people who were interested in learning something that you already know.)
>
> —Young boy from a participating family, interview

For this young boy, who is accustomed to having older people teach him, having this group of students needing and wanting to learn something he already knows, this is the first time he ever thought about his own resources. In this exchange program, the ones accustomed to giving (the "haves") become the ones in need of receiving, and the ones accustomed to needing (the "have nots") realize they have something valuable to

---

[28] Grassi and Castro, "Learning from Our Neighbors," 10.

[29] Paulo Freire, "Education As the Practice of Freedom," *Education for Critical Consciousness*, ed. Paulo Freire (New York: Continuum, 1973).

give. This young boy's father expresses the sense of learning from each other:

> Me gustó mucho la experiencia porque pudimos aprender nosotros también de ellas como ellas aprendieron de nosotros. (I liked the experience very much because we were able to learn from them in the same way they learned from us.)
>
> —Participating father, interview

The first encounter at the family's home is unnerving for our students. They are guests in this family's house: a family that, under normal circumstances, our students would have never had the opportunity to meet, let alone be invited into their home. This constitutes a true role reversal situation. The "haves" become the "learners" and those accustomed to being labeled as the ones who "need service," provide invaluable service to our university students.

Some Sense of Comfort and Commonality

Not knowing what to expect, being afraid of an unfamiliar environment, and not having the linguistic tools necessary to communicate, make students feel they do not belong, but soon enough they start to reach a comfort zone:

> I first was really nervous. Now they are like my second family in Denver.
>
> —Student participant, interview

As the visits progress we see a clear change in our students' perspectives. This interdisciplinary and multicultural/multilingual program initiates a paradigm shift in our students' perception of the "other" and leads our students through a journey of discovery. In the process, our students have managed to allow "the other" into their hearts.

There is no longer a feeling of awkwardness because specific cultural norms have now been acquired, and they are now comfortable with each other. Everyday activities, like setting the table, have gone from specific cultural peculiarities to the common set of actions happening in every house. The relationship has gone from one of difference to one of commonality. Our students and the families may belong to different cultures, but they have found a common ground.

The next step in their intercultural development is to recognize that although they come from different worlds and respond automatically to different symbols, they can accept, adapt, and integrate each other's ideas. Michael Bennett's Development Model of Intercultural Sensitivity helps explain the stages of the process our students are going through.[30] This theory sees the development of intercultural sensitivity as a continuum where learners move from ethnocentric to ethnorelative worldviews. Ethnocentric worldviews include stages such as "denial," where cultural differences are not identified as something real; "defense," where some cultural differences are identified but other cultures are considered as not safe to our own culture; and "reversal" where other cultures are seen as better than ours. After the ethnocentric period, learners move into a somewhat transitional stage called "minimization." In this stage of the continuum, learners are aware that cultural differences do exist, but tend to emphasize commonalities and "minimize" differences. Learners have moved into ethnorelative stages when they show signs of "acceptance," where they are capable of not only recognizing but also accepting cultural differences. In the following stages, "adaptation" and "integration," learners are also capable of modifying their behavior to adapt and integrate cultural differences. Students participating in our project have gone from the initial stages of denial and defense/reversal to minimization in quite a short time span. They still need to dig deeper to get at substantial differences while learning how to integrate them into their own cultural sensibility.

Some of our students are able to integrate and adapt when higher-level differences are encountered, but a majority remain at minimization. This is a good place to be when compared with a vast majority of human beings, who seldom move across the continuum. Nevertheless, our students still need to be able to accept the fact that, as humans, we might confront the same circumstances, but we will all react differently, we are all intrinsically different; we are not exact copies of each other: we are not the "same." Although journal reflections and assessment measures have allowed us to see these changes in our students, the results also tell us that we need to intentionally design specific activities geared at looking

---

[30] Michael J. Bennett, "A Developmental Approach to Training for Intercultural Sensitivity," *International Journal of Intercultural Relations* 10 (1986): 179–96; "Towards Ethnorelativism: A Developmental Model of Intercultural Sensitivity," *Education for the Intercultural Experience*, ed. R. M. Paige (Yarmouth, ME: Intercultural Press, 1993), 27–71.

at difference more in depth to help our students move to higher levels of adaptation and integration of cultural differences.

Empathy

> She works in a part time job in which she is told that she is only allowed to speak English. Therefore, she admitted that she is a "mute" at work.
>
> —Student participant, first visit

The first day they visit their host family most of our students experience how it feels not to have the linguistic and cultural competencies to be able to communicate. While experiencing this lack of abilities themselves, our students can relate with the difficulty this woman encounters every day at work. Our students now have the sensitivity to understand what it means exactly to have been dispossessed of language: to have their communicative abilities taken away. They still do not have a complete understanding of what it means to feel like you have no choice because you need the work to support your family, but they are getting closer.

A Deeper Understanding

As a result of these experiences, understanding, previously alien to our students, starts to develop:

> I've never studied abroad, so this is the closest I have ever felt to "culture shock." I can't imagine how nerve racking it must be to come to another country, not knowing the language, not knowing the societal rules, and not knowing how you were going to support your family. Visiting with my family gave me a very real understanding of how difficult it is to come into this country and try to live.
>
> —Student participant, third reflective essay

It is quite revealing that this student does not say "the family" or "this family" he says "my family." This group of people is no longer alien. Our students have acquired a new dimension of immigration and immigrants. Their perspective does not reflect the typical version of "needy people," "trouble makers," or people who come to this country to "take away jobs," or "break the law." Their new perspective looks at immigrants' struggles and how difficult it is to make a living when you do not know the language and have a family to support. Realizing that this is more common than what they had previously thought is very powerful.

> Coming from a foreign country experience where you are the foreigner, you realize how big that is. And now being back in the States you realize that no matter where you are in the US there are thousands of people going through the same experience. They live down the street from my university. They are everywhere. It's awesome how diverse Denver is.
>
> —Student participant, interview

The Invisible Becomes Visible

Being a foreigner in a foreign land can be difficult. This difficulty is caused, among other things, by the sense that life is considered to be easier when we are surrounded by sameness. It is somehow surprising to find this perspective of foreignness in the United States: a country of immigrants.

> I leave that house and they give me CDs of Mariachi music. Here is this guy from Denver who did not know any better five years ago, jamming Mariachi and cruising down Federal. This whole integral experience within what you know as home for people who did not necessarily were born here, don't speak the language. It's mindboggling and when I am with them, even though I am in Denver. I've been raised in Denver, and with all their friends, now I feel like the foreigner. This dynamic is just infinite how many possibilities of mixes you can make with relationships and people and realizing how small you are in that whole connection. It's just incredible.[31]
>
> —Student participant, interview

This student has discovered a side of "home" he did not know was there. He used to walk past it without noticing its existence. These people and this world were invisible to him. However, by visiting the families, he has adapted to a new world and has integrated it by "cruising down Federal" listening to mariachi music but still feels like a foreigner. This feeling refers not to his inability to adapt, but to his awareness and integration of the "other's" cultural differences while being able to maintain his own.

---

[31] All quotes from students are literal transcriptions from English, or literal translations from Spanish.

> The greatest thing about this—especially in a university with the demographics Regis has—is that it is opening up the consciousness of all the students as to what reality can look like: it's an expansion of understanding the community of people of the US and just how you build relationships with people who are completely different from you. You are dealing with human relationships, with people.
>
> —Student participant, interview

Teachers Becoming Learners

Student participants in the CB-SEEP develop an authentic love of learning inspired by the newly acquired awareness of the situation.

> It's about learning. You don't have to do the assignment just because it is for class you do it because you are building relationships with people.
>
> —Student participant, interview

Consequently, they are ready to transfer that love to their students as they prepare to provide challenging opportunities for them.

> They don't know the language, the "cultura," but learning has to happen. Learning from different people; students immersed in the experience of learning. Being comfortable with challenge and making students comfortable with challenge and push them and support in that direction.
>
> —Student participant, interview

This student participant, a future teacher, has discovered that learning does not happen in prepackaged lessons to be repeated endlessly. Learning happens when we are able and open to learn from different groups, from different styles, and from different environments. This future teacher understands the challenges and is willing to face those challenges and have his students grow from them, while he keeps growing at the same time.

> I think these visits show me how important, fun, valuable, etc. a family visit could and would be as a teacher. I want to get to know the people I am going to teach. I want to know how they make dinner, the fun that goes into it. The joy that comes at knowing you have created something. I want to know how they eat together, how they

talk over dinner, how they clean up together. I think that there is some essential learning in eating a meal together that cannot and will not be gathered simply from a classroom.

—Student participant, third reflective essay

We can see in the words above an expression of the need for eucharistic engagement. The need to experience communion together becomes part of the student's transformational journey. At the same time, we also see the motivation to become members of a shared community and a commitment to help each other.

As the Spanish family has shown me, I need to live as a type of cultural broker. It becomes my responsibility to reach out to families and make sure that they know they can come to me with questions. It is also my responsibility to make sure that their children learn the "American" culture and way of doing things while still embracing their own culture.[32]

—Student participant, third reflective essay

Stereotypes Change

I think being from a diverse background sometimes carried a bad connotation in school but I can see how smart these children really are and there is a lot more to it than I realized.

—Student participant, first reflective essay

To see how intrinsically our identification of "difference" is associated with negative ideas of "not as good," "not standard," "not as smart" is a big step in the process of understanding culturally different groups. For this student, the realization that diversity is not equated with "not being smart" is a huge undertaking. To actually realize "how smart these children are" constitutes a huge leap from previously preconceived notions.

For some reason young Mexican mothers seem to have an unfair stereotype about not being good moms. She [the mother], on the other hand, obviously cares very much about her children's education and wants to make the journey with them.

—Student participant, first reflective essay

[32] Also cited in Grassi and Castro, "Learning from Our Neighbors," 11.

This comment shows us that the student is challenging her preconceived stereotypes of young Mexican mothers. The family experience allows her to see a reality that contradicts her previous perceptions. The next step for this student will be to ask herself where the stereotypes originated in her own culture; by doing so she will get closer to a non-polarizing conceptualization of "difference."

The "Other" Becomes "Us," and a Deep Transformation Happens

> I have always thought that I am "helping" the M. family, (. . .) and that I am bringing something to the table to better their lives. Going to the house more and more I am seeing that I am learning just as much as they are, probably more.
>
> —Student participant, third reflective essay

It is only through human interaction that transformation can happen. Bernard Cooke talked about the experiential component of sacraments as being the base of their transformative power.[33] "Fundamentally, sacraments are human experiences that transform our perspectives, meaning, and action."[34] There are countless ways of providing a service to others but just a few where a profound interaction with the "other" allows us to acquire a knowledge of humanity that would be otherwise invisible.

> I think back on all the cultural walls and language differences that separated "me" from "them." Now the words "me" from "them" sound harsh and cold because the family is no longer the other, rather they are an intricate part of the culture that makes America so great. The experience gave me a perspective on another culture that I commonly critiqued and allowed me to look at my own culture and critique it.[35]
>
> —Student participant, last reflective essay

This student has not only been able to see the commonalities with the "other," but she is now ready to contrast and compare the peculiarities

---

[33] Bernard Cooke, *Sacraments and* Sacramentality, rev. ed. (Mystic, CT: Twenty Third Publications, 1994).

[34] Barbara J. Fleischer and Gerald M. Fagin, "The Sacramentality of Friendship and Its Implications for Ministry," In *A Sacramental Life: A Festschrift Honoring Bernard Cooke,* ed. Michael Horace Barnes and William P. Roberts (Milwaukee, WI: Marquette University Press, 2003), 231–51.

[35] Also quoted in Grassi and Castro, "Learning from Our Neighbors," 11; and Armon and Grassi, "Developing Justice-Oriented Teachers," 74.

of the family's culture to her own and learn from the differences. This student has been able to identify the innate goodness in difference. Now she can look back at her own culture with a better understanding of its principles and behaviors.

> My personal beliefs have been changed because it is no longer a faceless "other" that is suffering; it is my family that lives in fear and is treated as less than. It is crucial that all people be confronted with the reality of racism in the world today.
>
> —Student participant, fourth reflective essay

The "other" has become "my family." This communion with the other and profound knowledge of the other has brought up a feeling of love and a cry for social justice.[36] This student is now ready to begin identifying areas for needed change and find proactive ways to make it happen. Hopefully, she will be part of the solution, not the problem.

The following student summed up very well the achievements of this program:

> I derive great self-satisfaction from this process because I genuinely love the experience, not particularly because it is a "service," but more on the basis of the great relationships you establish. (. . .) This summer I am going to help my Spanish brother apply to college. What a privilege! To pass on knowledge I have acquired through my time here, and in turn, to learn from an amazing group of people.
>
> —Student participant, program evaluation

This student, like many others in this project, had the opportunity to identify himself as part of a group while establishing relationships with another as an individual. In this process, he came to understand a different but similar world and found a way to make connections. It is in this "dealing with human relationships" where our students encounter the essence of sacramentality. Bernard Cooke represented human friendship as the Basic Sacrament.[37] Developing strong relationships with a previously unfamiliar group made the invisible visible and transcendent for our students. According to Himes "the whole sacramental life is a

---

[36] See Armon and Grassi, "Developing Justice-Oriented Teachers."
[37] Bernard Cooke, *Sacraments and Sacramentality*.

training to be beholders."[38] By uncovering the unfamiliar in familiar places, our students were given the gift of grace to become "sacramental beholders."[39]

The student above was able to make clear contributions to this newfound world. However, these contributions did not come through as charity, handouts, or a contribution made only once to a faceless other. Rather, this was a thank you–like response: "You have given me so much; it is only natural that I give you something in return." There is a sense of self-transcendence or self-reflexive insight that points to spiritual recognition. He is now able to see the world with the eyes of his heart. He allows himself to be affected by unique experiences that give him new insight.

Giving Something Back

Besides making clear individual progress as indicated by trend analysis and assessment results, our students have also contributed to the world they visited. We have found that one of the biggest contributions our students make to the families is their presence in their house as university students. Our students spend a lot of time answering questions and explaining the "rules of the game" for college admission to the families. They have also brought the families on campus to show them around.

> You have to teach them the "secret rules." You realize that there is a crisis about minority students in the area and you realize that they are not because they are not smart, but because they don't know the rules.
>
> —Student participant, interview

We have found that this program has evolved into a true exchange— our students learn to be more compassionate human beings, and the families gain the cultural capital they need to negotiate a system they long to be involved in. In the end, both groups gained a more profound understanding of shared humanity.

---

[38] Himes, "Finding God in All Things," 100.
[39] Ibid.

"Do unto Others"[40]

At the end of the program, our students experience a feeling of elation because they sense they have been given a gift. The relationships established are an act of grace, a unique experience our students will take with them the rest of their lives. It will help them connect with others. It will take them away from their individual selves, from their self-selected groups, and make them part of a bigger group; similar but different. The meeting of these two groups once a week for ten weeks takes on a dimension of a sacramental communicative act. Sharing food, words, problems, sentiments, music, games, jokes . . . becomes the gift of sharing humanity. The principle of "do unto others . . ." is no longer a command, but instead it has been appropriated as a personal desire to share the goodness. One of our students said it very well:

> I hope I am doing as much for them as they are doing for me.[41]
>
> —Student participant, interview

Bibliography

Armon, Joan, et al. "Developing Justice-Oriented Teachers: Personal Transformation through Relationships." *Jesuit Higher Education* 1, no. 1 (2012): 101–7.

Armon, Joan, and Elizabeth Grassi. "Developing Justice-Oriented Teachers." *Jesuit Higher Education* 1, no. 2 (2012): 72–81.

Bennett, M. J. "A Developmental Approach to Training for Intercultural Sensitivity." *International Journal of Intercultural Relations* 10 (1986): 179–96.

———. "Towards Ethnorelativism: A Developmental Model of Intercultural Sensitivity." In *Education for the Intercultural Experience*, edited by R. M. Paige, 27–71. Yarmouth, ME: Intercultural Press, 1993.

Castro, Obdulia, and Elizabeth Grassi. "The Community-Based Cultural and Linguistic Acquisition Project." *The Voice of Hispanic Higher Education* 15, no. 3 (2006): 4–5.

Chauvet, Louis Marie. *The Sacraments: The Word of God at the Mercy of the Body*. Collegeville, MN: Liturgical Press, 2001.

---

[40] Matthew 7:12.
[41] Also quoted in Grassi and Castro, "Learning from Our Neighbors," 11.

Cooke, Bernard: *Sacraments and Sacramentality*. Rev. ed. Mystic, CT: Twenty Third Publications, 1994.

Crites, Stephen. "The Narrative Quality of Experience." *Journal of the American Academy of Religion* 39 (1971): 291–311.

Fleischer, Barbara J., and Gerald Fagin. "The Sacramentality of Friendship and Its Implications for Ministry." *A Sacramental Life: A Festschrift Honoring Bernard Cooke*. Edited by Michael Horace Barnes and William P. Roberts. Milwaukee, WI: Marquette University Press, 2003. 231–51.

Freire, Paulo. *Education as the Practice of Freedom*. In *Education for Critical Consciousness*. New York: Continuum, 1973.

———. *Pedagogy of the Oppressed*. Harmondsworth: Penguin, 1972.

Grassi, Elizabeth, and Obdulia Castro. "Learning from Our Neighbors: Teachers Studying 'Abroad' with Local Immigrant Families." *AccELLerate! Quarterly Review of the National Clearinghouse for English Language Acquisition* 4, no. 1 (2011): 10–12.

Hammer, M. R., M. J. Bennett, and R. Wiseman. "The Intercultural Development Inventory: A Measure of Intercultural Sensitivity." In *International Journal of Intercultural Relations*. Guest edited by Michael Paige. 7, no. 4 (2003): 421–43.

Himes, Michael. "Living Conversation: Higher Education in a Catholic Context." *Conversations in Higher Jesuit Education* 8 (Fall 1995).

———. "Finding God in All Things: A Sacramental Worldview and Its Effects." In *As Leaven in the World*. Edited by Thomas Landy. Franklin, WI: Sheed & Ward, 2001.

International Commission on the Apostolate of Jesuit Education (ICAJE). *Ignatian Pedagogy: A Practical Approach*. World Union of Jesuit Alumni, 1993.

Jorge, Ethel. "The Intergenerational Aspects of an Undergraduate Community-Based Spanish Learning Program." *Journal of Intergenerational Relationships* 9, no. 3 (August 2011).

———. "Assessing the Value of a Community-Based Approach to Language and Cultural Learning: A Longitudinal Study." *Journal of Scholarship of Teaching and Learning* 11, no. 1 (January 2011).

———. "Where's the Community?" *Hispania* 93, no. 1 (March 2010).

———. "Moving beyond the Classroom: Creating Community-Based Learning Opportunities to Enhance Language Learning." *Hispania* 91, no. 1 (March 2008).

————. "Community-Based Spanish Language and Culture Program." In *First-Year Civic Engagement: Sound Foundations for College, Citizenship and Democracy*. Edited by Martha J. Labare. New York: *New York Times* and The National Resource Center for the First-Year Experience and Students in Transition, 2007.

————. "Outcomes for Community Partners in an Unmediated Service-Learning Program." *Michigan Journal of Community Service Learning* 10, no. 1 (Fall 2003): 28–38.

Kuh, G. D., J. Kinzie, J. H. Schuh, E. J. Whitt, and Associates. *Student Success in College: Creating Conditions That Matter*. San Francisco: Jossey-Bass, 2005.

López, Sylvia, and Richard Raschio. "The Latino Connection: Designing Service-Learning Programs for Community-Enhanced Language Learning." A workshop co-presented at the AATSP Annual Conference, New York, July–August 2005.

Minnesota Language Proficiency Assessment (Listening, Spanish). Minneapolis: Regents University of Minnesota, 2000.

Nussbaum, Martha. "The Old Education and the Think Academy." In *Cultivating Humanity: A Classical Defense of Reform in Liberal Education*. Cambridge, MA: Harvard University Press, 1997.

————. "Democratic Citizenship and the Narrative Imagination." In *Yearbook of the National Society for the Study of Education* (2008). Chapter 10: 107: 143–57. doi: 10.1111/j.1744-7984.2008.00138.x.

————. *Not for Profit: Why Democracy Needs the Humanities*. Princeton, NJ: Princeton University Press, 2010.

Pascarella, Ernest T. "How College Affects Students: Ten Directions for Future Research." *Journal of College Student Development* (2006): 508–20.

Pascarella, Ernest T., and P. T. Terenzini. *How College Affects Students*. Vol. 2, *A Third Decade of Research*. San Francisco: Jossey-Bass, 2005.

Potowski, Kim. "Experiences of Spanish Heritage Speakers in University Foreign Language Courses and Implications for Teacher Training." *Association of Departments of Foreign Languages Bulletin*, 2002. http://www.adfl.org/bulletin/V33N3/333035.htm.

Ratio atque Institutio Studiorum Societatis Iesu. Volume 5 of the *Monumenta Paedagogica Societatis Iesu*. Edited by Ladislaus Lukàcs. Volume 129 of the series *Monumenta Historica Societatis Iesu*, 357–454. Rome: Institutum Historicum Societatis Iesu, 1986.

Ratio Studiorum: The Official Plan for Jesuit Education (*Ratio atque Institutio Studiorum Societatis Iesu*). Translated by Claude Pavur. Saint Louis: Institute of Jesuit Resources, 2005.

Ricoeur, Paul. *Figuring the Sacred: Religion, Narrative, and Imagination*. Translated by David Pellauer. Edited by Mark I. Wallace. Minneapolis, MN: Fortress Press, 1995.

Staszak, Fean-François. "Other/Otherness." In *International Encyclopedia of Human Geography*. Amsterdam, Netherlands: Elsevier, 2008.

Stoddart, Eric. "Spirituality and Citizenship: Sacramentality in a Parable." *Theological Studies* 68 (2007).

Tilley-Lubbs, Gresilda A., Richard Raschio, Ethel Jorge, and Sylvia López. "Service-Learning: Taking Language Learning into the Real World." *Hispania* 88, no. 1 (March 2005): 160–67.

Von Wright, Moira. "Narrative Imagination and Taking the Perspective of Others." *Studies in Philosophy and Education* 21, nos. 4–5 (July–September 2002): 407–16.

Ward, Colleen. "Psychological Theories of Culture Contact and Their Implications for Intercultural Training and Interventions." In *Handbook of Intercultural Training*, 3rd ed., edited by Dan Landis, Janet M. Bennett, and Milton J. Bennett, 185–216. Thousand Oaks, CA: Sage, 2003.

Ward, Colleen, Stephen Bochner, and Adrian Furnham. *The Psychology of Culture Shock*, 2nd ed. Philadelphia, PA: Routledge, 2001.

Dialogues of Discernment:
Science for Social Justice

Audrey A. Friedman

Overview

Each person's *vocational discernment journey* navigates and negotiates multiple pathways as well as critical and not-so-critical episodes and intersections that inform how one comes to develop, warrant, and justify knowledge claims about academic, personal, and spiritual dilemmas in the context of commitment to self, others, and society writ large. Critical reflection essential to effective personal discernment and cognizance of God in all things demands recursive examination of the significant and seemingly mundane episodes that occur throughout one's life journey and explicit analyses of the connectedness of these personal, academic, and spiritual episodes. This discussion describes the effectiveness of a significant pedagogical strategy, "Dialogue Journals" implemented in a senior "capstone" seminar, Science for Social Justice. Students worked through several iterations of nine journals/dialogues that addressed how significant personal relationships, special "work" experiences, physical/health situations, social alliances/allegiances, unexpected events, episodes of spiritual clarity and wisdom, dreams, and roads not taken culminating in a final reflection that identified significant patterns of influence in their journey of discernment and seeing God in all things.

Discerning Self via Discerning God in All Things

In explaining Augustine's theology of grace, Donald Burt observes, "Left to themselves, humans can only sin. This is so not simply because they need instruction on what to do, but even more because they need the power to delight in and to love the things of God."[1] Grace, for Augustine, is the freedom of God to love beyond human understanding or control. In essence, we need God to see God. Robert Barron further elaborates the necessity of this power in reaching *ordo*—social order—which leads to peace. "Augustine insists that when such a God is worshipped, a fundamentally different form of social order comes into existence, one based upon connection, compassion, forgiveness, and nonviolence."[2] It is only when we truly see our connection with all, genuinely feel compassion for all, selflessly forgive all, and peacefully coexist with all, that we reach a social and political plane of order that improves the human condition and creates God's "community of relationality."[3]

Yet humankind's nature to sin and serve self makes it difficult to accept and use essential grace to see God in all things. Buddhists have long since interrogated the problem that plagued Augustine: humankind's "bondage to ego-clinging and vice, which prevents an ethical response."[4] It is this bondage to an erroneous perception/construction of self that causes us to "misreact to others unawares, reacting to our projections instead of to persons. We thereby contribute moment by moment, in little or big ways, to the communal cocreation of a world of fear, confusion, greed, and violence."[5] Open, authentic, unbiased, and selfless interactions with others also dispose one toward developing epistemic cognition, which can lead to higher stages of reflective judgment.

St. Augustine and St. Ignatius: In Service of Others through Action

Augustinian and Ignatian spirituality are grounded in a community of compassion, forgiveness, relationality, and action. In both, actions speak volumes; deeds triumph over words; others replace self. Like Augustine, Ignatius believed that God could be found in all things and

---

[1] Donald X. Burt, *Augustine's World: An Introduction into His Speculative Philosophy* (Lanham, MD: University Press, 1996), 151.

[2] Robert Barron, "Augustine's Questions: Why the Augustinian Theology of God Matters Today," *Logos: A Journal of Catholic Thought and Culture* 10, no. 4 (2007): 51.

[3] Ibid., 45.

[4] John Maransky, "Buddhist Analogues of Sin and Grace: A Dialogue with Augustine," *Thagaste Symposium, Center for Augustinian Study Merrimack College* (2001), 4.

[5] Ibid.

that by serving others and immersing ourselves in the continuum of the human condition, we would become more fully human, enabling others to realize their own humanity. Being a person for others extends far beyond simple service but is instantiated in the belief that service, grounded in faith and a belief that God exists in all things, enriches our understanding of how all humankind is part of God's plan for the world. This understanding is critical to teaching, living, and acting for social justice, a tenet of Jesuit teachings and student formation.

Intellectual, Social, and Spiritual Dimensions of Student Formation

Student formation in the Jesuit context nurtures three dimensions: intellectual, social, and spiritual. Rigorous inquiry into the essential questions of the discipline not only exposes enduring understandings of the discipline but also develops an intellectually curious habit of mind that can deepen one's passion for subject. Intellectual inquiry accompanied by critical reflection leads to epistemic cognition, an ability to reason about ill-defined, moral-cognitive dilemmas through rigorous and systematic evaluation of evidence, expertise, and experience, resulting in genuine consideration of multiple perspectives across multiple contexts. The intellectual dimension expands openness and understanding, hones talents and abilities, and connects us to intellectual traditions, past and present, sustaining a critical awareness beyond self.

Although the social dimension certainly encompasses day-to-day relationships in students' lives, the goal of this aspect of formation is to challenge preconceived notions of and prejudices about the "other," to develop adults who use intellect and talents to improve the life chances of the disenfranchised, and to create a community grounded in collaboration, compassion, and selflessness, a community of men and women for others.

Inherent in the developmental journey is the mission to find meaning and relevance in the old and the new. Critiquing prior beliefs, experiences, and upbringing, and assimilating new beliefs and experiences into a developing worldview has a spiritual dimension in the Jesuit context. For students who come from a faith-based perspective, experiences that help them process and interrogate beliefs will hopefully deepen spiritual maturity and commitment to faith and community. For others, "discovering how to live authentically in the world"[6] is part of formation's spiritual mission.

Coalescence of these dimensions leads to discerning citizens who work to live authentically in the world, see God's existence in all things, understand their relationality with others in genuine community, and commit their passions and talents to helping others—especially the marginalized—realize their own humanity in a just way. In a university setting, context and pedagogy are critical to nurturing such coalescence. The following discussion describes the effectiveness of one significant pedagogical strategy implemented in a senior capstone seminar, Science for Social Justice: Dialogue Journals in Promoting Discernment, Formation, and the Coalescence of the Intellectual, Social, and Spiritual Dimensions.

Context: Science for Social Justice, A Capstone Experience

In the capstone tradition, Science for Social Justice is a seminar offered to seniors with the goals of vocational discernment through critical reflection about commitment to self, others, career, society "writ large," and spirituality. Identifying the various ways individuals come to warrant and justify knowledge claims in decision-making about academics, moral-cognitive dilemmas, relationships, and spirituality, students explore critical events, personal talents, gifts, passions, and their commitment to social justice and the enhancement of life chances of others.

Seeing God in all things and being a person for others through genuine action require complex thinking that challenges personal assumptions, considers and evaluates multiple perspectives across multiple contexts, connects us to intellectual traditions, past and present, and ultimately sustains a critical awareness beyond self. Thus, knowing and understanding are dynamic processes that change as individuals develop and modify worldviews toward interdependence and interconnectedness.

Pedagogy: Dialogue Journals

Although coursework integrated dialogue journals, debates, visualizations, and silent conversations, the following discussion focuses on one pedagogical strategy: dialogue journals. The pedagogy is described and

---

[6] *Journey into Adulthood: Understanding Student Formation*, Intersections Program (Boston: Boston College, 2007): 11.

elaborated using students' responses. These responses are analyzed in the context of Augustinian and Ignatian precepts.

Ira Progoff observed, "spiritual contact is the awareness of the profounder meanings of life which can only be experienced in the silence of privacy"[7] and that one of the most effective ways of exploring "life's meanings" was through intensive journaling. Intensive journaling not only deepens one's awareness of self but also enhances one's ability to interrogate assumptions, explore passions, and consider self in relation to others. As a result, Progoff developed an intensive journal system, a series of dialogue journals, in which persons explore and interrogate critical and mundane events and memories.

As part of students' journey to develop intellectually, spiritually, and relationally, students completed dialogue journals, to which I responded with probing questions and comments in the effort to promote more rigorous inquiry, not only into the event but also into its relationship to deepening spiritual maturity and commitment to faith and community. Most students explored each question through three to five iterative journals, which addressed but were not limited to questions such as:

1. How have you come to believe this?

2. What evidence do you have to support your claim?

3. What specifically challenged you about . . . ?

4. If you assumed the perspective of . . . how might your inferences change?

5. Why do you think you made that choice at that point in your life?

6. What are other ways to look at this?

7. How do you think . . . viewed this event?

8. What assumptions are you making about . . . ?

9. What biases and preconceived notions informed your analysis of this experience?

10. What specific examples of change in your thinking about . . . can you provide?

11. What did you learn about yourself as a result?

12. What did you learn about others as a result?

[7] Ira Progoff, *At a Journal Workshop: Writing to Access the Power of the Unconscious and Evoke Creative Ability* (New York: Penguin, 1992), 5.

13. Why do you believe . . . thinks and acts the way s/he does?

14. What different or similar action might you take at this point in your life?

Additional comments asked for elaboration, detail, and more analytical and evaluative thinking.

Dialogues, Descriptions, and Analysis of Responses

The following discussion identifies specific dialogue prompts and specific excerpts from students' dialogues and offers analyses of these responses in light of how students' reflections demonstrate how they see God in all things. The students' names are pseudonyms.

1. Dialogue with Person: *What were/are the significant events or relationships with persons that have impacted your vocational discernment? Focus not only on the dramatic relationships and abrupt changes in your life, but examine also the everyday relationships that have marked your journey.*

Ruth identified her internship experience in Ghana and specifically her mentors Adwoa and Charity as people who challenged her assumptions about others and moved her toward serving and finding God and goodness in others. She observed, "There is much to be thankful for and appreciated about Ghana. I was blessed to have Adwoa keep me from indulging in my attitude of American exceptionalism when I was frustrated at some of the cultural differences I encountered." Recognizing that self-indulgent arrogance and materialism clouded her ability to see Ghana and its cultural differences as beautiful, Ruth took a critical step in expanding the complexity of her worldview and affirming goodness in the cultural other. "Moved" by Charity, a woman who "had lost her job due to a deteriorating immune system (HIV) and who despite her misfortune wowed her community with her continued strength and perseverance, caring for ailing family and community members," Ruth developed a "sense of purpose to learn how [she] could serve others like Charity" and returned to Africa after graduation. This critical experience forced Ruth to negotiate what Tillich calls the "tension between estrangement and participation, which leads to authentic ultimate concern."[8]

---

[8] Paul Tillich, *The Dynamics of Faith* (New York: Harper & Row, 1957), 116.

Mandy acknowledged, "I had never understood the purpose of faith but exposure to the Jesuits and their inspiring link between faith, learning, and service and other students who had similar ideals inspired me to continue to seek a life that would do good in the context of a social justice-driven career." It was in a philosophy course, Values in Social Services and Healthcare, where Mandy was exposed to speakers who ran nonprofits, established a school system in the Sudan, or worked in a Haitian orphanage. "Their stories opened my eyes to the many ways I could do good in the world." As a result, she too decided to serve in Ghana for a semester. Although Mandy entered college with the goal of becoming a physician, she realized significant ways she could "serve others, doctor or not." Learning and serving in community with others clarified her understanding of faith and intensified her relationality to others. Tisdell (2000) observes that when teachers who taught and acted for social justice experienced critical or challenging events, they suffered "grief moments," which eventually became "graced moments."[9]

Seth commented that, "Emulating the characteristics I admire in others is a way that I have been trying to learn about and appreciate others," in particular, his grandfather. "By far the friendliest and most outgoing person I know. He never has a mean word to say about anyone, and wherever he goes he always manages to find a new friend." Inspired by his example, Seth's goal was to be able "to strike up a sincere and meaningful conversation with a stranger off the street." Although simple and personal, Seth recognized and appreciated his grandfather's genuine sense of authenticity. Conversation with strangers suggests an openness to difference, a willingness to hear others' perspectives, and a realization of complexity: qualities that expand one's worldview and acceptance of others.

2. Dialogue with Works: *What were the external activities that became a focus for you, or held inner meaning for you during this period of vocational discernment? These may be projects or works that were completed, begun but not completed, or planned but never actually started.*

Zach worked in South Korea during summer vacation of his sophomore year. He helped out at a "daycare" center located in a Red Light District next to a US army base. In essence, this was "night care" for children of prostitutes. Although he helped out only a short while, his

---

[9] Elizabeth J. Tisdell, "Spirituality and Emancipatory Adult Education in Women Adult Educators for Social Change," *Adult Education Quarterly* 50 (2000): 322.

time there "helped [him] see the harsh reality of these children's lives, and that even through all the hardships they had to endure, these children laughed and smiled like any other child." Finding this behavior uplifting and encouraging, Zach eventually served as a camp counselor for children from broken homes. Admitting that he was "in over his head, twenty-four-seven," he attributed these experiences as influencing his goal to become a pediatrician. Upon graduation, Zach returned to South Korea to teach English to native South Korean children. As a result of this sudden turn in his discernment journey, Zach discovered a passion to improve the lives of others, especially children. Purposefully seeking out experiences that challenged personal biases and beliefs, Zach developed empathy and understanding, enabling him to see beauty in harsh reality and connect "with the largeness of life."[10]

Much to his surprise, Peter found his experience as a teaching assistant in freshman chemistry to be an agent of change in his perspective about learning. "Creating the open-ended lab experiment that I experienced in general chemistry as a sophomore opened my eyes about the relationship between teaching and learning." Peter required students to design their own experiments to address a specific problem, participating in a completely open-ended performance assessment. "Students and I were able to learn from our mistakes: they redesigned their experiments; I redesigned my teaching." This example suggests collaboration and relationality, a willingness to modify self to help others. Teaching is an act of ultimate concern and requires service to others to develop self-fulfillment. Peter's self-inquiry, which led to modification in order to serve his students more effectively, reflects Tillich's definition of ultimate concern: "the interdependency of agape (service to others) and eros (self-fulfillment)."[11]

3. Dialogue with the Body: *What were/are the occurrences or situations that were especially related to the physical aspects of your life? These may include illness, health programs, athletics, sexuality, drugs, indulgences or addictions of any kind.*

Noah acknowledged, "I have been blessed with a healthy, working body and I think because of my heart surgery I am able to appreciate

---

[10] Parker Palmer, *Let Your Life Speak: Listening for the Voice of Vocation* (San Francisco, CA: Jossey-Bass, 1999), 8.

[11] Tillich, *The Dynamics of Faith*, 118.

that fully." Born with a congenital birth defect that resulted in four car-
diac abnormalities, Noah must have surgery every twelve to fifteen years,
but as he has aged, people have inquired more and more about his health,
demonstrating fear and concern. Although his condition has forced him
to alter his lifestyle, he observes, "I am thankful that modern medicine
has allowed me to lead such a normal life, where even just decades prior
I could have been dead by the age of one." He comments that "in the
grand scheme of things, it could be so much worse so I don't take that
for granted." Noah has not only learned to accept "self" as fortunate
rather than handicapped but also accepts others' fear and concern as
gestures of kindness and care.

Body image and ambition often make students lose sight of what is
important. Experiencing the "jeers and bullying that comes with being
the short guy" firsthand, Stephen constantly grappled with body image
throughout high school and participated in athletics to "enhance his
image." Stephen's wish to compete in the state wrestling championships
during high school was realized at the expense of his health. Succumbing
to "an incredibly unhealthy diet and essentially starving [himself],"
Stephen tipped the scales at 112 pounds after losing one-sixth of his body
weight. He observes, "Blinded by ambition I made the wrong decision.
I looked incredibly skinny both on and off the wrestling mat, and comments from my friends and teachers about how unhealthy I looked became a part of my daily routine." This decision seriously impacted his
life on and off the mat. He lost the title, endured failing health, was
generally unhappy, but more importantly lost faith in himself. Interrogating this experience five years later, Stephen recognized that much of
his self-worth was embedded in society's construct of beauty and success.
During a third iteration of this dialogue journal Stephen shared, "Something that I think might surprise you is the fact that I have a cross, which
I designed myself, tattooed on my right upper back to remind me not to
get too caught up in my own life and to always be conscious of others."
When asked what motivated this action, Stephen reiterated what he
considered the most poignant tenet of his faith: "remembering Jesus'
message of communal interconnectedness and concern for others."

4. Dialogue with Society: *During the periods discussed in Dialogue 3, did
you deepen or diminish your relation to groups or institutions that have a
fundamental connection to your existence? Consider your allegiances to political
party, country, or religion. Are you redefining your identification with race,
family, or social group? Were there events that posed serious questions to personal*

commitment to academics, others, institutions? During this time did you become deeply involved in literary, scientific, or art works that forced a profound consideration of human existence?

What is intriguing about students' responses to Dialogue with Society is that all but one probed their relationship to *religion*. Ben's response is the most illustrative of how these young men and women were grappling with "organized religion." In most entries, students observed the more personal nature of this dialogue. That all discussed their relationship to religion instead of politics, clubs, or service trips, suggests that grappling with faith was significant. Of course the very nature of capstone may have elicited this response, but as other choices were provided, this theme, which is representative of stages of faith, is more apparent.

Ben began, "I must preface this by saying that these topics certainly get more personal! However, I have no problem discussing the disillusionment I have progressively developed over the past few years with the religious tradition of my family: Catholicism." Ben noted that there is an "inextricable link between religion and history and politics" and questions whether or not, due in part to the church's ambiguous teachings, it is the "Church rather than God or Jesus" that has had "a pivotal role in peoples' lives." He observed that "God loves everyone, but if someone 'commits' homosexual acts, he will have sinned" and what "the Church did to hide what is terribly wrong is reprehensible." Ben concluded that "the most important person is the one right next to you," and that "We believe that a man died in order to save an entire people. The argument is not whether or not the story is true, but how we can live a life of sacrifice just like Him." Astley might describe Ben's grappling with religious teachings as reflective of an emerging sense of maturity and autonomy or what Fowler would call Stage 4: "Individuative-Reflective Faith."[12] Ben is overtly evaluating what he has been taught and attempting to take responsibility for his commitments and beliefs, but there is a hint of arrogance in his response. What is critical, however, is that Ben recognizes that he is responsible for the "person next to him" and that "living a life of sacrifice" is essential to his self-worth.

[12] Jeff Astley, *Empirical Theology in Texts and Tables: Qualitative, Quantitative and Comparative Perspectives* (Leiden, Netherlands: Brill, 2009), 11.

5. Dialogue with Events: *What unexpected or unexplained events have occurred in your life? Describe the situations when you felt that life was testing you with pain, physical accidents, pleasure, or unusual good fortune. What were the difficult or challenging, inner or outer pressures that forced you to grapple with problems of human existence?*

Students discussed events that created dissonance in their lives rather than positive or pleasurable episodes. What is telling is that most students worked to transform these challenging experiences into authentic concern. Anna identified her father's alcoholism as a "source of a lot of anger and strain in my relationship with him." Assuming limited responsibility as a father even before her parents' divorce, he relied on her sister and her to make him happy; thus, Anna decided that it was her responsibility "to set her own personal development in motion." Yet in response to "his incredible loneliness and depression, [she] struggled to mask [her] anger and maintain a relationship with him based on compassion." The summer before Anna's senior year, her dad took her out for ice cream and admitted his addiction and began a first step to rehab. Anna marked this as the "first chapter of honesty" between them, and although she is still angry, this event taught her "the importance of family and loving those who are suffering even when it is the most difficult thing you could imagine doing. Human existence is marred by imperfections." Himes observes that, "God's love is like a verb. It is to find and appreciate God in all things. Therefore, God is what is done, not the one who does it, nor the one to whom it is done. God is the doing, the loving."[13] Despite her anger and pain, Anna exemplifies finding God in relationship based on authentic concern.

The stress and self-doubt Lisa experienced in a particularly difficult premed course load was exacerbated by the death of her grandmother, which she recounts caused a profound "downward emotional spiral." Kairos and Companion retreats, which helped her overcome that stress, came at precisely the right time to turn her tough year around. She states, "It could be so-called 'good fortune,' but I believe that God had a hand in those crucial experiences because He knew that I really needed them to learn how to handle such stress and unhappiness." Lisa's thinking reflects the union of agape and eros. By participating in God's community

---

[13] Michael Himes, "Living Conversation," *Conversations on Jesuit Education* 8, no. 1 (1995): 17, accessed October 11, 2013, http://epublications.marquette.edu/conversations/vol8/iss1/5.

(Kairos and Companion Retreats), Lisa realized fulfillment through interdependence and recognized these experiences as God's grace(ious) "hand in those crucial experiences."

6. *Dialogue with Inner Wisdom and Spirituality:* *What experiences do you recall in which you recognized a profound truth of human existence that was new to you at the time? You may not have reached an ultimate answer, but what question persists in your thoughts? What persons played a critical role in deepening or challenging your thoughts and feelings? Were there persons with whom you had direct contact or works that challenged your beliefs, values, and understanding? Or were there persons whose reality is beyond history in the symbolism of religion or philosophy?*

Cynthia, a biologist, grounded her responses to these questions in a quotation that appeared in an assigned reading: "Most people wake up in the morning trying to reduce what they have to worry about. Environmentalists wake up trying to increase it" (Michael Shellenberger, *The Death of Environmentalism*). Cyntha writes, "In an evolutionary sense his quote says, people prioritize what they need to do to survive. You can fight evolution, which is why it is profound when an individual goes out of his or her way to take on another individual's worries." What Cynthia suggests is that despite humankind's innate need to survive, it is "these acts of generosity, this altruism that makes us human."

In our struggle to survive and evolve, Cynthia elaborates that even though other people's worries and hardships may not threaten our personal survival, it is "devoting energy to something that doesn't promote our survival that is the profound truth of *human* existence." When probed as to why she thought some humans responded in this way, she observed: "I think spirituality is what makes us more than just organisms that are struggling to survive. The soul and body *are* inextricably linked but they are also distinct parts. So we are both spiritual beings and biological organisms." Of all students' dialogues, Cynthia's is the most complex as she finds a critical theme that integrates a quotation, belief in evolution, human acts of kindness and compassion, and behavior counterintuitive to personal survival to assume others' worries that she identifies as spirituality. Her reasoning, although primarily grounded in evolutionary biology (one perspective), suggests movement toward reflective thinking as she identifies humans as biological organisms driven to survive, but then assimilates spirituality into her view, attributing acts of human kindness and compassion and assumption of others' worries as profoundly human and spiritual. Her thinking connects past, present, and future and ultimately reflects a critical awareness beyond self.

7. *Dialogue with Dreams Past and Present:* *Do you remember dreams that impacted you in a strong way or dreams that you could not forget? In retrospect did these dreams have any prophetic value? Did they make you change behavior in any way?*

Although as a facilitator I found this dialogue's focus incongruent, I was surprised by a theme that pervaded most responses: dreams (or nightmares) enhanced appreciation of family and closeness to others. Frank reports a recurring nightmare in which he dreams that his little brother is dying. "This nightmare would make me so upset. As a result, I was more protective of my little brother." In a subsequent iteration, Frank recalled that this dream impacted his frame of mind, as he flipped out when an older kid in the neighborhood was bullying his little brother. Jenna echoed a similar reaction to a dream in which she dropped a pen which rolled into the street. When her dad chased after the pen into the street, a car hit and killed him. She remembers that this dream seemed so real at the time that "she woke up in tears and in a terrible state of panic." Upon analysis, she recognized that "this dream in general just made me appreciate my family a lot more. I was in such a terrible state thinking that one of them had died and it really shocked me into knowing how much they mean to me." Ben observes that a dream of betrayal gave him "incredible angst" reminding him "of how important a friend is to [him] and how important it is not to betray others." Realizing the importance of immediate community and their connectedness to community, students recognized interdependence with family and friends, an initial step toward valuing and connecting to the larger community.

8. *Dialogue with Roads Not Taken:* *Have you come to crossroads of decision-making that impacted the course of future events in a fundamental way? Were these decisions that you made or actions that you failed to take? Were there decisions that were forced upon you rather than within your discretion? In either case, the fact that you took one road meant that another was not pursued. Has this untaken road remained a possibility of life that has not been lived?*

Ruth observes that after returning from Ghana it was "clear that further decision making was out of my control and best left alone." So determined to return to Africa she decided to forego acceptance to law school and to pursue a Fulbright to Malawi, which she received. For Ruth, the initial road taken had led her to other roads that she had to take. Although this dialogue does not directly address spirituality, it suggests that Ruth's return to Africa addresses a sociocultural dimension of spirituality. Fueled by mission like the teachers in Tisdell's study, Ruth integrated her spirituality with her work for social change in Africa; her decision emerged from her service to others which enabled self-fulfillment, causing her to reject what she called "profound parental and peer pressure to pursue law," a road she would definitely not take. For Ruth, ultimate concern and authentic faith are identical.

Stephen seriously regrets a road not taken but acknowledges that this mistake prepared him to seize a similar road later in college. "One choice that I wish I had made differently during my freshman year at BC is my decision not to go on a forty-eight hour retreat, but on the bright side, I have been selected to attend BC's Kairos Retreat. Kairos is an experience that allows us to share our fears and hopes in a supportive, spiritual, and compassionate community." As retreat members often do not know each other, this unfamiliarity can enhance one's vulnerability, but God's love is found in relationship, and therefore in authentic ultimate concern, discovered in authentic loving communion between people. Stephen's refusal to take a potentially significant road in his life later caused him to seize a second chance to explore an even more critical path.

Authentic Ultimate Concern

Authentic ultimate concern creates tension between participation and estrangement, which in turn creates a dynamic of true faith. "Without some participation in the object of one's ultimate concern, it is not possible to be concerned about it."[14] In large and small ways, these students more often than not opted for "participation." Putting aside her views of American exceptionalism, a variable of estrangement, Ruth worked to appreciate cultural difference and focused her energy on finding ways to participate in the work of her Ghanaian mentors. Returning to Malawi deepened her commitment to others, allowing her to integrate more fully the sociocultural dimension of her spirituality with a mission of social change. Zach's experience working in "night care for children of prostitutes," in South Korea suggests an innate sense of participation, but

---

[14] Tillich, *The Dynamics of Faith*, 116.

interrogating that experience enabled him to set aside preconceived notions of intellectual estrangement. Assuming that children of prostitutes could only be unhappy given their harsh surroundings, Zach learned that despite the hardships they endured, "these children laughed and smiled like any other child." While participation is commendable, participation without genuine respect for, interconnectedness with, and relationality to others suggests a mission of rescue rather than a mission of ultimate concern. Understanding and appreciating the resilience of these children, Zach moved on to working with children from broken homes, even though he was "in over his head, twenty-four-seven." No longer intellectually estranged, but truly empathetic and cognizant, Zach saw beauty in harsh reality and connected "with the largeness of life."[15] Stories of representatives from nonprofits, Sudan schools, and a Haitian orphanage, opened Mandy's eyes to the many ways [she] could do good in the world." Learning and serving in community with others clarified her understanding of faith and intensified her relationality to others. Mandy also went to Ghana to manifest her faith and commitment. Although humans are "endlessly caught in a web of decisions among partial goods,"[16] these students took the risk of "discerning the good and acting upon it insofar as you can see the good, knowing that you never see it with perfect clarity."[17]

Community and Interconnectedness

Tillich notes that when humans give themselves to others for the benefit of the community, they derive self-fulfillment because they are truly participating in God's community. Authentic love derives from the unity of agape (self-surrender) and eros (self-fulfillment). Naturally, service experiences offer students rich opportunities to interact with others in community, but often students enter these experiences as self-perceived rescuers or saviors, believing that their mission is to elevate the status of those they serve, suggesting that they are in a position of dominance. What is critical about these experiences, however, is that they hopefully become events of authentic interconnectedness and community, where members learn to leave the comfort of personal frames

[15] Palmer, *Let Your Life Speak: Listening for the Voice of Vocation*, 8.
[16] Himes, "Living Conversation," 60.
[17] Ibid.

of reference and social contexts and act differently in their personal and professional lives. For these students, community was found in several venues and places.

Lisa found support and understanding though Kairos and Compassion Retreats. They lifted her from "an emotional downward spiral" and offered a sounding board to examine personal vocational discernment. Stephen viewed his forthcoming Kairos as a place "to share fears and hopes in a supportive, spiritual, and compassionate community." Ruth observed that the call to return to Africa was so powerful it essentially took decision-making out of her hands, moving her to give herself away for the benefit of the community, simultaneously providing her fulfillment, demonstrating authentic faith. Zach's initial experience in South Korea set him on a search for interconnectedness and community. From "night care" to "campus counseling for children from broken homes," to "teaching English in South Korea," Zach's involvement has become more personal, more connected, and more communal, reinforcing his decision not to become a pediatrician at this time, but rather to deepen the relationship between agape and eros.

Becoming More Knowing in the Genuine Sense

Recognizing goodness in others requires one to interrogate and challenge personal biases and beliefs. Cynthia not only interrogates premises of survival of the fittest in evolutionary biology but also observes that despite humankind's innate need to survive, it is "these acts of generosity, this altruism that makes us human." Noting that, "devoting energy to something that doesn't promote our survival is the profound truth of *human* existence." Cynthia reasons at a complex level, integrating concepts of biology, acts of compassion, human existence, the soul, body, and spirituality. Her worldview reflects a more developed way of knowing and a genuine commitment to seeing goodness in others. Her thinking connects past, present, and future and ultimately reflects a critical awareness beyond self. Likewise Anna's renewed connection to her alcoholic father suggests clear growth and change. Understanding that humans are imperfect, Anna's realization that loving family and those who are truly suffering (her father) was most important, she negotiated her anger, becoming more knowing and accepting. Ruth's autonomy was demonstrated by a decision to forego acceptance to law school to pursue a Fulbright to Malawi, thereby rejecting "profound parental and peer pressure to pursue law." Ruth's return to Africa not only addresses a sociocultural dimension of spirituality but also a commitment to making the most justifiable decision based on dimensions of spirituality, service, faith, and fulfillment.

Conclusion

Discerning self requires discerning God in all things. It is only when we truly see our connection with all, genuinely feel compassion for all, selflessly forgive all, and peacefully coexist with all, that we reach a social and political plane of order that improves the human condition and creates God's "community of relationality."[18] Throughout this capstone experience, students interrogated beliefs, actions, relationships, events, and experiences. Open, authentic, unbiased, and selfless interactions with others disposed them to develop epistemic cognition, leading to higher levels of complex reasoning. Although not all students articulated the role of faith and spirituality in their lives or engaged with others to the degree we would desire for all of us, their actions were grounded in community, compassion, forgiveness, action, and relationality. Serving others and immersing themselves in the continuum of the human condition, they began and continued their journey to become more fully human and to enable others to realize their own humanity.

Formation is grounded in spiritual, social, and intellectual dimensions. As people for others, these students' involvement extended far beyond simple service but was instantiated in the belief that service, grounded in faith and a belief that God exists in all things, enriched their understanding of how all humankind is part of God's plan for the world.

Bibliography

Astley, Jeff. *Empirical Theology in Texts and Tables: Qualitative, Quantitative and Comparative Perspectives*. Leiden: Brill, 2009.

Barron, Robert. (2007). "Augustine's Questions: Why the Augustinian theology of God Matters Today." *Logos: A Journal of Catholic Thought and Culture* 10, no. 4 (2007): 35–54.

[18] Barron, "Augustine's Questions," 45.

Boston College Intersections Program. *Journey into Adulthood: Understanding Student Formation*. 2007.

Burt, Donald X. *Augustine's World: An Introduction to His Speculative Philosophy*. Lanham, MD: University Press, 1996.

Hansen, David T. "Teaching and the Sense of Vocation." *Educational Theory* 44 (1994): 259–75.

Himes, Michael. "Living Conversation." *Conversations on Jesuit Education* 8, no. 1 (1995). Available at: http://epublications.marquette.edu/conversations /vol8/iss1/5. Accessed 8 July 2011.

King, Patricia, and Karen S. Kitchener. *The Development of Reflective Judgment: Theory, Research, and Educational Applications*. San Francisco, CA: Jossey-Bass, 1994.

Maransky, John. *Buddhist Analogues of Sin and Grace: A Dialogue with Augustine*. Thagaste Symposium, Center for Augustinian Study Merrimack College from which this essay issued, 2001.

Palmer, Parker. J. *Let Your Life Speak: Listening for the Voice of Vocation*. San Francisco, CA: Jossey-Bass. 1999.

Progoff, Ira. *At a Journal Workshop: Writing to Access the Power of the Unconscious and Evoke Creative Ability*. New York: Penguin, 1975/1995.

Tillich, Paul. *The Dynamics of Faith*. New York: Harper & Row, 1957.

Tisdell, Elizabeth J. "Spirituality and Emancipatory Adult Education in Women Adult Educators for Social Change." *Adult Education Quarterly* 50 (2000): 308–35.

Cultivating Empathy and Mindfulness: Religious Praxis[1]

Angela Kim Harkins

One of the goals of Jesuit education is to transform students into men and women for others. My hope is that the courses that I teach contribute in meaningful ways to this end. Teaching is a ministry that challenges me to meet my students where they are and equip them with the skills to be authentic persons in a changing and religiously diverse world. I designed the following journal assignment to create experiential-learning moments of religious praxis that will give students a glimpse of meditation and mindfulness and ultimately an opportunity for reflection and transformation. The journal assignment asks students to take on a religious practice and to be committed to it for a week while abstaining from distracting forms of social technology. This assignment is designed to cultivate empathy among college students for diverse expressions of religion in America and offers a small taste of the different religious practices that foster mindfulness—practices that students report to be especially challenging.

One of the difficulties of teaching religious studies is that students come into the class with many assumptions and expectations about religion that are based on their everyday experience of the world. Students today are "plugged-in" to the world of social media and technology and juggle many different roles and responsibilities. This context develops habits of perception that can make learning about religion challenging

[1] This essay is dedicated to all of my students from fall 2010. I am grateful for their openness to learning about religion.

because it encourages an expectation that religious practices, like a switch on a computer, produce an instantaneous effect. This assumption is difficult for students to unlearn. I designed this assignment to help students examine their assumptions about religion and to invite them to learn experientially that mindfulness, like a habit, is a way of being that is cultivated over a long period of time. Meditation and contemplation are not switches that can be turned on and off, and spirituality cannot be downloaded and accessed instantaneously. The human person is formed into these religious habits of mindfulness through embodied practices.

The assignment described in this essay asks students to reflect upon how practices in the ordinary material world can be a site for religious experience.[2] The operative premise is that for the major religious traditions that are discussed in the course, e.g., Christianity, Judaism, and Islam, the bodily performance of religious practices serves in profound ways to cultivate and generate religious individuals. Amy Hollywood writes, "[i]t is through bodily practices that subjectivities are formed, virtues inculcated, and beliefs embodied."[3] This theoretical point is difficult for students to grasp, many of whom hold onto an outdated notion of Cartesian dualism of the mind and the body operating independently from one another—in such a model, oftentimes what is imagined is that belief happens first and then the body follows suit.[4] Stated otherwise, religious praxis, that is, reiterated performative ritual practices, generate spiritual and religious subjectivities. Students are invited to learn this experientially by engaging their ordinary world through praxis, ulti-

---

[2] Joanna E. Ziegler, "Practice Makes Reception: The Role of Contemplative Ritual in Approaching Art," in *As Leaven in the World: Catholic Perspectives on Faith, Vocation, and the Intellectual Life*, ed. Thomas M. Landy (Franklin, WI: Sheed & Ward, 2001), 31–42.

[3] Amy Hollywood, "Towards a Feminist Philosophy of Ritual and Bodily Practice," in *Difference in Philosophy of Religion*, ed. Philip Goodchild (Aldershot, UK: Ashgate, 2003), 73–83. This theoretical point is related to theoretical poststructuralist understandings of subjectivity and citationality, and performance studies associated with Jacques Derrida.

[4] Ritual practices that engage the body and arouse the emotions can be understood within this context as generating religious subjectivities. On the relationship between the "mind and body," understood as cognition and emotion, see Justin Storbeck and Gerald L. Clore, "On the Interdependence of Cognition and Emotion," *Cognition and Emotion* 21 (2007): 1212–37; and Antonio Damasio, *Looking for Spinoza: Joy, Sorrow, and the Feeling Brain* (New York: Harcourt, 2003); Antonio Damasio, *The Feeling of What Happens: Body and Emotion in the Making of Consciousness* (New York: Harcourt, 1999); Antonio Damasio, *Descartes' Error: Emotions, Reason, and the Human Brain* (New York: Avon Books, 1994).

mately with the goal of gaining a sympathetic understanding of religion from the perspective of people who are themselves religious.

I. Institutional and Course Contexts

At Fairfield University, religious studies falls under the "Engaging Traditions" area of the core curriculum. This is one of six core pathways that is described in the following way:

> Liberal education in the Catholic and Jesuit tradition has always had, at its core, the act of retrieving the manifold traditions of human reflection—philosophical schools, religious traditions of faith and practice, historical accounts of peoples and cultures, and the oral and literary traditions that shape these in all their richness and diversity.[5]

All undergraduate students are required to take courses in religious studies as part of the core curriculum at my university. The practice in my department has been to allow faculty members to have some flexibility and freedom in designing the entry level course, provided that we abide by the following learning objectives: (1) to teach students the foundations of major religious traditions; (2) to teach critical skills needed by professionals in the field of religious studies; and (3) to apply scholarly approaches to religion to actual lived experiences of religion in cultural contexts.[6] In the case of the first objective goal, the journal assignment asks students to learn in an experiential way about religious praxis. Student mastery of this objective engages a basic aspect of religion and reinforces the discipline-specific language with which we discuss religious experience in the classroom. The assignment also provides the opportunity to examine the relationship between religion and culture, especially in the lived context of a Jesuit university campus.

[5] http://www.fairfield.edu/documents/academic/cae_core_pathways_bro.pdf; see p. 4 of that file. The other core pathways are: creative and aesthetic engagement, global citizenship, rhetoric and reflection, quantitative reasoning, and scientific reasoning.
[6] These learning goals more or less correspond with the IDEA Center learning objectives: (1) "gaining factual knowledge (terminology, classifications, methods, trends)"; (2) "developing specific skills, competencies, and points of view needed by professionals in the field most closely related to this course"; (3) "learning to apply course material (to improve thinking, problem solving, and decisions)."

Above all, the assignment focuses on the lived-experience of religion within a specific religious tradition. While a textbook presentation of religion is useful for generating a common understanding of religious experience, religion is a human experience that is always embedded in specific contexts. The journal assignment is designed to cultivate empathy about the human experience of religion. Empathy is a lifelong goal that I have for each of my students and a skill that must be practiced before it can be mastered. I tell my students on the first day of class that being able to imagine yourself in the shoes of another will serve them well in whatever they do in life; whether their goal is to be a health-care professional, a marketing executive, a good friend, parent, or spouse. The capacity for empathy makes us more fully human. In light of the department's learning goals for the religious studies core, I designed a short assignment for students to help them to practice thinking about religion in a way that is sympathetic to the experiences of religious people and to give them an opportunity to think more deeply about how religion is experienced today in their own cultural context. This assignment, called the "Action Element Project," is structured to help students learn experientially about religion in the American culture, and to give students an opportunity to develop their capacity to empathize with the experiences of religious people who practice their faith.

The idea for this assignment is based on a *New York Times* best-seller by A. J. Jacobs, *The Year of Living Biblically*.[7] In this book, Jacobs, an agnostic, nonpracticing cultural Jew, chronicles his experience of following one religious law each day for 365 days. Jacobs gives many brief glimpses of different religious traditions in New York City. They provide interesting vignettes of encounters that Jacobs has with actual religious people in a variety of contemporary contexts. Jacobs is a self-professed atheist who, like some of my students, favors the idea of the spiritual but not the idea of the religious. Jacobs describes himself in this way:

> I grew up in an extremely secular home in New York City. I am officially Jewish, but I'm Jewish in the same way the Olive Garden is an Italian restaurant. Which is to say: not very. I attended no Hebrew school, ate no matzoh. The closest my family came to observing Judaism was a paradoxical classic of assimilation: a Star of David on top of our Christmas tree.[8]

---

[7] A. J. Jacobs, *The Year of Living Biblically: One Man's Humble Quest to Follow the Bible as Literally as Possible* (New York: Simon & Schuster, 2007).

[8] Ibid., 4.

The book blurbs promised a great deal: "extremely funny" (*The Providence Journal*); "Engagingly written chronicle" (*Los Angeles Times*); "Throughout his journey, Jacobs comes across as a generous and thoughtful (and yes, slightly neurotic) participant observer, lacing his story with absurdly funny cultural commentary" (*Publishers Weekly*). Jacobs makes the topic of the Bible exciting and vibrant in an accessible way. I decided to use Jacobs's book because it showcases biblical law in a contemporary way that is interesting to a nonspecialist reader. I hoped that Jacobs would spark student curiosity about the Bible, religious traditions, and the complex relationship between religion and culture. Indirectly, I hoped that the book would reinforce learning about foundational knowledge of ritual practice, Judaism and Christianity, and the idea of the Law.[9]

The overwhelming majority of students at Fairfield University come from a Christian tradition where the Jewish idea of the Law is conceptually difficult for them to understand and appreciate. Some of this is due to Christian antinomian understandings of the Law rooted in Pauline theology. Many of the biblical laws that Jacobs engages are laws that must be creatively reimagined in a modern, twenty-first-century world. For example, Jacobs describes the law about stoning an adulterer, which he decides to actualize in the twenty-first century by throwing pebbles at a stranger in a park; an act that was, needless to say, most unwelcome. Students appreciate this comical way of observing the law, and it affords an opportunity to discuss the need for laws to be interpreted and actualized by living communities in each generation. I am careful to emphasize that Jacobs is not himself a member of a religious Jewish community, as that is conventionally understood, and he does not necessarily exemplify what it is to be Jewish. In the assignment I state:

> Jacobs is not being presented as a model of how to be religious today; instead, his comical experiences highlight interesting relationships between religion and culture, the ancient sacred text and contemporary contexts, and an amazing variety of ways of being Jewish and Christian. All of these aspects of Jacobs's book are worth discussing in light of the other course readings.

---

[9] In the RS 151 course that semester, I used *The Year of Living Biblically* as a supplemental text to the biblical text (NRSV). Our primary textbook that semester was Marc Zvi Brettler, *How to Read the Bible* (New York: Jewish Publication Society, 2005) with selections from Timothy K. Beal, *Religion and Its Monsters* (New York: Routledge, 2002).

The Jacobs book was used selectively in the course. I reserved about ten to fifteen minutes of each seventy-five-minute class period to discuss or highlight details in Jacobs's book about his encounters with actual religious communities, insofar as they dovetailed with our other course readings.

II. The Journal Assignment

The journal assignment was piloted in one core section of a non-majors course on sacred texts in fall 2010 and in the following semester. I used it in two sections of my introductory course as a low-stakes assignment (5 percent) about the phenomenal experience of religion today. The "action element" or the "doing of religion" is a significant experience of religion for Judaism, Christianity, and Islam.[10] The journal assignment asked students to devote one week during the semester to practicing a handful of different religious rituals or laws of their own choosing. During the week that they complete the assignment, students are asked to refrain from all forms of social technology (e.g., texting, Facebook, cell phones). Putting aside social technology clears a space so that they could practice mindfulness, and surprisingly, students actually did this. One student commented: "I went about my Saturday night without any social devices, just as I did for most of the week to the best of my ability. This was so hard to do. I left my dorm room to go out tonight and *literally felt naked*."

Students are given a list of twenty different religious observances or practices taken from Jacobs's book, and they are free to choose any five to observe for at least seven consecutive days. Some of the choices are clearly ethical (e.g., do not covet; do not gossip); others relate to the practice of mindfulness and prayer (e.g., praying throughout the day—in the morning and at night; praying before meals; meditating). Many of these are not explicitly religious. There was also the option of not mixing cotton and wool fibers in their clothing, an actual Jewish practice that Jacobs discusses at length and that offers an opportunity for mindfulness. After a week's worth of journaling, the students were asked to write a concluding reflection about what they learned about themselves and about religious practices.

I also gave students the freedom to pursue other laws of their choosing, either ones that Jacobs engages or ones that they choose entirely on their own. No one chose this option in the upper level RS 151, but one

---

[10] Lawrence Cunningham and John Kelsay, *The Sacred Quest: An Invitation to the Study of Religion*, 5th ed. (Upper Saddle River, NJ: Prentice Hall, 2010), 14, 71–83.

student in the RS 10 course chose to observe practices specific to Islam: "I figured that I would attempt to do various rituals that were doable for me from the three different religions that we are studying in this course. I decided to imitate the Muslim practice of praying five times a day. I will not be praying to Allah, I will just pray at the same times that they do so that I can see what it is like." This student had chosen to take on the Muslim practice of praying five times a day and did so because he had many Muslim friends in high school who did this. He reported the following: "I feel like I understand a tiny bit more about the religion of Islam, more so than I had before the course. I respect the prayer practices that they do, in the degree of difficulty that is demanded in order to stay true to their religious beliefs. The dedication that people have to their religions is an amazing thing." Another student who chose her own religious law to follow selected intercessory prayer and wrote: "Putting my focus on others helped me to contemplate the suffering of others and how many opportunities have been available to me. . . . While I was praying I realized prayer could be the catalyst for action." These students who chose their own set of religious laws were the exception. The majority of students selected practices from the list of twenty that I provided them. Certain practices were chosen with a great frequency by the students and allowed me to engage students in common themes during our in-class discussion.

III. Commonly Chosen Religious Practices

Students in all three classes tended to choose very similar religious practices, and the most commonly chosen practices were related to mindfulness and public expressions of prayer.

A. *Challenges of Practicing Mindfulness*

> *Thou shalt not covet* (Exod 20:17); *Don't go around as a gossiper* (Lev 19:16); *and Nor shall there come upon you a garment of cloth made of two kinds of stuff* (Lev 19:19).

The specific laws that I discuss in this section are ones that are not necessarily religious: they have to do with not coveting, not gossiping, and not wearing mixed fibers. Each of them posed challenges for students and helped them to be more aware of their day-to-day actions and behaviors.

Fairfield University is a private university in the northeast and many—not all—students come from affluent backgrounds. A number of students, both male and female, chose the particular law, "thou shall not covet" (Exod 20:17). All students who chose this law commented on how challenging it was to practice even for one full day. One student wrote:

> Wanting the things that I cannot have is a bad habit that I have. When I am bored, I constantly search the Internet or look in magazines for things that I want, but could never afford, whether it is guitars or expensive sneakers. Like Jacobs, it is a commandment that I break every day, making it the most difficult day for me. He also mentioned the whole commandment, which states that you shall not covet "anything that is your neighbor's" which, as Jacob says, leaves "no wiggle room." I think that it is simply human nature to want the things that a friend has that you do not have. I think the most difficult part of this commandment is that I have to covet something first to realize that I want it, and then consciously not covet it, finding that I just covet it more when I try to not want it. It is a vicious cycle. I agree with Jacobs when he says that it is the most difficult commandment to follow.

Students often described the extent to which they struggled to be mindful of not coveting things belonging to other people on campus or things that they see advertised. A biblical law that was chosen by an overwhelmingly large group of students was one that was not specifically religious—the law prohibiting gossiping (Lev 19:16). One student writes, "one of the biggest things I noticed today was . . . that I was conscious of everything I said and did. . . . When I hang out with my friends, every single conversation turns to talking about other people. . . . I made a conscious effort not to talk negatively about anybody." Many students commented that they came to realize how routine it was to spread stories about their friends and other people whom they know, with little regard for whether or not the stories were true. Because of the assignment, some students found that not participating in the gossip was "refreshing." It felt good to them to take a break from this kind of talk.

The third example of commonly chosen practice that cultivates mindfulness is an actual biblical law that prohibits the mixing of fibers. In its practical application, it could be described as seeking to cultivate a mindful ordering of the world by the religious person, although the actual rationale for why this law exists in the Bible is not clearly given. Some understand this law as relating to the religious worldview of ancient Israel to be set apart and to maintain orderly distinctions—in this case, in the realm of clothing by distinguishing between plant (cotton) and animal fibers (wool). I included this law among the laws that students could choose from because not all students are religious and there is no explicitly moral or religious motivation for this law. Students who chose this law described at length how they were forced to dress in all cotton; "I was left with regular white cotton t-shirts and sweats." Another person wrote, "I feel more confident when I put time into how I look and dress, so I felt naked in some respect by not feeling up to par with my outfit. It is humbling." Another student reflected on the fiber regulation and the observance of kosher laws:

> I have not been aware of the clothes I have been wearing or the food I have been eating. These are things that, on normal occasion, I do rather instinctively. I eat whatever is available to me when I am hungry at home or in public. I wear, quite frankly, whatever I feel in the mood to wear for that day. But, for the Judeans, even these seemingly pivotal [sic] things are something that they took great consideration in. They did not wear clothes of mixed threads, or mix foods together that were not parallel [sic] with kosher laws. It is rather amazing how much thought is actually necessary to effectively practice this law. It seems as if almost every aspect of life, even down to the clothes you wear and the food you eat, are guided by some sort of religious regulation. I can only image how great a level of self-awareness these practices bring to those who truly practice these laws in their everyday lives.

Students who observed special food laws frequently reported forgetting and finding themselves eating meat and dairy together. They reflected upon this in their journal and commented on how their food choices in the cafeteria tend to be made mindlessly.

After the journals were collected, we discussed in class the public aspect of clothing and how members of religious traditions may choose to wear certain fibers and/or modest clothing or eat certain types of food. There are practices that have a public dimension which identify them as religious individuals (Orthodox Jews and Muslims). The assignment also dovetailed nicely with a timely controversy in France about the public veiling of the face by observant Muslims. In class we discuss how difficult the practice of mindfulness is. Students commented on how easily they forgot to follow the dietary laws or how they found themselves falling into old habits of coveting unconsciously.

B. *Religious Practices: Prayers of Thanksgiving (Deut 8:10)*

Certain laws that I specified for this assignment were explicitly religious laws that had to do with prayer. One commonly chosen law is from Deuteronomy 8:10—"and you shall eat and be full, and you shall bless the Lord your God for the good land He has given you."[11] A great majority of students who chose to observe this practice did so by praying before meals in the cafeteria. Students who chose to pray before meals in the cafeteria commented on how uncomfortable they felt and how they were mocked or ridiculed by their peers. While the law doesn't specify how they should pray, students often prayed in a way that fit their family's religious tradition, e.g., students from a Catholic tradition made the sign of the cross. I noticed that several students wrote in their journals that when they explained their assignment to their friends, one then immediately responded: "Are you seriously going to do this?!" as if it would be preferable to fabricate the data—not something that I expected as a professor!

All students who chose this public religious practice expressed strong discomfort. One student wrote:

> I felt uncomfortable praying to God in the dining hall, because I just felt incredibly self-conscious and didn't want to be pegged as some off-beat religion fanatic. Praying in Barone (Campus Center) actually made me really anxious, so I kind of revised it and instead of bowing my head, closing my eyes, and folding my hands, I took a more meditative approach and folded my hands and placed my head on top of them. Once I was in that position, I would reflect and thank God for the food I was about to receive.

Another student wrote: "I found myself looking around before I blessed myself and said a quick prayer. It is definitely uncommon to do this and I feel like people are looking at me." This same student wrote later:

> [A]gain I said a prayer before eating but this time my roommate caught me doing this. After being questioned about what I was doing, I answered that I was doing a project and was attempting to pray before every meal. He was very understanding, but I can see other people looking at me and it still made me uncomfortable. Just like Jacobs was getting stared at for reading the Bible on the subway,

---

[11] Jacobs, *The Year of Living Biblically*, 94–96.

I was getting looked at for praying in public. I suppose it isn't normal but what is the big deal!

Another student wrote: "Even a silent prayer to myself followed by the sign of the cross before I ate would get weird looks from my friends. This was not an especially difficult day living according to Deuteronomy, but it was definitely the most socially awkward." Similar experiences were had by students who chose to pray in their rooms and similar conversations were had between them and their roommates.

In class we discussed the experience of prayer and how many of them felt awkward or uncomfortable about praying in public. This topic also helped students to learn experientially that performing religious actions in public brings strong feelings of anxiety. Their experience of discomfort while performing this religious practice is one that helps to explain why in more religiously diverse contexts like the Northeast, people can be reluctant to practice outward demonstrations of religion and prefer instead to prioritize inward contemplative experiences. In our class discussion, I used this example as a way to think about our culture's assumptions about religion (e.g., "off-beat religion fanatic") and also to invite them to think *empathetically* about the experiences of the religious person who *chooses* to perform public prayer practices or to wear clothing that would publically identify them as religious. In the discussion I was able to steer their attention to the need to create safe spaces on campus for people who are religious and ask them to think about small and specific ways they can foster a warmer climate on campus for people who are religious.

Closing Reflections and Conclusion

Teaching religious studies challenges me as a professor to continually reflect upon the material and how it might be experienced by the non-specialist student in the class. I not only seek to design assignments that might help them learn the objectives of the course in an experiential way; I want to offer readings that are stimulating and showcase religion as having a contemporary context. I chose the Jacobs book because as an atheist, Jacobs offers an intriguing glimpse of what religion and religious practices look like to someone who is unfamiliar with them—a perspective that I need to be continually reminded of as a professor of introductory courses in religion! Jacobs does so in a way that is friendly and empathetic to the experience of religion without being religious himself. In this way, he models a generous and genuine curiosity about religion that I hope my students will remember and imitate. For many of my students, even those who come from a religious tradition, certain aspects of religion, even elements from their own religious tradition, can be foreign and unfamiliar to them. Jacobs offers a model for how to inquire about religion without being threatened by it or becoming polemical. As an atheist, Jacobs demonstrates a generosity toward religion and a deep desire to understand those who are different—values I hope students will embody after taking my class. The religious people whom Jacobs encounters in New York City are vividly depicted and enrich our sense of what the lived experience of religion is like.

As a professor, the assignment also gave me insight into my students: what they care about and what their lives are like outside of the classroom. I am reminded of how complex this period of emerging adulthood can be. I am given a rare glimpse of what it is like to be a student and to negotiate questions of identity—both public and private—during the one week of journaling that I am able to read. The journals are surprisingly honest about how students spend their time (work, video gaming, golfing, looking at Facebook, studying), the specific challenges they face socially, and the many demands that are placed on them by school, friends, sports, clubs, volunteer work, and employment. The cultivation of mindfulness is especially challenging for students because of these competing obligations. Several students chose to follow the "Remember the Sabbath day, to Keep it holy" (Exod 20:8).

> Today is Palm Sunday and I have decided to attend Mass as I have the past few weeks. Today was special because of the recitation of the passion and the death of Christ. The Mass was nice but I felt as though it may be hard to devote the entire day to God as it is said in Exodus 20:8, "Remember the Sabbath Day, to keep it holy," because I had a few things on my agenda that I needed to do. The scripture says to us that we should not pursue our own goals on this day because it is a day of rest. For the most part, I just relaxed and did not do anything strenuous besides going to dinner. I wanted to go outside and play baseball however, I felt as though this action would not be considered as resting. This was most likely the most challenging day because having the entire day of rest was much harder than I had anticipated.

Students wrote in their journals that the observance of this practice to not work on the "Sabbath" generated a surprisingly high level of distress and anxiety within them. At the same time, others reported having no problem with letting the day go by with no work.

In the journals, students write that the observance of these practices was difficult. Mindfulness or paying attention was a significant challenge for students. Providing students with a structured opportunity to cultivate empathy and mindfulness aims at the larger life goal I have for students—namely, to become men and women for others. One student wrote about the transformative aspects that mindfulness and paying attention can have in his relationships with others:

> Today I decided to start the day off with Morning Prayer. It is something I did my whole life, and all through high school. For some reason I stopped doing it (i.e., prayer) when I came to school. I should have known that it would put me in an amazing mood to kick off the morning. I had history class, Chambers, and Glee club, and in between everything I tried to spend time catching up with friends I have been able to talk to this semester. Instead of the meaningless small talk that I make so often in passing when I see people, I had actual conversations and tried to focus on the person I was actually talking to. I know it has nothing to do with being religious, but it all links together for me because not only do I want to strengthen my faith relationship, I also want to develop stronger relationships with my friends. . . . After I finished up for the night, I stopped in the chapel for a few minutes. Everything was dark and peaceful. I was able to sit in the silent chapel and just think about this project. I am glad that I chose to do it during Lent, because it goes hand-in-hand with what Lent is all about: preparation. . . . Being conscious of the small things helps to keep it all in perspective, and being charitable in everything I do makes it easier to make bigger sacrifices as well.

Bodily practices that cultivate mindfulness—such as religious practices—or practices that focus attention on one's studies can cultivate a predisposition to respond in an authentic and genuine way to another. Religious practices that foster mindfulness can cultivate the capacity to love and be transformed by the things of this world. The sacramental aspect of mindfulness practices is expressed by Simone Weil, the French philosopher and activist, who writes:

> The solution of a geometry problem does not in itself constitute a precious gift, but the same law applies to it because it is the image of something precious. Being a little fragment of particular truth, it

is a pure image of the unique, eternal, and living Truth. . . . Every
school exercise, thought of in this way, is like a sacrament.[12]

According to Weil, the ability to focus one's attention is something that
is not only needed for an individual to pray, it allows one to become
more *fully* human. Weil's observation about the sacramental role of paying attention is very Augustinian in how it understands the things of
this world to assist the individual in a deeper contemplation of the sacred.
The person who is mindful is one who is able to give his or her full attention to the one who suffers. Weil writes, "The capacity to give one's attention to a sufferer is a very rare and difficult thing; it is almost a miracle;
it is a miracle. Nearly all those who think they have this capacity do not
possess it. Warmth of heart, impulsiveness, pity are not enough."[13]

When I designed the Action Element assignment, I had no idea what
I might find in the student reflections. I designed it to be a low-stakes
assignment that provided an opportunity for experiential learning about
religion and the action element of religion. I was surprised at the student
reflections and the honesty with which the students pursued the project.
Lest the reader think that all students were deeply spiritual, I want to
make clear that this was not the case. Many students wrote simply about
their greater self-awareness of their actions and behaviors. For the students, however, who already had a predisposition to spirituality, I believe
that this experiential learning assignment afforded them the structured
time to reflect upon their experience here at a Jesuit and Catholic college
campus and to deepen their understanding of those Ignatian questions
of who they are and who they are called to be—in refreshing solitude.[14]
As a professor, it also helped me not only to recognize the complexity
and rich diversity in their experiences but also to help me to think more
deeply about my vocation as a teacher: What do I want students to know
and care about? And what kind of people do I want them to become
after taking my class? Ultimately, I hope that my class will help them to
live more fully human lives and help them examine the world in which
they live.

---

[12] Simone Weil, "Reflections on the Right Use of School Studies with a View to the
Love of God," in *Waiting for God*, trans. Emma Craufurd (New York: Putnam, 1951),
57–65.

[13] Ibid., 64.

[14] William P. George, "Learning Alone: Solitude and Undergraduate Education,"
America: The National Catholic Review 199, no. 7 (September 15, 2008): 16–18.

This I Believe:
Linking the Mathematical Axiomatic Method with Personal Belief Systems

Stephanie Anne Salomone

Mathematics is not usually associated with faith. In fact, in a typical mathematics course, the notion of belief *not* based on proof is billed as antithetical to the content and pedagogical underpinnings of the course itself. Mathematicians, and hence mathematics students, are generally trained to use only those mathematical theorems for which they have seen (but not necessarily understood) a rigorous proof. Math students mistakenly believe, therefore, that *all* results must be proven. Furthermore, most students believe that pure mathematics exists in an academic bubble, that it is unrelated to any other subject or to real life. It is not surprising, given these common beliefs, that students tend to disassociate faith from abstract mathematics.

Rigorous mathematical proof rests on the axiomatic method, which is an "orderly development of theorems with proofs about abstract entities."[1] The method, developed as early as the sixth century BC in Greece but systematized by Euclid of Alexandria in 330 BC,[2] relies on the mathematician's acceptance of certain statements, called axioms, *without justification*. These axioms must be carefully selected so as not to contradict each other, simple enough to be believable without proof, and robust

---

[1] Marvin Jay Greenberg, *Euclidean and Non-Euclidean Geometries: Development and History*, 4th ed. (New York: W. H. Freeman and Company, 2008), 3.
[2] Ibid., 7–9.

enough to support the mountain of mathematical facts that can be logically deduced from them.

The axioms we choose to believe are, in a sense, the mathematical equivalent of a moral code, in that they dictate what is legal (and perhaps ethical) in the mathematical world, and how that world functions around us. I claim we could, and should, encourage mathematics students, particularly those at universities where both academic content and formation of the self are held in high regard, to see the link between belief in self-evident mathematical "facts" and personal belief systems. Both are the building blocks of a worldview, be it mathematical or personal. One change to a set of axioms has an effect on the mathematical world it supports, just as a change in a student's core beliefs can rock the foundation of his world.

One way in which we can show our students that faith and mathematics intersect is to help students see that the process of accepting axioms and building theorems and proofs from these axioms is the same process they follow when they accept some small piece of their own moral code and then construct a life in which they follow that code. Furthermore, an integration of faith in the form of expression of core beliefs and of science in the form of a deep understanding of different sets of mathematical axioms makes both pieces less abstract. Can students understand the ramifications of changing one mathematical axiom without talking about personal morality? Of course. But I believe that they understand the effect of small changes better, and are better able to explain and apply the effect, once they've experienced this link themselves.

Modern Geometry is a course in which students study the axiomatic method. It is a foundations course in which students learn how mathematical ideas grow and evolve. Students see how changing just one of the basic axioms changes the geometric world that is built from them. Much of our study is based around the controversial parallel postulate, stated by Euclid, and the consistent geometrical worlds that result when this axiom is negated. Students learn to question all geometric facts, many of which they've taken for granted since they were children, and many of which they've believed because someone in authority told them to and because they were never presented with other options. The material is extremely abstract, and in many cases it is impossible to create accurate visuals to help students see the concepts. (In fact, there are sections of the course devoted to the danger of reliance on diagrams.)

As part of the course, my students complete several written journal assignments, some of which seem at first unrelated to the course content. Most notably, students write a "This I Believe" essay, following the format of NPR's segment of the same title, which is based on the Edward R. Murrow program from the 1950s.[3] Students write about one of their core beliefs, and in all cases, the finished products are thoughtful, kind, and show that the students value family, friends, learning, and service to the community. Students also reflect on how the assignment relates to the geometry course itself. Based on their reflections, I claim that students get the point—that as thoughtful humans, we each have a set of core beliefs, "facts" which we take as true without proof. Altering one of these beliefs can change the way we interact with the world and the way we view the world around us. Mathematics works the same way.

Though this is a theoretical mathematics course, it is also a course about faith, about choosing which axioms we believe in, and seeing what we can build from those ideas. Rather than looking only at the axiomatic method as it pertains to geometry, through this journal assignment students look inward and connect the axiomatic method to their lives.

In the sections that follow, I will explain why, in layman's terms, modern geometry is the perfect class for students to explore the links between faith and mathematics, by giving an example of a surprising conclusion that comes from changing one geometric axiom. I will also offer some of the mechanics behind the journal-writing my students complete in this class, and will offer some examples of student essays and discussion points.

Modern Geometry and Belief in a Different Set of Axioms

As he wrote in the translator's introduction to Lobachevski's *The Theory of Parallels*, George Halsted explains the importance of belief in axioms in the following way: " 'Prove all things, hold fast that which is good,' does not mean demonstrate everything. From nothing assumed, nothing can be proved."[4] In modern geometry, we look critically at the ancient axioms of Euclid, the centuries-long debate over his fifth axiom, and the rise of non-Euclidean geometries in the mid-1800s. Given the

---

[3] "About This I Believe," accessed October 11, 2013, http://thisibelieve.com/about.

[4] Nicholas Lobachevski, *The Theory of Parallels*, trans. George Halstead (Chicago: Open Court Publishing Co., 1914), 5.

above description, I imagine most students' eyes start to glaze over before class even begins. However, I like to follow it with, "Your geometry teachers have lied to you. The measure of the angles of a triangle do not have to add up to 180 degrees." This tends to pique their interest.

Euclidean geometry is the geometry students learn in high school, and it is based on the *Elements*, thirteen volumes written by Euclid of Alexandria around 300 BC, covering what was known then about plane and solid geometry and number theory.[5] Euclid's contribution to mathematics, however, is more than just a textbook on geometric and algebraic facts. Euclid, more so than any mathematician who preceded him, provided us with "a model of how 'pure mathematics' should be written, with well thought out axioms, precise definitions, carefully stated theorems, and logically coherent proofs."[6]

Euclid stated five "common notions" on magnitudes that he assumed without proof, and five geometric axioms or postulates (modern mathematicians do not distinguish between these two terms, though some ancient ones did[7]). The first four of these postulates are easily assumed because they are both demonstrable and intuitively true. For example, Euclid's first postulate, rephrased, states "for every point P and every point Q not equal to P there exists a unique line that passes through P and Q."[8] Any student with a pencil and straightedge could convince himself of the obvious truth of this statement by drawing two dots and connecting them with a straight line segment. Because we must start with *some* set of assumptions, it is not a stretch to accept this one without proof.

The fifth postulate (known nicely as the parallel postulate and less nicely as the "vicious assumption"[9]) is impossible to demonstrate physically because we cannot draw lines that extend forever. Whether or not it should be accepted on faith as an axiom was the subject of much controversy for over two thousand years. Its translation is difficult to parse, and so to avoid that difficulty, we will look at an equivalent statement called Playfair's Postulate.[10]

[5] Greenberg, *Euclidean and Non-Euclidean Geometries*, 7–9.

[6] Victor J. Katz, *A History of Mathematics* (New York: HarperCollins College Publishers, 1993), 54.

[7] Carl B. Boyer, *A History of Mathematics*, 2nd ed. (New York: John Wiley & Sons, 1991), 105.

[8] Greenberg, *Euclidean and Non-Euclidean Geometries*, 15.

[9] Lobachevski, *The Theory of Parallels*, 8.

[10] Greenberg, *Euclidean and Non-Euclidean Geometries*, 20–21.

Playfair's Postulate

> For any line *l* and for any point *P* that does not lie on *l*, there exists a unique line *m* through *P* that is parallel to *l*.

Though Euclid described what he meant by "line," it is a word that modern geometers take as an undefined term. Like an axiom, an undefined term is understood in an intuitive way, and we assume that by "line" we mean the shortest distance between two points on a surface (in this case, a plane). Two lines are parallel if they do not intersect. What Playfair's postulate tells us is best illustrated in the following diagram:

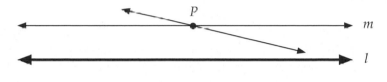

Figure 1. A diagram of Playfair's Postulate

Most people would agree that lines *m* and *l* look as though they will not meet, and that any other line through *P* will intersect *l* somewhere. That is, Playfair's postulate *does* seem to be intuitively true (particularly to any person who has been trained only in Euclidean geometry). However, because we cannot extend lines *l* and *m* forever to show conclusively that they do not meet, we simply cannot be sure that the statement is true. That Euclid did not use his version of the parallel postulate in proofs of his first twenty-eight propositions suggests that perhaps even he was skeptical that this was obviously true and that it could be taken as an axiom.[11] He was not alone. Mathematicians tried unsuccessfully for 2,100 years to prove the parallel postulate as a theorem (rather than assuming it), using only the other four postulates and the common notions as axioms. An explanation for their lack of success is simple to state but difficult to prove: it is possible to construct legitimate, consistent geometric worlds where we assume the *negation* of Euclid's parallel postulate. That is, we can choose to accept Euclid's parallel postulate on faith, or we can accept that no two lines are parallel, or we can accept that we can have multiple parallels. The mathematical world we get, however, depends on our initial choice of parallel axiom.

[11] Ibid., 23.

What was (and is) difficult about accepting a different parallel axiom to the one that Euclid posed was that the new worlds that followed logically from the axiom contradicted mathematicians' observations of the physical (flat, Euclidean) world. Further, the mathematical facts that are supported by a different axiomatic system are sometimes new and unexpected, contradicting earlier teachings. However, once mathematicians, namely, Gauss, Bolyai, Lobachevski, and Riemann, laid out the new non-Euclidean geometries, it was easier to accept that Euclid's parallel postulate is neither intuitively true nor false—it is simply not *necessarily* true.[12]

Elliptic geometry is based on acceptance of a new parallel axiom that states that given any two lines on a surface, these lines will meet eventually. That is, there are no parallel lines. *This*, I agree, is at first glance contrary to our physical experience. However, in elliptic geometry, space is not flat as it is in Euclidean geometry. Instead, the mathematical world exists on the surface of a sphere. Lines, which still need to indicate the shortest distance between two points on the sphere, are great circles. To those students who are still skeptical that this is a valid approach to looking for a geometry that correctly measures the world, I reply, a little sarcastically, "If only we lived on the surface of a sphere." As well, we must accept that a straight line (i.e., a great circle) is boundless, as we could walk on one without finding an end, without having an infinite length.

We *actually can* visualize this mathematical world using a schoolroom globe as our model. The Equator is a "line," as are all lines of longitude, as they are all great circles.

Figure 2. "Lines" on a sphere are Great Circles.

---

[12] Jan Gullberg, *Mathematics from the Birth of Numbers* (New York: W. W. Norton & Company, 1997), 381–82.

All lines of longitude meet at the North Pole and the South Pole. Any longitudinal line intersects the Equator, and what's more, these two great circles meet at a 90-degree angle. There are other great circles, and it's true that if you consider any pair of them, they will intersect. Students often point out that two "lines" of latitude are parallel because they don't intersect. However, since the Equator is the only line of latitude that is also a great circle, it is the only one that counts as a line in this mathematical world.

It can be difficult to stomach that there could be a mathematical world in which "no parallel lines" is taken as an axiom, particularly because it presents a challenge to Euclid's parallel postulate, which most students have taken on faith since they studied high school geometry. However, as Jan Gullberg states in *Mathematics from the Birth of Numbers*, "There is no such thing as one unassailable, mathematically true, geometry. From a mathematical viewpoint, any geometry—or any other branch of mathematics—that does not produce contradictions is acceptable."[13] Elliptic geometry is one option.

It is not just the notion of a new axiom that is hard to accept, but the resulting geometric facts which follow from the new set of foundational truths can, and often do, contradict those "facts" which have been long believed to be true. For example, students believe, because it is true in Euclidean geometry, that the sum of the measures of the angles of a triangle is 180 degrees. However, in elliptic geometry, it's easy to construct a triangle for which the sum of the measures of its angles is greater than 180 degrees.

In the plane, we make a triangle by drawing three points that do not all lie on one line and connecting the points with line segments. We do the same thing on the sphere, only our line segments are pieces of great circles. Again, we can use the globe as a model. Our three points can be the North Pole (90°N, 0°W), the point on both the Equator and the Prime Meridian (0°N, 0°W), and the point on both the Equator and the 90°W line of longitude (0°N, 90°W). If we connect these points with sections of great circles (which happen to be the Equator, the Prime Meridian, and the 90°W line of longitude), we get a triangle on the sphere. Because lines of longitude intersect the Equator at a 90-degree angle, the angles of the triangle that sit on the Equator are 90 degrees each. The angle at

---

[13] Gullberg, *Mathematics from the Birth of Numbers*, 384.

the North Pole is also 90 degrees, so the sum of the measures of the angles of this triangle is 270 degrees.

Students, and perhaps any reader of this book, may read the above description and assume that some mathematical hocus-pocus is at play. However, the above construction is completely legitimate, following logically from the definition of a triangle and the set of axioms for elliptic geometry.

While it can be upsetting that a long-held belief about a geometric "fact" may not be true, what I hope students take away from this example is that our choice of axioms absolutely determines the way in which the resulting mathematical world is constructed. When we change what we choose to believe without proof, the world that results changes. That no single set of geometric axioms can be called "correct," that we cannot say that one set definitely describes our world, can be upsetting as well, as students of mathematics tend to believe that there is a single right answer to any mathematical question. My students want the mathematical world to be made of absolute truths, and in modern geometry, they learn that their ability to prove "facts" depends on the assumptions they make to begin with. They learn to accept the gray area between "true" and "false." We are inching toward the world of faith.

The "This I Believe" Challenge

I teach my courses in an institution governed by the Congregation of Holy Cross. As Blessed Basil Moreau, founder of the Congregation of the Holy Cross, wrote, "We shall always place education side by side with instruction; the mind will not be cultivated at the expense of the heart." [14] In the case of modern geometry, the mind is certainly well-cultivated. The heart is a different matter entirely, and in most mathematics classes, it is ignored, to the detriment (I believe) of both the student and his understanding of the mathematical curriculum at hand.

My students claim, during a discussion on the first day of class, that they arrived at the University of Portland with a set of personal core beliefs that help them make decisions about how they view and act in the world around them. Though not all of our students are Catholic, most of them see themselves as spiritual in some way, and each of them

---

[14] Basil Moreau, CSC, *Circular Letters of the Very Reverend Basil Anthony Mary Moreau, Number Thirty-Six* (Notre Dame, IN: Ave Maria Press, 1943), 162.

has a set of beliefs that he or she holds sacred and makes up the foundation for his or her moral, ethical, and spiritual life. Our job as educators of the heart is to guide students as they explain, question, change, and truly accept their core beliefs. Brian Doyle, a colleague at the University of Portland, beautifully explained the need for us to play this role in the following way, "Unquestioned faith is a jacket; questioned faith is maybe a skin."[15] That, as I suggest, we can support students as they grapple with big questions while also introducing course content, makes both types of work more valuable and worthwhile.

In an effort to bring "the heart" back to the abstract mathematics classroom, I have asked students to delve into their personal beliefs with a writing assignment that ties back to the content of the modern geometry course itself. The assignment has two parts. First, students compose a "This I Believe" essay, which I will describe below, and second, they reflect on why I might assign such an essay. I am deliberately vague in the second part, for I hope that each student figures out the link between acknowledging and questioning personal core beliefs and accepting geometric axioms, and the similarities between building a worldview that is based on personal axioms and building a mathematical world that follows logically from geometric ones.

In addition to addressing the education of the heart, the essay assignment and reflection tie back to questions that are addressed in the University of Portland Core Curriculum. In fact, most of our students' core classes are lower-division. So once students have completed the core classes, they tend to forget that we expect them to continue to grapple with the key questions about living good, compassionate, and hopeful lives. This assignment gives the students an opportunity to reflect on their past answers and possibly consider new and different answers to the "big questions" of the core: Who am I? Who am I becoming? How does the world work? How could the world work better? Who or what is God? What is a good life?[16]

According to the "This I Believe" website, "This I Believe is an international organization engaging people in writing and sharing essays describing the core values that guide their daily lives. . . . The project is based on the popular 1950s radio series of the same name hosted by

---

[15] Brian Doyle, letter to the author, September 11, 2009.

[16] "College of Arts and Sciences: Core Curriculum," accessed October 11, 2013, http://college.up.edu/default.aspx?cid=9335&pid=4351.

Edward R. Murrow."[17] Each writer starts with a premise and describes how he or she came to accept that premise, or how his or her life is changed, molded from, or built upon that axiom. People from all walks of life—celebrities, teachers, drug addicts, scientists, singers, and stay-at-home moms—have contributed over 90,000 essays to the website.[18] Topics range from the seemingly mundane ("I believe in picking up trash"[19]) to the profound ("The most beautiful thing we can experience is the mysterious—the knowledge of the existence of something unfathomable to us, the manifestation of the most profound reason coupled with the most brilliant beauty"[20]). The essays are short, usually fewer than five hundred words, and yet each intimate piece gives a glimpse into the personal philosophy of its author.

I ask my students to read the guidelines and to read a few of the essays online to get a taste for their format and scope. I point them to the curriculum guides and brochures.[21] Then, without much guidance (at first), I tell them to write.

It is not easy to express a profound thought in so few words, but my students, all of whom are mathematics majors (and therefore often reticent writers), succeed beautifully. Some need more guidance than others. They write several drafts over four or five weeks, but because it is so different from the proof-writing that makes up the course content, because they appreciate the opportunity to be creative, and because they've never been asked so specifically to write about a single personal belief, students report that they enjoy the assignment and learn from it. One recent student commented, "My favorite journal was 'This I Believe.' I have a set of beliefs that I live by and rely on to aid me in making choices big and small. The idea of someone coming along and proving to me that one of my foundational beliefs was wrong would be devastating. Pinpointing one of our beliefs, writing about it, and relating it back to math was rewarding."

[17] "This I Believe," accessed August 23, 2011, http://thisibelieve.org/.

[18] Ibid.

[19] Mark Olmstead, "The Serenity to Change the Things I Can," accessed August 23, 2011, http://thisibelieve.org/essay/39990/.

[20] Albert Einstein, "An Ideal of Service to Our Fellow Man," accessed August 23, 2011, http://thisibelieve.org/essay/16465/.

[21] "This I Believe in the Classroom," accessed August 23, 2011, http://thisibelieve.org/educators/.

Examples of Student Essays

I share the following two essays as examples of student work. They exemplify both the commitment to family and community that we hope to see in our students, and the depth of feeling, approaching transcendence, which our students can convey.

> When I was nine years old, my father bought a plot of land in northern Wisconsin. It was four years after my parents had divorced and my siblings and I were living a split life between our mother's suburban household and our father's inner-city duplex. For as long as I could remember, my father had been talking about this piece of land and his dream house. I will never forget the elation on his face when he picked us up from our mom's house to take us up for our first look at our land.
>
> For me, these twenty acres of forest just outside of Florence, Wisconsin represented freedom, happiness, and a return to my childhood. For the first year and a half our disjointed family spent everyother summer weekend cutting down the birch trees that covered the plot of land that was our home. The four of us lived in a trailer parked in a newly cleared space as together we leveled the earth and poured the cement that was to be the foundation for the first phase our new homestead. By October 2001, the building that was to be the garage was completely built and insulated so as to serve as a temporary house.
>
> For years even before the land was purchased, my father had been calling our new home "Broken Arrow" after his favorite Neil Young song. In the fall of 2001, as we christened our land with a sign bearing that title and all of our names, our new home could not have felt more like a broken arrow. My brother was going away to college and my sister and I were being moved seventy-three miles away from the city we had grown up in.
>
> It has been eight years since my father, brother, sister and I established our homestead together. Since then, both my father and mother have been remarried. My brother graduated college and I moved halfway across the country. This fall, the plumbing, insulation, and drywall are all going into the real house and next summer we will be able to live in it. Things have changed, and by no means have things been easy.
>
> But whenever I go home to visit for Christmas or summer, the first thing I want to do is visit my home up north. I know it is a simple notion, but above all, I believe in home.

❖   ❖   ❖

Someone once said, "To whom much is given much is expected." When I first heard that, I immediately searched for a pen so I could write it down. That turned out to be unnecessary because like most important things, I memorized the quote upon hearing it. I put it right up there with SOH-CAH-TOA and Stop, Drop, and Roll.

The reason this quote has stuck with me is because I am one of those to whom much has been given. Throughout my entire life I have been handed things, opportunities, and responsibilities, mostly because of who my parents are and where I have lived, making much of my privilege unearned. The only way I can think of to balance this out is, first, to specifically acknowledge my own privilege and, second, use what I have been given for the forces of good, not evil.

My academic career has been particularly privileged. I went to fairly rigorous public schools where I was taught by mostly white teachers and had mostly white peers. My high school had money for a new science building, a strong athletics department, and art, theatre, and music programs. My parents helped me apply to college, and now they are helping me pay for it. I attend a pricey private university, which is also predominantly white, where I struggle only slightly more than I did in high school. While I don't yet have a specific plan for the future, some sort of graduate school is certainly on the horizon. With all this great education, I feel I have a moral responsibility to spend some portion of my life teaching. This will be part of my giving back to the world.

Even now in my everyday life I try to identify signs of privilege and start conversations with people about them. When a professor refers to a group of female students as "guys," or when someone uses "gay" as an insult, or when an entire class is taught from the prospective of dead white men, a flip switches in my brain and I am in "world-changing mode." For me, teaching falls under the category of world changing, and good teachers helps students find their own world-changing mode. In my experience, once you start trying to change the world, it becomes increasingly difficult to stop. Thank goodness.

The Reflection and Follow-Up Conversation

In addition to asking them to write the essay, I ask students to reflect on why they think I might have made this challenging assignment in the first place. Their answers surprise me as much as their actual essays do. It is not just that they figure out that personal and mathematical axioms have similarities, but that they come up with new reasons, ones which never occurred to me, for writing about personal beliefs in a pure mathematics class.

One student writes, "This assignment asks people to reveal their personal axioms, the beliefs they instantly assume without thinking or asking questions. When people are not absolutely clear and specific about these things, problems can arise. Exactly the same is true for math. We must say what we mean and mean what we say in math as much as in life." Another student gets at the heart of the link in the following way:

> I think that you had us do this assignment to make us identify the personal axioms from which we have built up our life theorems. Although it is a pretty nerdy metaphor, it turns out that mathematics is a pretty good model of life. . . . My beliefs about myself and the world around me are the only resources I have to help me conquer the questions and problems of life. Armed with this personal set of axioms, I should, theoretically, be able to build up a sound, logical world of truth. So far it's going pretty well; there have been some tough things I've had to figure out and prove along the way, but I know I can trust in my beliefs as I move through life.[22]

Students comment on the difficulty in choosing which core belief to highlight, and their difficulties stem from two places, picking one belief above all others, and picking something which they believe *others* will also see as intuitively true. Many of them mention that it would be devastating to find out that one of their long-held beliefs was considered wrong. Most of the students note that the assignment helps them to see that mathematics does not exist in a bubble, that there is some aspect of faith in mathematics class (and some point out, there may therefore be faith in all things scientific).

Our classroom discussions also reveal that students need and appreciate the opportunity to use the essay as a metaphor for the axiomatic system and vice versa, that they can explain their own moral code and the lives they choose to lead using the language of mathematics. Sometimes this is easier, they tell me, than explaining it in any other terms. Students mention as the course progresses that it is easier to accept the

---

[22] Mary Clare Metscher, e-mail to the author, September 29, 2009.

existence of a non-Euclidean geometry (because it is simply the result of a change of one axiom) once they have written the essay and reflected on how a change in their axioms would change their outlooks and ultimately change their lives. And vice versa, they appreciate learning about new geometries in part because knowing that the world can be described mathematically in different but logically sound ways helps them to understand and accept that another person's worldview, though different from their own, can be correct without making theirs wrong. It all depends, they learn, on the choice of axioms.

Conclusion

Modern Geometry is a foundations course in that students work to build a body of knowledge and facts stemming from a few basic common notions and axioms. It is also foundational in that it can be a course in which students question what they believe and why they believe it. Learning to identify which so-called facts are true (and to question why) is essential to learning to write rigorous proofs. It is also essential to forming a personal moral code and learning to justify behavior based on that code. Because students use both a mathematical lens and a personal lens through which to view axioms, they link faith and reason and, I believe, further understand the value of both.

One question that students and colleagues ask me when I talk to them about this assignment and the Modern Geometry course in general is whether or not I participate by writing my own essay. I do. I see great value in engaging students in conversations about faith in general and in faith as it relates to our academic pursuits. Such conversations, however, are sometimes difficult to start because I do not come from the same point on the belief spectrum as many of my students. I am not Catholic, nor do I subscribe to any other system of religious belief. Nonetheless, I believe that we are all "believers," that we all operate on faith, and that we can, and should, explore the consequences of that faith. I share my own essay to demonstrate concretely my dedication to examining my version of faith, and my commitment to sharing, questioning, and discussing the axioms we believe without proof and the world that results from those axioms. Additionally, because it is an opportunity for me to express my appreciation for the Holy Cross commitment to collaboration, my dedication to creating a supportive learning environment for my students and colleagues, and my understanding that sometimes when times are hard, we must rely on others to pull us through, I share the following essay with my students.

I believe that any person can complete a marathon, and that no person can complete a marathon alone.

Years and bodies and many ankle injuries ago, I was a long-distance runner. I wasn't fast, but I was a persistent mathematics graduate student with anxiety that could only be cured by feet pounding pavement.

There were not many academic triumphs of note for me in graduate school. Despite an enduring passion for learning mathematics, and despite the thrill of proving new facts, it was a long, hard slog through days when I felt like I was never going to finish, and nights when I was positive of this, peppered with little moments of insight that made it into my dissertation.

But my personal triumphs were many, and what made them more amazing and special and life-altering was that we—the few of us who banded together for emotional and intellectual support—shared them with each other. No one was left alone to flounder. Some of us found life partners, some of us found partners-in-crime, but all of us found a community that worked to hold up its members against sometimes impossible odds.

It was in the middle of this maelstrom of friendship and higher mathematics that I decided to become a marathon runner. I was up every morning at four to run, and then I'd swim for forty-five minutes, take a shower, and go to class. It was not a schedule that I could keep forever, but it was my sanity held together by rubber-soled shoes and the daily triumph of passing the ROTC cadets as we all ran uphill.

My third marathon in as many months was in Los Angeles, where I lived and studied. At mile three, I rounded a curve to see a gaggle of mathematicians. At mile ten, I ran into them again, but this time, my pal Keith jumped into the fray and ran next to me. Keith figured (in his usual, math-smart-but-maybe-not-so-street-smart way) he'd run for a while, and the rest of the math gang would drive along the marathon route in LA traffic and we'd find them a few miles up the road. It wasn't that he jumped in without a plan, he just jumped in without a *good* plan. I don't think it ever entered Keith's mind that there was a possibility that he'd have to complete over sixteen miles in the LA heat.

He jumped in to run beside me, and at first, he wouldn't take the water I offered, or the goo, the food, the candy. He'd jumped in to cheer me on, and he was fresh, he figured, and didn't need that stuff.

We talked about math. We talked about teaching math to students who were underprepared. He tried to convince me around mile seventeen that I should just leave him and he'd wait for our friends. His legs were too heavy, he said. He was unprepared, he said. I told him that I couldn't leave him, a skinny math kid with no ID and no money, in Compton, to wait. It didn't matter how tired we were; it didn't matter how hot it was. What mattered was getting to the end. We walked all of mile twenty-three. At that point, walking a mile felt as good as taking a long nap in a warm bed. With kittens. Keith picked me up when I tripped and fell at the mile twenty-five water station. Eventually, he took my offers of candy and power bars, and we feasted as we ran. We inspired each other. At mile twenty-six, one block from the end of the course in downtown Los Angeles, we found our friends, and we crossed the finish line, a pack of sprinting mathematicians.

Looking back on this, I'm certain Keith couldn't have finished without me. I'm also certain that without him and others like him, I would never have had the courage to start.

Mutual Benefice:
Helping Students Find God in a
Research Methods Course

Jonathan M. Bowman

A narrow discipline-specific focus with which today's scholar must struggle is relatively new in the world of the academy. Historically, the Renaissance tradition of enlightened education had highlighted a broad range of interdisciplinary engagement, and that engagement had been encouraged across traditions to include an extensive knowledge of faith.[1] Even more recently, issues of faith were considered a part of the search for truth in the early American education system,[2] with the understanding that the holistic scholar would use each one to infuse the other. Yet a modern academic perspective that encourages scholars to be incredibly focused and competent in a (mostly) single line of inquiry has also shaped the manner in which we engage and train those young minds to which we have sworn our fealty and discipleship. Scholarly breadth is rare; while my graduate program encouraged me to be deeply trained in two separate areas of communication research in the social science tradition, I also spent much time voraciously reading texts about faith and spirituality. I was often teased by friends at other institutions for the large range of knowledge I was expected to master before I was able to

---

[1] Indeed, faith often *was* intellectual engagement. An interesting overview of this period can be found in R. Po-Chia Hsia, *The World of Catholic Renewal, 1540–1770* (Cambridge, UK: Cambridge University Press, 2005).

[2] Sharon Daloz Parks, *Big Questions, Worthy Dreams* (San Francisco: Jossey-Bass, 2000), 10–11.

have my final commencement, let alone my self-guided extracurricular pursuit of knowledge about spirituality. Such a broad education was considered, it seems, overkill.

Not only that, but viewing education as a sacramental endeavor and using the terms "discipleship" or "fealty" seems surprising in the modern system. After all, aren't young scholars often encouraged to think of educating undergraduates as simply something that is done between research projects or—even more insidiously—in order to get tenure? I speak somewhat in jest, but there is some truth to the statement. I distinctly remember a renowned scholar at another institution quite seriously referring to his undergraduate teaching load as a "distraction" that would be better left to graduate students and other people who are not senior scholars. However, aren't we—either as Catholic scholars or as scholars at Catholic institutions—responsible to encourage students to engage their world around them? It is far too easy to accomplish one's graduation requirements at a Catholic institution without ever engaging the greater community of individuals in which one finds oneself.

Efficacious Boredom

Indeed, in my own work I began to note a greater separation between my educational, communal, and sacramental life. Having taught the same research methods course thirty-three times in less than eight years allowed me the opportunity to get somewhat bored, forcing me to re-evaluate that experience. Fortunately, I found myself at an early career crossroads where I was encouraged to reflect upon my teaching experiences. The course, Introductory Communication Research Methods, is not that different from similar "service" courses in other disciplines in that the material is important, essential for future coursework, and yet oftentimes seemingly boring. For that particular course, no longer was teaching a sacramental activity. While I may personally get somewhat excited about statistics and research design, a class full of students admittedly scared of math does not easily lend itself well to a sustained level of in-class excitement, regardless of one's approach to the content. As such, my redesign of the course and my interest in getting back to the basics of a more holistic education stemmed from a somewhat selfish place. What would make me get excited about this course again, particularly since I was slated to teach it regularly until my retirement, decades away? How could I engage the material in such a way that it was sacramental?

Obviously, a careful and intentional rethinking of any educational approach needed inspiration of some sort. As a scholar at a Catholic institution and as a person of faith with a high commitment to my community, I wondered how I could make this specific course more relevant and actively engaging for the students and community members with whom I came into contact. John Stott points out that "Christianity is no mere passive acquiescence in a series of propositions,"[3] and I desired to figure out how to help students engage issues of social justice with a similar efficacy. I hoped to continue to learn more about Catholic social thought, an essential core of my university's social justice mission. And more importantly, I wanted to answer the "so what" of education: What is someone who is excited about my course topic going to do to impact their world, and how can I make sure that they are effective in that as they move through their subsequent life experiences?

Mutual Benefice[4]

The answer to this question, to me, was to develop an experiential education activity that incorporated both a focus on others and an engagement with Catholic social thought. As an educator, I could encourage students to treat issues of community and diversity and justice as fertile opportunities for self-discovery. At some institutions, I have heard students refer to research methods courses as "just one of those things that you have to get through in order to graduate." This project would focus on getting students to consider practical, real-world research questions and to move beyond the typical "hypothetical" research experience. Typically, the best instructors will have a capstone project that demonstrates student learning of methodological processes, often through a comprehensive student proposal for research in which students are expected to imagine creative solutions to hypothetical research questions, with a summary of the methods that they would likely use if they were to carry out a project and a detailed description of the analyses that would be most appropriate for these methods. Indeed, this was the

---

[3] John R. W. Stott, *Basic Christianity* (London: InterVarsity Press, 1958), 107.

[4] Obviously, this play on the phrase "mutually beneficial" calls to mind the early church practice of a benefice, or a permanent appointment through the church where land or income are provided in return for church duties. Here, the enlightened professor receives the ancillary benefits of perceived altruism in return for the performance of his now-modified teaching duties. *New Oxford American Dictionary*, 4th ed. (New York: Oxford University Press, 2010).

model at the university where I did my undergraduate study, at the university where I did both graduate degrees, and at the university where I had my first tenure-track position.

Moving beyond that intellectual exercise to something that is both practically applied and potentially sacramental, my students are now placed into groups and paired with a local nonprofit in the area. Because students are given some freedom in selecting a nonprofit, they become heavily invested in both the mission of the nonprofit as well as the individuals who serve at and/or benefit from that particular nonprofit. This is an essential practice: by allowing students to research and engage a nonprofit and to find people "who are different from themselves," they are forced to leave their spheres of influence and engage with people with whom, they learn, they actually have much in common. Also, this is an excellent opportunity to infuse the classroom experience with Catholic social thought by discussing documents such as *Pacem in Terris*, the encyclical letter of Pope John XXIII from 1963,[5] in which the intelligence and will, rights and duties of each human being are affirmed.

At this point, students could easily tend to defer to nonprofits that aren't "messy," such as the Humane Society or the SPCA, where promises of playful puppies and unconditional love from animals soften the injustices that the nonprofit seeks to overcome. However, allowing students to remain in their comfort zones will water down the perspective-taking goals of such an assignment. How can students learn to apply their discipline while affirming other humans when the bulk of their work does not focus on issues of human dignity?

Once students are paired up with a nonprofit that works with people significantly different from them, they are then immersed in the culture of the nonprofit in an attempt to explore and understand the needs of that nonprofit, and to set up a series of testable hypotheses to address those needs. Students create a method that can be carried out in groups and actually test the hypotheses in a real-world setting. Adding to this foundational knowledge, the key element of civic engagement comes from the students' selection of their practical research question: myriad local nonprofit organizations identified key research questions that were important to the success of the organization but were unanswerable due to constraints of time and/or personnel. When students found a research question that was emotionally and practically appealing, they created a

---

[5] For an overview, see Edward P. DeBerri and James E. Hug, *Catholic Social Teaching: Our Best Kept Secret*, 4th ed. (Washington, DC: Center of Concern, 2003), 58–61.

project that in some way benefitted that local nonprofit and experienced a transcendent teachable moment as they learned to think outside themselves while they simultaneously pursued their own goals.

Exemplar Student Projects

Before discussing the sacramental benefits of this project, it is crucial to note that the endeavor also produces demonstrable outcomes that are worthwhile in their own right by engaging the community, bringing service to the local area, and even promoting the name of the university while simultaneously providing actual benefit to nonprofits and the people they help.

To begin, one group of students wanted to determine the best way to recruit and retain volunteers for a university student organization. That organization was founded to work with adults with severe intellectual disabilities in one of the most impoverished areas of our region. Interestingly, after providing research results and a list of interested student volunteers to the organization's leadership team, some of the students themselves became active volunteers. The group members' self-described standoffish attitudes and preconceived notions were each shifted as they interacted with people who had severe intellectual disabilities.

Another group of students with a love of the ocean worked directly with a local nonprofit whose mission is "to improve the health, well-being and self-reliance of people living in isolated regions connected to us through surfing."[6] Students determined the best way the organization could use electronic media and an incentive structure to communicate information about themselves in order to increase charitable contributions to the organization. After working directly with the nonprofit leadership, students were able to point to an organizational interest in restructuring their web presence and an interest in getting more involved with the organization directly.

The last example of a demonstrable student outcome is derived from a group of individuals interested in determining the best communication strategies for securing donations for an area food bank. In tackling this question, the group set up a complex factorial design testing the efficacy of different compliance-gaining strategies. In the test of these strategies,

[6] Surf Aid International website, accessed October 11, 2013, http://www.surfaid international.org.

students actually organized a canned food drive over multiple days (with the permission of the organization) and presented the findings (and the canned/monetary proceeds) to the organization at the end of the semester. Apparently, the organization has now changed its public communication strategy in part as a result of the students' findings. These students were quite pleased to have made a difference that they encounter in local advertising strategies.

Now, however, it becomes important to address why this and other exercises like it are sacramental in nature, and how they instill a desire for larger, more transcendent moments in the students as they move through their educational experience.

Opportunity One: Self-Reflection

First, we all know college as an inherently selfish time. For even the most enlightened student, there is something self-serving about pausing one's life to work on self-betterment. Now, I expect that I'll hear a lot of push-back on this point. One can think of numerous reasons why one can use one's education for the greater good of others, rather than oneself; an educated person can bring greater knowledge and depth of experience to their community. An education affords one the ability to make money and receive benefits that are sustaining and life-giving to one's family. An education can allow someone to learn skill sets like medicine or sustainable agriculture or conflict mediation that can transform the lives of the impoverished or underserved. An education can teach people how to engage in behaviors that will ultimately change the world for better. An education can even simply increase one's earning potential so that they have more finances to give to their churches, schools, communities, and other philanthropic endeavors. All of these things are true. Yet, there is an inherent self-reflection that often comes during one's college years that is not present in any other time throughout one's life experience. Is it selfish? According to my understanding, yes. Does it have the potential for great selflessness to emerge as a result? Most certainly. As such, this is the best time to engage students so as to guide and shape their self-reflection.

How might the professor guide such self-reflection in this activity? I have come to believe that the professor must first provide *exposure*. Depending upon the institution, many Catholic colleges and universities hope to take relatively sheltered students and introduce them to the wider world around them. For many students, this educational environment provides one of the first opportunities to truly engage with people who are different than themselves. By placing students in situations where they are interacting with people and learning of their competencies and finding similarities in hope and goal and ambition despite differences in education or culture or socioeconomic background, the faculty member has the unique opportunity to shepherd students toward an interaction that may prove life-changing for some.

Opportunity Two: Vocational Discernment

During one's college years, self-reflection also tends toward issues of job or career. By interacting with the idealistic young professionals that often staff nonprofits at higher levels, students are also able to see the potential for leading a life of service. Some students will interact with professionals who have chosen to become full-time nonprofit staffers. Other students might encounter people who volunteer part-time in addition to their career or family responsibilities. Even other encounters may include people who are giving of their financial resources or taking advantage of corporate responsibility programs to give to that nonprofit. All students are likely to come into contact with individuals who are making some level of sacrifice to better the lives of others. This is, of course, a useful experience for someone who is trying to discern what their career might look like; a student trying to gain an experience that will help them choose a career might instead earn a vocation. Helping someone gain insight into who they want to *be* rather than just what they want to *do* is a significant side-effect of encouraging student interaction with nonprofit organizations, regardless of one's disciplinary background.

Opportunity Three: Tangible Service Outcomes

Finally, simply serving can prove to be a transcendent experience for our undergraduate students. The Catholic Catechism describes both grace and sacrament as inextricable and demonstrable, discussing "efficacious signs of grace, instituted by Christ and entrusted to the Church, by which divine life is dispensed to us. The visible rites by which the sacraments are celebrated signify and make present the graces proper to each sacrament. They bear fruit in those who receive them with the required dispositions."[7] During the college experience, there are many opportunities for service that go missed because of commitments and classes and courtship; by incorporating service into the course require- ments, it is mandated that students take the time to briefly taste a mo- ment of actual, demonstrable, grace-filled service.

In a perfect world, such service would occur naturally and from purely altruistic origins. Indeed, an externally imposed moment of service does not necessarily provide an unambiguously clear experience of pure, selfless giving. However, activities that are good for the community and for the soul are important, regardless of origin. When a caregiver forces a petulant child to eat a vegetable before receiving dessert, does that child's unwilling spirit cause the broccoli to become any less nutritious? Does one's self-realization of the need in one's community become any less informative (and formative) because their professor helped them to learn it firsthand? In both cases, it seems unlikely.

A Charge

One student reflected on the experience, writing that his group "came to understand how it is within the human capacity to give to a worthy cause. The relationship between human communication—and the ability to give—provided us with our own opportunity to give." This comment proved to be a moment of grace for *me*. Will every student be dramati- cally changed by thinking outside themselves as a result of one insular, single classroom service experience? Probably not. However, by multiple faculty in multiple disciplines in multiple courses using experiential education to expose students to options and opportunities of sacramental self-transcendence, eventually the sum total of experience could prove dramatically changing to the culture in which we find ourselves. Is it easy to do the first time as a faculty member? No, but it gets easier. Is it something that will get you a line on your curriculum vitae that will help you get tenure or promotion or a performance increase in your paycheck? Not likely, although even that culture is changing at many of our Catholic institutions (and our service-minded cousins both public and private). Is incorporating such a service-based activity likely to

---

[7] *Catechism of the Catholic Church*, paragraph 1131.

change your academic life and reinfuse your teaching with purpose and clarity? Yes! At least, from personal experience, I can say that it has for me. By engaging students with the world around them, seasoning that engagement with essential Catholic social thought and sacramental service, and through the encouragement of reflection, I have reinvigorated *my own* experience of transcendence as I teach and mentor my undergraduate students.

About the Authors

Peter Alonzi is professor of economics at Dominican University, where his teaching excellence has been recognized by multiple awards. Since 1999 he has taught in Dominican's undergraduate and MBA economics and finance courses and is a mainstay of Dominican's International Executive MBA programs in Torun, Poland, and Brno, Czech Republic. Most recently, his research has focused on perverse incentives in financial markets.

Michael Bathgate is associate professor of religious studies at Saint Xavier University, where he teaches courses on the religions of Asia and the comparative study of religion. His scholarship addresses the uses and functions of popular literature in medieval Japan and the pedagogical implications of sharing that literature as part of the Catholic Liberal Arts. Among other pieces, he is the author of *The Fox's Craft in Japanese Religion and Folklore* and "Reading the Writing on the Wall: Visualizing One University's Mercy Mission in a Cosmopolitan World."

Kimberly P. Bowers is assistant professor of English at the University of Saint Francis in Fort Wayne, Indiana. She teaches Literature and the Natural Environment and a variety of other courses, including American Literature, Introduction to Theatre, and Literature by Women. She has presented papers at a number of national conferences, most recently the Association for the Study of Literature and the Environment, and has published an essay on the Dixie Chicks.

Jonathan M. Bowman is associate professor of communication studies and associate dean at the University of San Diego. The recipient of multiple teaching awards, he teaches courses in human communication processes. Bowman's research focuses on those behaviors associated with intimacy and close relationships, and his work has been published in a variety of scholarly journals and books. Bowman loves working directly with students and has been the director of the Social Justice Living-Learning Community at USD where he also works as an advisor and a mentor to undergraduates involved in Greek life, undergraduate research, and campus faith-based organizations.

Obdulia Castro has taught courses in Spanish language and culture, literature, linguistics, and teaching methodology at the graduate and undergraduate level at Georgetown University, George Mason University, St. Lawrence University, the University of Colorado at Boulder, and Regis University. She is currently chair and associate professor of Spanish in the Department of Modern and Classical Languages and Literature at Regis University in Denver, Colorado. She is the author of two books—*Galician Phonology and Morphology* and *Issues in Spanish Morphophonology: Implications for Language Acquisition*—and numerous scholarly articles.

James Corkery, SJ, is associate professor of systematic theology at the Milltown Institute of Theology and Philosophy in Dublin, Ireland. He is author of *Joseph Ratzinger's Theological Ideas: Wise Cautions and Legitimate Hopes* (Dublin: Dominican Publications and New York: Paulist Press) and coeditor of *The Papacy Since 1500: From Italian Prince to Universal Pastor* (Cambridge and New York: Cambridge University Press). He writes mainly in the areas of theological anthropology, spirituality and culture, social spirituality, and faith and justice.

Eric Cunningham is associate professor of history at Gonzaga University. He teaches and studies modern Japanese intellectual history, Zen Buddhism, Catholicism, eschatology, the history of consciousness, and psychedelia. His wide range of publications include these topics in popular films and media. He is a seeker of connections between Christianity, the various strands of ancient esoteric traditions, and modern "spirituality" worldwide.

Karen E. Eifler is professor of education at the University of Portland where she codirects the Garaventa Center for Catholic Intellectual Life and American Culture. A longtime contributor to Collegium, she has channeled lessons learned in that colloquy to her work with new and veteran college faculty members. She is the author of the collection of essays *A Month of Mondays: Spiritual Lessons from Catholic Classrooms*, and numerous scholarly articles.

Audrey A. Friedman is associate professor of education and assistant dean of the Lynch School of Education at Boston College. She probes the processes of adolescent and adult reflective judgment in her writing and teaching and explores meaningful alternative assessment strategies in K–12 classrooms. The Council for Advancement and Study of Education in the state of Massachusetts named her Professor of the Year in 2009.

Melissa A. Goldthwaite, professor of English at Saint Joseph's University, teaches creative writing (food writing, nature writing, creative nonfiction, poetry, and letter writing) and rhetorical theory. Recent works include *Books That Cook: The Making of a Literary Meal* (New York University Press), *The Norton Reader*, 13th ed. (W. W. Norton), and *The Norton Pocketbook of Writing by Students* (W. W. Norton). In 2009, she received a Fetzer Institute–funded Contemplative Practice Fellowship from the Center for Contemplative Mind in Society to develop her course on the rhetorics of silence.

Elizabeth Grassi is associate professor of linguistically and culturally diverse education at Regis University. Prior to joining the Regis faculty, Elizabeth was a K–12 teacher and coordinator of ESL/language acquisition programs in the United States and abroad.

Ann E. Green is professor of English and graduate director of the Writing Studies Program at Saint Joseph's University in Philadelphia and is the founding director of the SJU Writing Center. She currently chairs the American Association of University Professors committee on Women in the Profession, Committee W. She has published in *Writing on the Edge*, *Reflections: A Journal of Writing, Service-Learning, and Community Literacy*, and *College Composition and Communication*. Her most recent publication is "Local Politics and Voice: Speaking to be Heard," in *Academic Cultures: Professional Preparation and the Teaching Life*.

Angela Kim Harkins is associate professor of religious studies at Fairfield University, where she has been teaching since 2006. She frequently teaches Introduction to Religious Studies, Hebrew Bible/Old Testament, Women in the Bible, Religious Diversity in Early Judaism and Christianity in the core curriculum. She is the author of *Reading with an "I" to the Heavens* (Berlin: de Gruyter, 2012) and has published numerous articles on prayer in the Dead Sea Scrolls. She was a Fellow at the Wabash Center for Teaching and Learning in Theology and Religion in 2010, and in 2011 she was honored as the College of Arts and Sciences Distinguished Professor of the Year at Fairfield University. She is a member of the Lilly Fellows Program National Network Board. Angela is currently a Marie Curie International Incoming Fellow, funded by the European Commission, at the University of Birmingham, UK, for 2014–2016.

Michael J. Himes is a priest in the Archdiocese of New York and professor of theology at Boston College. Author of several books and many articles, he is a sought-after speaker and is a recipient of four honorary degrees.

Anita Houck teaches at Saint Mary's College, Notre Dame, Indiana, where she has served as associate professor and chair of the Department of Religious Studies and director of the Writing Proficiency Program. A former high-school teacher and parish pastoral associate, she studies humor in religion, spirituality of single life, and pedagogy, including educational assessment. She is the coeditor, with Mary Doak, of *Translating Religion* (Orbis, 2013).

Thomas M. Landy, a sociologist with a specialization in the sociology of religion and Catholicism, is director of the Rev. Michael C. McFarland, SJ, Center for Religion, Ethics and Culture at the College of the Holy Cross. In 1992 he founded Collegium, a colloquy on faith and intellectual life. Collegium sponsors highly regarded summer faculty development programs for faculty from sixty-five Catholic colleges and universities. He is editor of *As Leaven for the World: Catholic Reflections on Faith, Vocation, and the Intellectual Life* (Franklin, WI: Sheed & Ward, 2001). His latest project, "Catholics and Cultures," attempts to engage scholars in the study of Catholic practices and beliefs around the globe.

Rev. William M. Lies, CSC, is vice-president for mission engagement and church affairs at the University of Notre Dame. Fr. Lies is also a member of the Department of Political Science and a fellow of the Joan B. Kroc Institute for International Peace Studies and its Kellogg Institute for International Studies at Notre Dame. His research and teaching focus has been on the politics of poverty and Catholic social tradition. He is the author of many papers and publications on the consolidation of democracy, religion and politics, and religious freedom.

Michael P. Pagano is associate professor and graduate program director in the Department of Communication at Fairfield University. He has published four health communication–related books, numerous journal articles, and an e-novel. He also trained as a physician assistant. As professor and chair he developed and inaugurated the Physician Assistant Program at the University of Health Sciences/The Chicago Medical School, in North Chicago, Illinois. Today, he continues to practice as a PA and combines that profession with his twenty-five years of undergraduate and graduate teaching experience. In addition, he enjoys researching and writing about health-care provider education, as well as health, interpersonal, and organizational communication.

Michael Patella, OSB, is the chair of the Committee on Illumination and Text for *The Saint John's Bible*. A Benedictine monk of Saint John's Abbey in Collegeville, Minnesota, he is a professor of New Testament and teaches in both the undergraduate theology department and the graduate School of Theology·Seminary at Saint John's University, where he serves as seminary rector and the director of the graduate school's Holy Land Studies Program. He has published on Luke, Mark, and Paul, and he has a new book out on the hermeneutics of *The Saint John's Bible*.

William Purcell is the associate director for the Catholic Social Tradition and Practice at the Center for Social Concerns and codirects the minor in Catholic Social Tradition at the University of Notre Dame. He teaches community-based learning courses on poverty, with the biggest being Urban Plunge. Bill has written extensively on Catholic social teaching and is on various local and national committees for social justice issues.

Stephanie Anne Salomone is associate professor of mathematics at the University of Portland, where she earned the Outstanding Teaching Award in 2009. She is a mama of three, wife, and math professor in Portland, Oregon. No longer a long-distance runner, she completes weekly marathons in paper grading, toddler and baby wrangling, picking up Legos, and laundry folding. She wouldn't change a thing, though she'd really like a nap.

Susan Crawford Sullivan is associate professor of sociology and Edward Bennett Williams Fellow at the College of the Holy Cross. Her book, *Living Faith: Everyday Religion and Mothers in Poverty* (University of Chicago, 2011) explores the role of religion in the lives of low-income urban mothers. She has academic interests in religion, poverty and public policy, family, and community-based learning.

Joanna (Jody) Ziegler was a professor of art history at the College of the Holy Cross and served the college in many capacities before her too early passing from cancer in 2010. Her essay reprinted here, "Practice Makes Reception," earns raves each time it is studied at the annual Collegium colloquy, an enterprise she served with great zeal as friend, mentor, and board member.